Our Mission in Today's World

COUNCIL ON EVANGELISM
OFFICIAL PAPERS AND REPORTS

EDITORIAL COMMITTEE:
Richard Champion, chairman; Edward S. Caldwell; Gary Leggett

GOSPEL PUBLISHING HOUSE
Springfield, Missouri

2-563

CONTENTS

MORNING SEMINARS (Continued)

EVENING SEMINARS

INTRODUCTION

THE COUNCIL ON EVANGELISM, held in St Louis, Missouri, August 26-29, 1968, may well be recorded as one of the most significant meetings in the 54-year history of the Assemblies of God.

The Council was called as part of the Movement's intensive self-study program. The deep moving of the Holy Spirit on the sessions was fresh evidence that the Assemblies of God was moving in God's way at God's time.

A total of 7,072 persons registered for the Council. The number exceeded the registration at the 32nd biennial General Council held the year before in Long Beach, California.

This book contains a digest of the messages, reports, and seminars which, added together, stress the necessity of revival and evangelism.

The book begins with the white paper: "Why the Plan of Advance?" detailing the circumstances leading up to the Council.

Following this are the four major evening messages delivered at the Kiel Auditorium. The subject was the Church—its mission, mandate, message, and motivation. Because of the progression involved in these messages, they can best be studied as a unit.

Morning sessions of the Council were held at two St. Louis hotels: the Sheraton-Jefferson and the St. Louis Gateway. Themes for the united morning sessions were expositions of Biblical revivals—with six different speakers presenting a study of three different revivals. These six sermons are printed in the order in which they were presented at the Council. This accounts for sermons listed under the same subject but by different speakers.

Afternoon united sessions were held at the Kiel Auditorium. These involved a definition of the mission of the Assemblies of God in contemporary society as being to minister to the Lord, to the saints, and to the world. These three messages are presented in sequence in the book and should also be studied as a unit.

The afternoon sessions also featured guidelines for the Year of Revival (1969) and helps in maintaining spiritual priorities—two printed papers presented to the delegates. Both of these are reproduced in this volume.

A major portion of this book highlights a digest of the seminars.

Two-hour seminars were held each morning at both of the headquarters hotels. These followed a similar format: presentation of a paper by a speaker and a discussion led by a moderator and a panel. A recorder was assigned to retain the essence of the session.

Each morning session was repeated in a different hotel but involved the same personnel. In the book the panel discussion following the speaker's topic is a summation of both of those sessions.

There were 24 different seminars held in the mornings—a total of 48 sessions, since each was repeated.

Another 11 seminars, each an hour long, were

held just prior to the evening services. These were similar in format to the morning sessions but were abbreviated because of the shorter time allotted to them.

Almost all seminar sessions were well attended, with recorders frequently noting "standing room only" in their reports to the Committee on Advance.

The book presents the morning seminars, and then the evening seminars, in alphabetical order.

Recorders' notes of the seminars, which frequently were copious, were intended basically to guide the Committee on Advance in further deliberations. These reports have necessarily been condensed to bring out only the highlights of the discussion for this book.

Speakers for the general sessions and the seminars have been identified in an appendix to this book.

Concluding the Council on Evangelism was the "Declaration at St. Louis"—a statement of awareness and acceptance of mission. This Declaration concludes the material in the book.

When the Council on Evangelism was ended, General Superintendent T. F. Zimmerman declared that the meeting had effected a shift in the Assemblies of God position from "a defensive holding action to a dynamic offensive outreach." He further stated that the enthusiastic response from Council delegates made it possible for the Movement to formulate a program of progress for the days ahead. "This will let us project specific goals and objectives to help us meaningfully fulfill our mission in today's world and let us address ourselves to the needs and challenges of contemporary society," the General Superintendent declared.

And the spirit of the Council on Evangelism, catching fire throughout the churches of the Movement, gives new impetus to making the gospel relevant in a rapidly changing world—and to reaching men everywhere with the unchanging message of God's love and mercy.

WHY THE PLAN OF ADVANCE?

WHY THE PLAN OF ADVANCE?

WHITE PAPER

WHY A COUNCIL ON EVANGELISM? Why a Plan of Advance? These questions cannot be answered properly without an understanding of circumstances leading up to them.

A Sense of Concern

The 1963 session of the General Council manifested a profound sense of spiritual concern for the future of the Assemblies of God. This sense of concern, evident in the reports of various committees, resulted in a change of the organizational structure of the Assemblies of God. Evangelism was elevated above the rank of a department and assigned to the office of the General Superintendent.

As a result of this action, it became the responsibility of the General Superintendent's office to correlate the evangelistic thrust that reaches out through every department, district, and church.

There was commendation for initiation of regional spiritual life conventions in 1960 in response to an action of the 1959 General Council which called for "national, district, and local church conferences . . . as a means to point up the need for intensifying the spiritual life of our church."

How could the office of the General Superintendent best fulfill its responsibility to revitalize and deepen the spiritual life of the Movement and to lead the Movement forward in an aggressive thrust of evangelism? After prayerful consideration, the Spiritual Life—Evangelism Commission was formed. The purpose of the Commission is to ". . . coordinate the spiritual and evangelistic thrust of our Fellowship through all departments and to carry out the emphases drawn up by the Evangelism Committee."

The sense of concern about the spiritual life and the evangelistic efforts of the Assemblies of God continued to grow in all segments and at all levels of the Movement. The sense of concern was crystallized and articulated in the meeting of the full Executive Presbytery on May 31, 1967. The following quotation is taken from the minutes of that historic meeting.

"In view of the fact of the widespread outpouring of the Holy Spirit in the historic churches, together with the deep hunger for reality that is innate in the hearts of people everywhere, there is presented to the General Council of the Assemblies of God an opportunity to demonstrate leadership in projecting a Pentecostal witness in an hour of unprecedented need; and

"Notwithstanding we are beset with formidable adversaries in a day that is marked by secularism, materialism, amorality, and widespread apathy, we have a God-given charge to penetrate our culture with the dynamics of a full-gospel ministry; therefore, be it

"*Resolved*, That aggressive steps be taken to make an in-depth evaluation of our strengths and weaknesses with the objective of fortifying ourselves in order to demonstrate a virile witness to our generation; and be it further

"*Resolved*, That a Five-Year Program of Advance be tooled out so as to project goals and give a sense of direction for all our departments and ministries that personnel and material resources may be more fully utilized for the advancement of the cause of Christ."

On June 14, 1967, the action of the Executive Presbytery was reported by letter to the general presbyters:

"Possibly the most important item of business which claimed a major part of our time was the frank and prayerful evaluation of the evangelism and growth patterns that have obtained in the immediate past decade. After considerable deliberation, it was noted that we have many points that are most encouraging. It was the consensus, however, that the time is ripe for an in-depth study to be made of our strengths and weaknesses with an eye to projecting a Five-Year Plan of Advance, should Jesus tarry."

In the same letter a call for a special Council on Evangelism was issued:

"Under God, this can be the launching pad for an unprecedented era of advance and evangelism."

But how should such a study be carried out? A small scanning committee was called for and met two days, June 15 and 16. Members of the committee were: Thomas F. Zimmerman, T. E. Gannon, C. W. Denton, Gene Scott, Donald F. Johns, and Ralph W. Harris. This committee discussed possible procedures, personnel, and target dates for the in-depth study authorized by the Executive Presbytery. It was agreed that the study would have three major phases: diagnosis, evaluation, and projection.

On July 12, 1967, on behalf of the Executive Presbytery the General Superintendent appointed by letter 14 persons to serve with him on the study committee to be known as the Committee on Advance. Care was taken to insure that the committee membership would represent various types of ministry in the Movement, various areas of the country, and various levels of responsibility. Invited to serve with the General Superintendent were: Lowell Ashbrook, G. Raymond Carlson, C. W. Denton, T. E. Gannon, James E. Hamill, Ralph W. Harris, J. Philip Hogan, Cyril Homer, D. V. Hurst, Donald F. Johns, Harry Myers, Andrew Nellie, Gene Scott, and William Vickery.

On August 22, 1967, the action taken by the Executive Presbytery on May 31, 1967, was reported to the General Presbytery. The membership list and purpose of the Committee on Advance were presented. At that time, the need for diagnosis, evaluation, and projection was explained. Following this presentation special prayer was offered for this very important undertaking. An utterance in tongues with interpretation followed, and the season of prayer continued freely with the entire Presbytery joining in spontaneous prayer and praise.

The General Superintendent concluded the afternoon session with the following statement: "In the providence of the Lord we have had a historic session this afternoon. I think all of us are looking from time to time for a confirmation of . . . direction. . . . I feel reassurance in my own heart. I feel we can confidently go forward, and there are great and wonderful things in store if we will be humble and obedient to God. It is going to take these qualities. Before we can teach others, we must be taught ourselves. We are prime candidates for it."

At the 1967 General Council the appointment of the Committee on Advance was announced and its role in relation to the Council on Evangelism and the Plan of Advance was discussed. In reporting to the General Council, the Spiritual Life Committee heartily endorsed the proposed Five-Year Plan of Advance. The Committee report offered three observations:

"(a) We express appreciation for the very name *Advance* which we understand to mean that its driving objective is to move us forward in God.

"(b) An analysis of history shows that this is a very critical generation for our Movement. One of the problems that makes this generation critical is the tendency to forget our distinctive reason-for-being. We encourage the Committee on Advance to specifically give itself to rearticulate our purposes.

"(c) We hold the belief that those most effective in analyzing any movement are those on the inside who love the movement they might criticize. Growth and fruit come from within, not without. . . .

"This report reflects the thinking and heart-burden of each member of the Spiritual Life Committee. We wish to commend our Executive Presbytery for calling our Movement to rededication to the spiritual challenge of reaching the world for God."

The Council responded enthusiastically to the report of the Spiritual Life Committee:

"It was moved and seconded that this highly significant report be adopted. The motion was unanimously carried by a standing vote."

The Committee on Advance

The first meeting of the Committee on Advance was held at Long Beach, California, on August 26, 1967. General Superintendent Thomas F. Zimmerman indicated that in the years he has been associated with the Assemblies of God there has never been a matter about which he has felt a keener burden or which he has considered of greater importance than the work assigned to the Committee on Advance.

He expressed his personal belief that the Assemblies of God has reached an important crossroads. The Movement has before it two possible alternatives: it can content itself with maintaining the status quo, or it can accept the challenge under God of mobilizing all its resources to advance the cause for which it has been brought into existence. He reviewed briefly the circumstances leading up to the meeting and introduced Gene Scott who had been appointed to serve as research director.

Dr. Scott discussed the significance of the term *Advance* in relation to the proposed study and plan. He pointed out that to advance, the Movement must capitalize on its strengths and seek to eliminate its weaknesses. He pointed out the conviction of the scanning committee that such a study could best be undertaken by men who love the Movement and who are committed to its improvement. He briefly oriented the committee members to the research objectives and procedures. In the discussion which followed, various members of the committee expressed their awe at the magnitude of the committee assignment. Prior to adjournment some preliminary research assignments were made to various members of the committee.

The second meeting of the committee was September 25-28, 1967. At that meeting, Hardy W. Steinberg, who had been appointed to serve as secretary, joined the committee. Prior to undertaking any work the committee, burdened by the awesome sense of its responsibility and recognizing its need for utter dependence upon the Lord, met together for prayer and communion. In approaching the elements of the Lord's Supper, the committee adhered to the admonition of the apostle Paul, "Let a man examine himself..." (1 Corinthians 11:28). This typified the objective approach taken by the committee to in-depth self-analysis in spiritual perspective.

Subsequent meetings were held November 8-10, 1967; January 3-5, February 27-29, March 12-14, May 6-9, and June 11-13, 1968. In addition to these full committee meetings, there was a meeting of an important subcommittee on April 8-10, 1968. Throughout all meetings, the attendance of the members was excellent. Most of the time, either the full membership was present or all but one or two members.

Subcommittees

How should the committee proceed in order to fulfill its awesome responsibilities? It was obvious that much research would be necessary in several areas. Therefore, appropriate subcommittees were appointed.

If the Assemblies of God was to fulfill its God-given responsibility of advancing the cause of Christ, the advance must be firmly grounded on scriptural principles. Therefore, a subcommittee was formed to undertake a continuing study of the Scripture in the light of the overall assignment of the committee. The function of this subcommittee was to insure a Biblical perspective for the work of the committee.

It was also clear that the reasons which motivated the call for the first General Council and forming of the Fellowship would be most meaningful to any evaluation of its strengths and weaknesses and its development. These would be found in the Call of the Council, the records of the Council as well as subsequent Councils, and in related legal documents. Therefore, another subcommittee was appointed and assigned the responsibility to study the various official written statements of purpose in the legal documents of the Assemblies of God, including those statements found in the constitution and bylaws, minutes of the General Councils, and the charter. What were our first purposes? Were they clearly stated? Have legal interpretations of those purposes changed?

In addition to these official written statements of purpose recorded in legal documents, it was evident also that individuals might have personal, private understandings and interpretations of the purpose of the Assemblies of God. These private and personal understandings of purpose held by various persons within the Assemblies of God might or might not correspond to the purposes as stated in the legal documents. To ascertain how persons within the Fellowship presently view the purposes of the Movement, another subcommittee was formed. This subcommittee had as its assignment the analysis of subjectively-held opinions concerning the purposes of the Assemblies of God.

The action of the Executive Presbytery on May 31, 1967, called for "an in-depth evaluation of our strengths and weaknesses with an objective of fortifying ourselves in order to demonstrate a virile witness to our generation." To accomplish this purpose, it would be necessary to analyze the strengths and weaknesses of the Movement in order to capitalize on the strengths and to attack the weaknesses. Therefore, a subcommittee was formed to appraise the strengths and weaknesses of the Assemblies of God.

Further analysis revealed that the Plan of Advance, when finally formulated, could not be implemented in a vacuum. It would be necessary to take into consideration the nature of the Movement as it is today. What the Movement is today is partially a result of its legal structure and its legal documents, partially a result of the way it has developed historically, partially a result of self-understanding as set forth in its publications, and partially a result of its culture, those unwritten rules of behavior which in part determine how we think and act. Legal forces, history, publications, cultures—these are the controlling forces which must be understood before the Plan of Advance can be projected and implemented. A subcommittee was appointed to study controlling forces.

Thinking ahead, it became apparent that the Committee on Advance would want to communicate its findings to the Movement as a whole. Much of this communication would take place through printed materials. Therefore, an editorial subcommittee was appointed to assume responsibility for developing those materials when they proved necessary.

A procedural subcommittee was also appointed to coordinate the work of the various subcommittees with the committee as a whole.

The Research

The analysis of the legal statements of purpose of the General Council of the Assemblies of God revealed a degree of ambiguity.

Though all documents from the original Call to the present time were minutely examined by the Committee, intensive attention was given to the action of the General Council at Memphis, Tennessee, in 1963. This attention was necessary because the Memphis Council had expressed and made official a priority statement of purpose which superseded previous statements. At this time the Council identified evangelism as

"the entire work of the entire church" and "the whole work of the whole church" without delineating or defining in full what it meant by evangelism.

Since this action gave an official statement of priority purpose expressed by a single word, it became necessary to determine if a uniform understanding of meaning for the word *evangelism* existed in the thinking of our constituency. Our research clearly indicated that such a uniform understanding did not exist. Ambiguity in understood purpose thus existed.

To test the degree to which there exists in the Movement a genuine ambiguity about the meaning of the term *evangelism*, 758 questionnaires were sent to pastors; 86 to laymen; 169 to general presbyters and nonresident executives; 21 to missionaries and missionary evangelists; 48 to school personnel; and 8 to evangelists. An analysis of the returned questionnaires indicated the same ambiguity about the meaning of the term *evangelism* that was evident in the legal documents. The Committee on Advance observed that the Memphis Council recognized a need expressed by the word *evangelism*, but that there were different understandings on the part of the constituency about the meaning of the word *evangelism*. The committee concluded that the confusion caused by the observed ambiguity in the meaning of the term *evangelism* could be removed by defining the mission of our church in a way which would not require unanimous agreement for the meaning of one word. The committee therefore adopted for its use the following resolution of interpretation and statement of purpose:

"*Whereas,* The very name *Assemblies of God* implied the belief that this organization consists of a people who belong to the Lord and who exist as instruments of His purpose; and

"*Whereas,* The 1963 General Council in Memphis identified evangelism as 'the entire work of the entire church' and 'the whole work of the whole church' without delineating or defining in full what is meant by evangelism; and

"*Whereas,* It is the studied opinion of the Committee on Advance that the General Council action regarding evangelism should be interpreted to mean that the Assemblies of God should give priority emphasis to the purpose of God; and

"*Whereas,* We believe that God's purpose concerning man is:

"1. To seek and to save that which is lost,

"2. To be worshiped by man,

"3. To build a body of believers in the image of His Son;

"*Therefore, be it resolved,* That the Committee on Advance affirm the priority reason-for-being of the Assemblies of God is:

"1. To be an agency of God for evangelizing the world,

"2. To be a corporate body in which man may worship God,

"3. To be a channel of God's purpose to build a body of saints being perfected in the image of His Son; and be it

"*Further resolved,* That we affirm that the Assemblies of God exists expressly to give continuing emphasis to this reason-for-being in the New Testament apostolic pattern by teaching and encouraging believers to be baptized in the Holy Spirit which:

"1. Enables them to evangelize in the power of the Spirit with accompanying supernatural signs,

"2. Adds a necessary dimension to worshipful relationship with God,

"3. Enables them to respond to the full working of the Holy Spirit in expression of fruit and gifts and ministries as in New Testament times for the edifying of the body of Christ."

It will be noted that the resolution stresses the Pentecostal dimension of the reason-for-being of the Assemblies of God. It also provides a foundation for the *Declaration at St. Louis.*

The Plan of Advance

Prayerful consideration of the Scripture and the history of the Movement made the Committee increasingly aware of the importance of spiritual renewal as a necessary preparation for evangelistic outreach. The Committee recommended that the first year of the Five-Year Plan of Advance should be a year of revival emphasis. Only as the Movement brings itself into a fresh relationship to God will it be able to evangelize in the power of the Spirit with the accompanying supernatural signs. Only as the Movement brings itself into revived relationship to God will it be able to respond to the full working of the Holy Spirit in expression of fruit and gifts and ministries as in New Testament times for the edifying of the body of Christ.

The Committee on Advance believes that a clearly understood mission will motivate a definite plan of action. A five-year plan of implementation thus was presented on three afternoons of the Council on Evangelism as "The Report of the Committee on Advance."

Spiritual renewal, a clearly defined sense of mission, an intensive plan of action—these are the basic ingredients of the Plan of Advance as the Assemblies of God mobilizes to meet the challenge of the present hour.

EVENING MESSAGES

THE MISSION OF THE CHURCH

A Message Given Monday Night, August 26, 1968

T. F. ZIMMERMAN

INSCRIBED ON THE ARCHIVES BUILDING in Washington, D. C., is the very significant statement, "History is the prologue to the future." How true it is that every historical event has great significance for the future—either for good, or for evil. As we assemble for this Council on Evangelism, we are making history. It is our prayer that this historical event will be the prologue to the greatest Spirit-empowered fulfillment of mission our beloved Fellowship has ever accomplished.

One of the historical convocations of the Old Testament has great significance for us today. Just as Joshua and all Israel were gathered at the Jordan River to receive marching orders from God (Joshua 1:1-9), so we are gathered to hear God speak to us in a critical hour.

The first important lesson we can learn from the message Israel received is that God's people must

Go Forward

In Joshua 1:2 we read God's words to Joshua: "Now therefore arise, go over this Jordan, thou, and all this people, unto the land which I do give to them."

As we consider Israel's history, it is easy to see that the Israelites came to various plateaus in their relationship with God. As they encamped east of the Jordan River, they had come farther than ever before in the journey God had planned

for them. But Israel needed to remind itself that plateaus of achievement are not permanent stopping places. They are but steppingstones or springboards to greater accomplishments for God.

At an earlier time after Israel had compassed Mount Seir many days, God recognized the indication of complacency and spoke from heaven saying, "Ye have compassed this mountain long enough" (Deuteronomy 2:3). God was telling them it was time to go forward.

Plateaus are enjoyable experiences. They provide opportunities to look back and see the ascending levels to which God has brought His people. But plateaus of achievement can also be dangerous. God's people sin when they are content with past achievements and lose the burning desire to move forward.

This danger is illustrated by Israel's experience at Kadesh-barnea. After God had commanded Israel to go forward and enter the Promised Land, they flagrantly refused to obey. We all know the terrible consequence of their smugness and complacency. Instead of moving forward as an army terrible with banners, they perished in the wilderness. It was not until a new generation came along that they moved forward as God had commanded.

There is nothing more tragic than to see a group of God's people who have failed to keep in step with God. They may still have a form, but they no longer know the power of God.

A fable has been told of a flock of geese that lived in a barnyard. At regular occasions they would gather in a corner of the yard, and one of the eloquent ganders would speak of the greatness of their history. He would tell of the great exploits of their forefathers who flew thousands of miles. He would eulogize the Creator who had given the geese the urge to migrate and the unerring instinct to find their way through the trackless sky. He spoke of their stamina which had become legendary. As the geese listened to spellbinding accounts, they would nod their heads and even verbally indicate their appreciation for the accounts of their ancestoral accomplishments. They did everything proud geese should do—but they did not fly.

Each time when the meeting ended, they went back to the security of the barnyard where they enjoyed the good corn provided for them. You see, they had become so dependent upon the material provisions of the farmer that they had lost their ability to respond to their God-given instinct to soar through the heavens. God grant that the time will never come when our Fellowship substitutes happy memories for action.

The tendency to be content with past achievements is undoubtedly one reason throughout Israel's history God urged them to move forward. This is why it became necessary for God to command the new generation to cross the Jordan and possess the land. It would have been too easy for them to content themselves with a borderland experience!

As we compare the history of our Fellowship with Israel's experiences, we see points of similarity. There was persecution in early days. The time came when we needed organization. We have always enjoyed anointed leadership and worship in the freedom of the Spirit.

In my message I can only refer briefly to the way in which God has led our Fellowship. A comprehensive paper entitled, "Why the Plan of Advance," has been prepared which provides considerable detail. You will want to read this carefully. In essence this document outlines the steps which have brought us to this great Council. It tells why we believe God is asking our Fellowship to advance. You will find that the basic reason the Assemblies of God exists is to minister to the Lord, minister to the saints, and minister to the world.

Even though our Fellowship has much to be thankful for, let us never get the idea that God has brought us to our present plateau to termi-nate progress—His command is, "Go forward."

The second great lesson we can learn from God's message to Joshua is that His people must always

Go Forward Scripturally

In Joshua 1:8 we read these important words: "This book of the law shall not depart out of thy mouth; but thou shalt meditate therein day and night, that thou mayest observe to do according to all that is written therein: for then thou shalt make thy way prosperous, and then thou shalt have good success." In this command to Joshua Israel learned that God was not only interested in *what* the children of Israel did, but also in *how* they did it.

At the Jordan River God provided the pattern for progress as He had for others in earlier days. To Noah He gave very specific instructions concerning the building of an ark (Genesis 6:14-16). When God told Moses to build a tabernacle, He said: "According to all that I show thee, after the pattern of the tabernacle, and the pattern of all the instruments thereof, even so shall ye make it" (Exodus 25:9).

Now as Israel was commanded to go forward across the Jordan, God made it clear it should be in accordance with the *Book* (Joshua 1:8). This was the *only* way to make progress.

During the past months much thought has been given by many from across our Fellowship to what we feel to be God's will concerning a greater forward movement. We have asked for suggestions from pastors, from evangelists, from missionaries, from educators, and from laymen. These have all spoken from hearts full of the Word and the Spirit. It seems God has been speaking to many saying, "Go forward according to the Book."

After thousands of hours of careful study and seeking the face of God, it became clear to the Committee on Advance that the primary mission of our Fellowship is threefold. It includes: ministry to the Lord, ministry to the saints, and ministry to the world.

Let us think first about the importance of ministry to the Lord. As we read the Scriptures, there is frequent reference to ministry to the Lord. In the turbulent days of the first-century Church Luke indicated that the believers "ministered unto the Lord" (Acts 13:2). In the distressing days of Israel's transition from rule by judges to rule by kings, Samuel ministered unto the Lord (1 Samuel 2:18; 3:1). This is what Mary, the mother of Jesus, was doing as she worshiped in the Magnificat (Luke 2:46-56), and I think this is what Mary of Bethany was doing when she sat at the feet of Jesus (Luke 10:38-42).

These people were not ministering or working *for* the Lord: they were ministering *to* the Lord. It is so easy to continually ask God for favors, but possibly a very neglected quality in our lives is worship, praise, and communion. How God must long for our ministry to Him.

This ministry can be illustrated by an elderly lady who was ushered into the presence of Abraham Lincoln. Very kindly the President asked, "What can I do for you, madam?" After she had placed a covered basket on the table, she said, "Mr. President, I have not come here today to ask any favor for myself or anyone else. I heard that you were very fond of cookies, and I came to bring you this basket of cookies!"

It is said that tears trickled down the face of the President, and he was speechless for a moment. Then he said, "My good woman, your thoughtful and unselfish deed greatly moves me. Thousands have come into this office since I became President, and you are the first to come asking no favor." Without doubt, God is longing for believers to minister unto Him as His people have done in earlier days. If we would move forward scripturally, we must be faithful in ministering unto the Lord.

As we give consideration to the mission of the church, it is important to consider also the church's ministry to the saints. Once new converts have come into the fold, there is a definite obligation to help them "grow in grace, and in the knowledge of our Lord and Saviour Jesus Christ" (2 Peter 3:18).

The Bible has a great deal to say about ministry to the saints. The ministry gifts of Christ—apostles, prophets, evangelists, pastors and teachers are "for the perfecting of the saints" (Ephesians 4:11, 12). The gifts of the Spirit are for the profit of the entire body (1 Corinthians 12:7). It is because ministry to the saints is important that Paul charged Timothy to "preach the Word" (2 Timothy 4:2). And this is why elders were admonished to "feed the flock of God" (1 Peter 5:2). If we would move forward scripturally, we must be faithful in ministering to the saints.

The third aspect of our mission involves ministry to the world. May God help us to get a new vision of its importance. The church has an obligation to win the lost to Christ. This was the mission of Christ. He said, "The Son of man is come to seek and to save that which is lost." Scripture makes it clear that as the Father sent Christ, so He sends us. The Great Commission indicates that we are to make disciples of all nations. God has not sent the church to make the prodigal comfortable in the far country, but to bring the sinner back to God.

This discipling of all nations must be done everywhere and at all times. It must be done with people of all ages. It must be done now, for the longer they live the more difficult it seems to be for them to surrender to Christ. Dr. Robert G. Lee once observed: after age 25, one in 10,000 is saved; after age 35, one in 50,000; after age 45, one in 200,000; after age 55, one in 300,000; after age 65, one in 500,000; and after age 75, only one in 700,000 is saved.

When we think of the large percentage of our population made up of young people, we can realize the importance of our mission to the world. If they are not won now, it will become increasingly difficult to win them to Christ later. It is of greatest urgency that we be completely faithful in our ministry to the world.

This then is the mission of our fellowship: ministry to the Lord, to the saints, and to the world.

As we consider the tremendous mission of the church we are overwhelmed with a frightening sense of inadequacy. In ourselves we are not sufficient for this awesome task. But thank God for the assurance that with Him all things are possible. It is because we recognize the immensity of our threefold mission and because we recognize our continuing need of God's power that we are designating 1969 as "The Year of Revival." Let us earnestly pray that God will enable us to so yield ourselves to the Spirit that He will be able to move us on to greater victories. Only the power of the Holy Spirit will make us equal to our great mission in life. How encouraging to know we will always find the Spirit's power adequate!

The important thing for us to keep in mind as we pursue our mission is that we must always make ourselves available to the Holy Spirit. This great truth is illustrated by an episode in the life of the great preacher, Dr. J. H. Jowett. On one occasion when he wished to preach on the text, "The wind bloweth where it listeth," he decided to go down to the harbor to consult the sailors about the actions of the wind.

He approached a sailor and asked, "Can you tell me something about the wind?"

The sailor looked as if he thought the minister was demented and responded with a positive, "No."

"But you have been sailing the seas all your life; you must know something about the wind," Dr. Jowett continued.

The sailor said, "I repeat, sir, that I know nothing about the wind. All I know is that when I feel the wind blowing, I raise my sails and I am moved on to my port."

This was enough for Dr. Jowett. He hurried back to his study. He had his message.

The Holy Spirit like a rushing wind is moving all about us. May God help us to raise our sails to catch the power of the heavenly wind which will move us forward in this hour.

The third lesson we can learn from God's message to Joshua is that we must

Go Forward Courageously

God said to Joshua: "Be strong and of a good courage; be not afraid, neither be thou dismayed: for the Lord thy God is with thee whithersoever thou goest" (Joshua 1:9).

God was not unmindful of the problems Israel would face in going forward. He told them courage would be needed. God knew in advance about problems like the swollen Jordan River, walled cities like Jericho, internal failures like that of Achan, crafty enemies like the Gibeonites, and enemy alliances such as Adonizedec formed. God told Israel to go forward anyway. The God of Israel is not the victim of circumstances—He is the Master.

The Bible indicates that as long as Israel moved forward in faith and with courage, they were victorious. The only thing that could defeat them was their own sin and doubt.

Today God is aware that there will be problems ahead for those who want to serve Him faithfully. People have a tendency to look at circumstances and say it can't be done. But this is an hour to keep looking to the God of the supernatural.

History teaches that the church has always been glorious when it looked to God in simple faith—big problems meant big victories. When threatened believers said, "We cannot but speak the things which we have seen and heard" (Acts 4:20). When in prison they sang songs (Acts 16:25). When martyred they forgave (Acts 7:60). Under the most severe persecution and opposition, they could sing with Martin Luther:

A mighty fortress is our God
A bulwark never failing. . . .
And though this world, with devils filled,
Should threaten to undo us,

We will not fear, for God hath willed
His truth to triumph through us.

In 1857 the English historian, Thomas Macaulay, wrote about America, "Your republic will be fearfully plundered and laid waste by barbarians in the twentieth century as the Roman Empire was in the fifth, with this difference; the Huns and Vandals who ravaged the Roman Empire came from without, and your Huns and Vandals will have been engendered within your own country by your own institutions."

In some respects this more than one-hundred-year-old prediction is coming to pass in our day, and if there ever was an hour for a courageous church to rise to the occasion, that hour is now. Only the gospel can solve the desperate problems on every hand, and we must proclaim it in its fullness.

Like Israel we can go forward courageously because it is the Lord who commands it (Joshua 1:9). Our command is the Great Commission. Our responsibility is to go "into all the world, and preach the gospel to every creature" (Mark 16:15).

Like Israel we can go forward courageously because of the presence of the Lord (Joshua 1:9). After giving the Great Commission, Jesus said, "Lo, I am with you alway, even unto the end of the world" (Matthew 28:20). It doesn't make any difference what circumstances we meet as long as we know we are doing God's will and His presence is with us.

Conclusion

After God had given His instructions to Israel, there were two things they needed to do. These are given in Joshua 3:5. First, they had to sanctify themselves—that is, completely set themselves apart to do God's bidding. The second thing they had to do was to start looking for miracles. They were told, "Tomorrow the Lord will do wonders among you."

This is a dark time in the world's history, but there have been other dark times. And when God found dedicated persons, He was able to save entire nations from revolution and destruction.

The days of John Wesley were notably dark days. In the book *John Wesley, the Burning Heart*, A. Skevington Wood indicates the nation was on the verge of moral disintegration. National leaders lived in undisguised adultery. The state of matrimony was ridiculed by young ladies and young men alike. Entertainment was indecent and lewd. The popular taste in literature was completely demoralized. The nation had given itself over to the twin evils of drunkenness and gambling. There was widespread indulgence in cruel and degrading sports. There was general indifference to the things of God and lack of passion in the pulpit.

It was in such a dark hour that God called John Wesley. But Wesley found the power of God sufficient to bring a mighty revival to England which spared it from a revolution such as France suffered.

Today, conditions in our beloved country parallel some of the darkest times of human history. Sin of every kind is prevalent. Anarchy stalks the land. Only God knows what the future holds unless America has a great spiritual awakening.

Some will look to circumstances and say conditions are so bad there is nothing the church can do. Others will look to God and hear Him say, "Rededicate yourselves and I will do wonders among you." We have come to St. Louis to place ourselves at God's disposal for a great revival and ingathering of souls throughout our fellowship. Let us pray that this Council will mark the beginning of the greatest moving of God's Spirit the Church has known.

THE MANDATE OF THE CHURCH

A Message Given Tuesday Night, August 27, 1968

PAUL LOWENBERG

THE MANDATE OF THE CHURCH is generally considered in the words of Jesus: "Go ye into all the world, and preach the gospel to every creature." Mark recorded it: "He that believeth and is baptized shall be saved; but he that believeth not shall be damned." In Acts 1:8 it is stated: "Ye shall receive power, after that the Holy Ghost is come upon you: and ye shall be witnesses unto me both in Jerusalem, and in all Judea, and in Samaria, and unto the uttermost part of the earth." In John 20:21 Jesus said to His disciples, "As my Father hath sent me, even so send I you." This is the Great Commission—the mandate of the Church.

Webster says a mandate is "a formal order from a superior court to an inferior one: an authoritative command; an injunction or an order."

Our mandate is not a matter of interpretation; it is a matter of total obedience to the last will and testament of the Lord Jesus Christ. The mandate does not actually reside in the Church. It resides in the people of the Church. Individuals must hear the mandate; individuals must obey the mandate. God does not anoint churches; He anoints people. He does not call churches; He calls people. He does not send the church; He sends people who have heard the call of God, who are willing to obey God and pay the price.

The total earthly purpose of the New Testa-ment Church is summed up in these words, "Go ye into all the world, and preach the gos-pel." If we stop short in this path, we fail to justify our existence. Christ asks nothing more, but He accepts nothing less.

It is a little difficult to ascertain which part of the Great Commission the Church is fulfilling in joining in protest marches, civil disobedience, political lobbying, advising the United Nations, and participating in riots that have destroyed life and property. Is this the role Christ has planned for His Church in these last days? Are these the credentials of the New Testament Church bought with the blood of Christ, sealed with the Holy Ghost of God, given a mandate to take the gospel of the bleeding Son of God to the ends of the earth? The Great Commission of our Saviour is very explicit. We are told what to preach. I believe that we as individuals, as pastors, as leaders are here with the fervent prayer that we will hear the Lord of the Church speaking to us as He did to His disciples on the Mount of Olives, just prior to His ascension.

We are known as a praying and a preaching Movement. We had to preach. When the people did not come into the buildings to hear us, we went out on the street corners, into the fields, down to the lakes and beaches to tell them of Jesus Christ. Oh, that we might recapture the throb, the thrill, the drive of that anointing of the Holy Spirit! Oh, that we might hear Him tonight as He says, "Ye shall be witnesses . . . in Jerusalem, in Judea, in Samaria, and unto the uttermost part of the earth."

"Jerusalem" did the Master say? Not too long before they heard Him say, "Oh, Jerusalem, Jerusalem, thou that killest the prophets, and stonest them which are sent unto thee." Now He says, "Boys, it's back to Jerusalem; back to the city of blood; back to the city of intrigue; back to the city with its explosive religious bigotry and seering sectarianism; back to Jerusalem with its garden and its bitter cup."

Brethren, to Jerusalem! Preach the gospel of pardon, of forgiveness, of reconciliation, of restoration, of healing, of deliverance, of power, of anointing, of hope, and heaven.

Unto Judea, with its purer and gentler people, with its refinement. Preach the gospel—how that Christ died for our sins according to the Scriptures, was buried, and rose again the third day, according to the Scriptures.

Unto Samaria, gentlemen, with its riots and racial strife, with its slums and its ghettos, its immorality and sin, its poverty and filth. Go into the hedges and byways and tell them the Master has prepared a great supper and invites the poor, the maimed, the halt, and the blind.

And then, gentlemen, go unto the uttermost parts of the earth. Let neither sea nor mountain, languages, customs, color nor race, suffering nor sacrifice hinder you. Go preach wherever humans go—the highways where they walk, the ditches where they lie, the slums where they rot—and preach to them as your Saviour preached.

The entire life of our Lord Jesus Christ is epitomized in the terse language of John 4:4: "He must needs go through Samaria." Why must the Saviour go through Samaria? The total passion of Christ was motivated by a divine must. Love compels; love constrains; love calls. Love does not seek the easy and the popular route. "He must needs go through Samaria."

Heaven must meet hell that day. The holiest of all must meet the most defiled; the divine supply must meet the human need. From that personal encounter comes this jubilant testimony: "Come, see a man, which told me all things that ever I did." And Samaria comes to see, to listen, and to believe. Glory to God! The Head of the Church practices what He preaches. When He says, "Go," He Himself leads the way.

Did you ever stop and think what the disciples were doing during this time? They had gone downtown to buy bread; but instead of talking to the merchant about the bread of life,

I think they were haggling over the high prices and were so busy driving a hard bargain, they forgot to talk to the old storekeeper about Jesus Christ. An alien, defiled, and debauched woman brought the whole town—but His chosen, privileged, highly honored disciples brought no one!

J. Philip Hogan, the executive director of our Foreign Missions Department, jarred me when he said to the missionaries of the Assemblies of God and those of us at the School of Missions: "Sometime ago a leading national minister was asked by a visiting missions board executive which missionary was the most effective personal soul winner. The national leader said, 'Sir, I never think of a missionary as a personal soul winner.'"

We talk about great preachers, great orators, great theologians, gifted teachers, good pastors, but very seldom do people refer to us as good soul winners. Preaching the gospel and winning souls must be synonymous. These are not two aspects of the ministry. Brethren, they are inseparable.

If we follow Jesus Christ, we soon discover He was always preaching to win men to God. He fired no random shots. He didn't preach on Sunday morning because it was Sunday morning. He preached with one objective in view: to acquaint men and women with His loving heavenly Father.

While Jesus Christ preached to tremendous audiences, yet He never forgot the value of an individual soul. Check the record and see how many chapters in the Book of John are devoted to one soul. In chapter 2 you have an anonymous couple of lovers who got married. That does not seem to be so important; but Jesus wanted them to remember their wedding day with pleasure, so for one couple He performed a special miracle so their marriage could get off on the right foot. In John 3 one Nicodemus; in John 8 one woman taken in adultery; in chapter 9 one boy born blind; in John 11 one Lazarus. We read of one Bartimaeus, one Zacchaeus, one woman with an issue of blood, one blind man, one leper. Again and again and again the King of kings and Lord of lords turned His attention to individuals. These were the objects of His search and of His love.

Nowhere is the passion of Jesus more distinctly stated than in Luke 15, where we have one parable in four sections.

"What man of you, having a hundred sheep, if he lose one of them, doth not leave the ninety and nine . . . and go after that which is lost?"

Just one absent; ninety-nine percent of the enrollment here! That deserves headlines in *The Pentecostal Evangel*. Stop the presses! Ninety-nine percent of our entire enrollment was in church today! But the Master Shepherd said, "No, I cannot be at ease until that one stray sheep is brought back again. Ninety-nine percent is not enough. I must have a hundred percent; that absent one is worthy of me going to the canyon, out among the rocks and the cactus and the heat of the day and the cold of the night." He said, "I must find him."

The passion of Jesus Christ is wrapped up in the Great Commission which He passes on to you and to me. In the canyon, in the gulleys, in the ditches, in the sewers, in the beautiful halls and offices of the banks and businesses are sheep who have gone astray. Our commission is: "Find them!"

Brethren, would you send a report to *The Pentecostal Evangel* and say, "Folks, rejoice with me; we had a revival; one saved." The Master thinks enough of one sheep that He causes the choirs of heaven to sing, "One sheep has been brought home."

In the same story He says there was a coin lost in the house. A lady had ten pieces, but she lost one. The story is so rich in symbolism. The coin was out of circulation, paid no bills, bought no bread. It was genuine silver—the king's superscription was upon it—but it was lost, valueless. She lights a candle; she gets a broom; she opens up the windows. For a little while that house is a scene of excitement. One lady is trying to find a piece of lost silver.

There is a worthier coin lost tonight. Where? In the house. This coin was not out on the mountain. It was not in the canyon. This coin was lost in the home.

It was made in the image of God, capable of being the tabernacle of the Holy Ghost, a witness to others. Yet it was lost in the house, in the Sunday school department, in the CA's, in the choir, in the young adult class—lost.

While we complain about not reaching the masses, the ones upon which Jesus put a priority come to our churches every Sunday morning. The church is full of people like Colonel Sanders featured by C. M. Ward's book—church members, devout people, going to hell without Jesus Christ. Somehow we haven't gotten the message to these people that they must be born again. Brethren, it is time to light the candle!

In this convention the emphasis is on the Word of God—a lamp unto our feet and a light

to our pathway. Let's get back to Bible evangelism, Bible preaching, Bible teaching, a Bible kind of worship. This is the light that will illuminate the whole house.

Let's take the brooms of sanctification; let's get the cobwebs and the dust of multiplied thousands of pieces of machinery out of the way. In the dust and in the cobwebs souls lie buried and lost while we busy ourselves with a lot of machinery.

She opened up the windows. Let's let in a breath of heaven's fresh air; let's let the breezes of the Holy Ghost once more sweep through our sanctuary. Let's open the blinds and let the sunshine in until some lost, dying, distressed, troubled soul says, "There is something in this church giving life and light and salvation. This is where I am going to go."

In the same chapter Jesus told about the prodigal son. There were really two prodigals: one was lost in the beautiful orchard and the other was lost in the hog pen. But both were lost. The father invites one in; he goes to meet the other.

Gentlemen, have we forgotten that men without Christ are lost even though they are our friends, our financiers, salesmen, storekeepers, postmen—they are lost unless they are born again. Have we witnessed to them?

Have we lost the art of winning souls while cultivating the art of good preaching? This Council might not be as necessary if we had all been about our Master's business. We have lost that keen cutting edge of the Holy Spirit. We have lost that anointing, that burden, that concern, that passion the Master vouchsafed to us so long ago.

Our world is dying; shall we settle for the status quo? Shall we excuse our ineffectiveness? Shall we succumb to the fatalism of our day? Or shall we get hold of ourselves?

We need to recover the spirit of the day of the storefront, the brush arbor, the upstairs meeting, the street corner. Since we have moved to our air-conditioned sanctuaries with our beautifully robed choirs, we need more of the Spirit of God now than we did then. Oh, God, revive us! Oh, God, set us on fire! God, restore the years that the locust, the caterpillar, the cankerworm, and the palmerworm have eaten.

We have preached that there would be a falling away and lukewarmness, and people have believed it and have started practicing it!

I listen to our religious historians when they say history records the rise and the fall of every major evangelical denomination. History has told us where we came from, but history cannot dictate the future! Oh, let's get out of this rut of being a slave to history. Read words like this, "It shall come to pass in the last days, saith the Lord, I will pour out of my Spirit upon all flesh." If we would preach that as fervently and as zealously and with the same conviction that we preach history, we would not have to worry about the falling away in our churches. The only things that would be falling would be the power of the Holy Spirit, and the kingdom of the devil!

When Dr. Goodall accepted the pastorate of Calvary Methodist Church in New York City a good many years ago, he asked his board, "Gentlemen, when have you last had a revival here?"

They said, "We haven't had a revival in years. In fact, we believe that the age of revivals is passed."

Old Dr. Goodall looked at his board and said, "Brethren, we are either going to have a revival at Calvary Methodist Church or we are going to have a funeral in the parsonage."

When men become this desperate, something is going to happen. When we are willing to secure a revival with blood, with sweat and tears, I believe our God will still pour out the Holy Ghost.

Jesus said, "The kingdom of heaven suffereth violence, and the violent take it by force." Violence is everywhere—on radio, on TV, in some pulpits. They march the streets; they burn our cities; they destroy and kill; they spread hatred; they desecrate our flag. But where is the contrasting violence—the violence of agonizing intercession, the violence of personal heart-searching, the violence of white-hot prayers from a burdened and broken heart? Where is the violence of a passionate love? Where is the violence of the prayer room? Where is that prayer, "I'll not let You go; I'll not let You go!"

We must have revival. We must have a moving of the Spirit of God. We will not settle for anything less than a mighty explosion of the power of God.

Dr. Jowett said, "When we cease to bleed, we cease to bless." Let me ask you: Is there blood in our sermon preparation? Is there blood in our prayers? Is there blood in our preaching? Is there blood in our altar calls? When we no longer bleed, we lose the fellowship of the atoning Blood.

Christ died in Jerusalem; His servants must die on many fields. The sufferings need a herald; the story needs a teller; the gospel requires an evangelist; Gethsemane must be repeated ten thousand times over. Golgatha must become an experience in the life of everyone who carries a credential card if he would be worthy of the high calling of God. Christ can only multiply Himself through you and me. The spirit of Calvary must be duplicated in ten thousands of God's workers.

"As the Father hath sent me, even so send I you," He said. He came weeping; shall we follow Him dry-eyed? He came in abject poverty; shall we seek prosperity and affluence? He came to suffer and die; shall we seek security and ease?

Once more, brethren, the mandate is clear. We have no choice. The Commander says, "Go . . . preach . . . win."

Paul said, "Woe is unto me, if I preach not the gospel." He did not say, "Woe is unto me if I preach not." He said, "Woe is unto me, if I preach not *the gospel*." There is a lot of preaching that is not gospel. May God revive in us a consuming burden for Bible preaching, for Bible revivals that move men to God.

The end is in sight. We must redouble our efforts; we must renew our consecration; we must revive our zeal; we must hasten the return of our Lord. Every sign points to His soon coming.

Brethren, let us not count wages, working conditions, or hours; there is a harvest out there that needs to be garnered. As we are anointed by the Holy Ghost, filled with a consuming passion for a lost and dying world and an intense desire to fulfill the Great Commission, one day we will be able to sing:

"Thou dying Lamb, Thy precious blood
Shall never lose its power,
Till all the ransomed church of God
Are saved, to sin no more."

THE MESSAGE OF THE CHURCH

A Message Given Wednesday Night, August 28, 1968

GENE SCOTT

I TURN IN THE OLD TESTAMENT to 2 Samuel 7. God's Word has been the theme of this Council. I have often thought that God has enough to say to us that if He takes the trouble in His Word to say something more than once, I had better pay particular attention to that. So I have learned to major on what I have come to call God's repeatables—the things He says more than once in action or word. I would like to camp tonight for a few moments on an oft-repeated action of God as a prelude to stating that which is the theme, "The Message of the Church." I begin with David, but it is the repetition that drives the thought home.

David is at the peak of his career, and God sends a message to him and reminds him of his beginning. The prophet Nathan is to say, "I took thee from the sheepcote, from following the sheep, to be ruler over my people, over Israel: and I was with thee whithersoever thou wentest, and have cut off all thine enemies out of thy sight, and have made thee a great name, like unto the name of the great men that are in the earth" (2 Samuel 7:8, 9).

David, considering from whence he had come and the place to which God had lifted him, said, "Who am I, O Lord God? and what is my house, that thou hast brought me hitherto?" (2 Samuel 7:18).

If it had been my responsibility to pick a leader for Israel, I would not have picked David as he followed the sheep.

If I were on a pulpit committee, I would not have picked Elijah as my preacher. Judging by outward appearance, he had no formal training to qualify him as a spokesman for God. But God picked him, and Elijah was a man who prayed, and it quit raining. He prayed again, and the rain came down. Prior to that he prayed, and the widow's son was raised from the dead. He prayed, and the fire fell from heaven. Of all those that God might have picked to be with the Lord on the Mount of Transfiguration, He picks Elijah to stand there with Moses. God's ways are not my ways.

Look at Amos. Amos was a herdsman and a tender of sycamore trees by trade. And again, if I were on a committee for picking a preacher, I probably would have passed Amos. No formal training, nothing that stands out in the natural. But God picked him. Amos will tell you more about God's heart in regard to sin than any other man in the Old Testament.

Look at Jeremiah in the twentieth chapter of his book. He gets so upset he curses the day he was born and is sorry he ever became a prophet. In the eighteenth chapter he gets so mad at those who oppose God that he prays God will destroy every one of them. And mark this, he prayed that God would not even forgive them for what they have done. You would boot old Jeremiah out of your pulpit, but God picked him to write part of the eternal Word of God.

In my mind, I say pick a fellow who is master

of the language, a grammarian, with finesse, with a vocabulary that enables him to express himself. But God picked a bunch of fishermen who slaughtered the Aramaic and did worse with the Greek.

Whom did He choose to tell the story of heaven? John. And just about everyone agrees he was the most limited in vocabulary; a great logician—but to describe the beauties of heaven? Again and again human judgment might determine another person, but God confounds my judgment and picks them one after another and places them in prominence in His service.

Let you and me sit as the judges on the qualifications of the Lord's disciples as he picks them. On their shoulders will rest the entire future of the Kingdom of heaven. To them He will give all that He comes to bring. My mind says, "Pick the best." So let us help Him pick them.

Here comes one; he smells like fish. Everytime he opens his mouth, you can tell he is not very learned; he is unstable in his nature. One moment he swears he will never betray his Lord if they kill him; shortly thereafter he denies Him three times. When things go wrong for Peter, he runs back to his fish boat. He can't join the band.

The next two are high-tempered. They too smell like fish; their language gives away their lack of training, and on top of that they are self-centered and selfish; they want the best seats in the Kingdom, and the rascals don't have courage to ask for it themselves—but send their mother to do it. So out go James and John.

The next decision is easy. The fellow's a cheat. He makes his living charging an excess on the taxes and that from his own brethren! Out goes Matthew.

The next fellow wants to fight. He is a Zealot. He lives to fight the Romans. And when he hears Jesus teach turn the other cheek, and render to Caesar that which is Caesar's, he goes running off after another revolutionary looking for a fight. Out goes Simon.

Not everybody will appreciate Thomas the way I did. I am a preacher's kid who watched my dad healed from a coma of rheumatic fever in 1936. God raised him up, and I have known other miracles. But during the period of my college life I couldn't help it because I had some questions that needed to be answered, and I didn't find it easy to believe everything the way some thought I should. During that period I thanked God for the choice of Thomas.

Now go through that entire list and see that it is not just something of interest but a repeti-tion written in God's Book—God confounding my judgment in the choice of those He uses.

I am not suggesting that God prefers the ignorant or that He prefers the unlearned and the "have-nots." In the days of the Old Testament Moses was learned in all the wisdom of Egypt; the apostle Paul was needed to do the task that God assigned to him. But I am saying that the key which unlocks a place or a position in God's program is not to be found in a commonalty of natural training, skills, or attitudes.

I backed up in God's Book and I began to look at every one of these lives again, trying to find a common denominator, a thread that would weave them all on the same line, something each had in common. I didn't find it in the natural area, but I did find it in the spiritual dimension, the way in which a man relates himself to God.

In First and Second Samuel you can see again and again that little extra plus dimension in David. The Lord said; David went and did. There were thousands in David's day who kept all the rituals, some arising at daylight, listening to the Pentateuch being recited. There were thousands who kept all of the rules, and there were thousands who could articulate the creed; but David went a little farther to a living relationship with an invisible person—God. That is the note written into every one of his Psalms.

What made Elijah different? Read 1 Kings 17. See Elijah the Tishbite standing in the court of the king. He says, "As the Lord God of Israel liveth. . . ." There is the creed. Here is the plus factor: ". . . in whose presence I stand." Living awareness of God as a Person.

What made the disciples different? Jesus passed by and said, "Follow Me." And to use Mark's words, "They straightway forsook their nets, and followed him" (Mark 1:18). Look at the starting point of those disciples we referred to in the third chapter. "And he ordained twelve, that they should be with him" (Mark 3:14). Watch that word *with*. Years later, praying in John 17, Jesus says, "While I was with them in the world, I kept them" (John 17:12).

A Person is at the heart of Christianity. *Christian* literally means "a follower of Christ." It is a relationship with a Person.

The Word was made flesh and dwelt among them. The picture of *dwelt* in Greek is to pitch a tent and move into it. That invisible One who was of the same essence and who could tell us all we needed to know about God, came out of the invisible dimension to pitch a tent in human flesh and walk the roads of history. He told out in word and deed and action what God is like and then left and sent the Spirit back.

The heart of Christianity is a relationship with a Person. "And this is life eternal, that they might know thee the only true God, and Jesus Christ, whom thou hast sent" (John 17:3).

There is a generation rejecting Christ, and they have never met Him. Experts on Christianity, disillusioned with disciples—but do they know Him?

Many pastors are worried about the message for this generation. So many questions on science, so many questions on psychology, so many questions on this and that. I say, the message has not changed. Preach Christ and Him crucified. This is life eternal, that a man know the one true God and Jesus Christ whom He has sent!

As ministers in today's world we can be forgiven if we are not the town's greatest expert on science, on history, on psychiatry, and on counseling. But I doubt if we can be forgiven unless we are trying to be the best expert on what the Word reveals about Christ.

Bond Bowman once said Jesus was in Jerusalem and He saw a blind man and He spit on some mud and made a little mud patty and healed a man. Now those who saw this act built a spit-and-mudball healing church, and they started doing what Jesus did.

Jesus went on to another section of Jerusalem. He saw another blind man. He touched the blind man, and he was healed. So there was the touch-and-heal church.

He went to another section of Jerusalem, saw another blind man, and He spoke, and the man was healed. So there was the speak-and-be-healed church.

They were all doing what they had seen Jesus do until those speak-and-be-healed people heard about the touch-and-be-healed people. Then they forgot all about blind eyes and went into the arguments of showing that you had to speak to bring healing instead of touching to have the healing.

Let me ask you what you think a sermon is. Do you know where the word *sermon* comes from? It comes from the Latin word *sermo*. And the Latin Bible opens John's Gospel with these words, "In the beginning was the *sermo;* the *sermo* was with God; the *sermo* was God.... The *sermo* was made flesh and dwelt among us."

Christ is the sermon. There is a world of difference between preaching Christ and some homiletical oration. Our mission in today's world is to preach Christ. And the Holy Spirit experience that we hold so dear and real is given for one purpose—to testify of Christ" (John 15:26).

Secondly, this world today needs to *feel* this message. A. W. Tozer has said that this generation is so afraid of its emotions in religious expressions that it reminds him of a people that throw a cordon of policemen around the graveyard for fear they will have a political rally.

I don't practice the presence of God; God is present no matter what I practice. But what I have learned to practice is an awareness of His presence. And there are those times when the Spirit moves in and you know the Lord is present because you feel something.

That which is the message of the Assemblies of God is the reality of the Person of the Spirit which can be known in experience. We need in this world to hear the message and we need to feel it as the oldtimers knew what it was to be raised from the deathbed.

But thirdly, our mission in today's world is to let this message be *seen*. That which is missing in today's pragmatic society is that glimpse Peter talked about when he said in 1 Peter 5 to the elders: "Let them be ensamples to the flock." The word *ensamples* is a picture of an imprint left after a blow has been struck. Our mission is to let the beauty of Jesus be seen in us.

Last December I caught a glimpse from the pages of gospel history of that which has done more to transform my life than anything that has ever happened to me. I went again in Rome to that little hole in the ground that was Paul's prison. It is beneath the street, across from the old Roman Forum. I went down in that hole, came out, and asked Al Perna to take me back the next day. I went down in it, stood there, and I read 2 Timothy, which Paul wrote from that prison. "I know *whom* I have believed,"—not what I believed, not where I have been or what I have done; "I know whom I have believed, and am persuaded that he is able to keep that which I have committed unto him against that day" (2 Timothy 1:12). "I have fought a good fight, I have finished my course, I have kept the faith: henceforth there is laid up for me a crown of righteousness, which the Lord, the righteous judge, shall give at that day" (2 Timothy 4:7, 8).

I had gone to Athens, looked at the ruins. Paul left Athens without much accomplished in this city, determining to preach Christ and Him crucified. I stood there one sundown and looked at the Acropolis. It was great in Paul's day. Now just a bunch of ruins.

As the sun went down, I reflected that the sun has never set in this day on the words that Paul wrote: "Who shall separate us from the love of Christ? shall tribulation, or distress, or persecution, or famine, or nakedness, or peril, or sword? Nay, in all these things we are more than conquerors...." How? "Through him" a Person again! "...through him that loved us. For I am persuaded, that neither death, nor life, nor angels, nor principalities, nor powers, nor things present, nor things to come, nor height, nor depth, nor any other creature, shall be able to separate us from the love of God, which is in Christ Jesus our Lord" (Romans 8:35, 37-39).

I looked at the ruins of Corinth. I walked out to the Bema Rock and remembered Paul sitting there had his eyes on our Blessed Hope. And I wept unashamedly.

I have complained about getting tired; I have complained about other things; but I have never gone through what Paul went through. Standing in the darkness I said, "God, help me never again to just pray, 'Lord, help me preach.'" But I prayed, "God, help me to be the ensample that those who look at me get a little glimpse of what I see in Paul—a dedication that in a dying position, in a hole in the ground, can say, 'I know whom I have believed.'"

That's the message. The message of a Person—Jesus Christ and Him crucified. It needs to be told from the Word and it needs to be experienced and it needs to be seen.

We have a danger in this generation as young people. The churches are built; the pulpits are there. And we come out of Bible school saying, "Give me a pulpit; I am ready to preach." We need to do some internship in a dark place like Paul to find out where our anchor is.

The smallest population group in the ministry in our Movement is under the age of forty. We are not reproducing ourselves! It has haunted me since I found it.

The next generation of teen-agers needs to see some men in our pulpits and in our churches like the men that preceded us, who like Paul know whom they have believed.

THE MOTIVATION OF THE CHURCH

A Message Given Thursday Night, August 29, 1968

JAMES E. HAMILL

THE CHURCH IS A DIVINE INSTITUTION. Conceived in the heart of God and implemented by the Lord Jesus Christ, it is administered by the Holy Spirit.

The Church is a fellowship of believers, the fellowship of the redeemed, the people of God, the society of those who have trusted in Him—those who have been redeemed, reconciled, and regenerated through faith in Christ and obedience to God.

The Church has a divine plan, a divine program, and a divine purpose. The Church has a God-given mission, a God-given message, and a God-given method of accomplishing that mission.

God's plan for the Church is (1) that it may be a means by which God can be revealed to man in a personal experience—a personal encounter with His Son, Jesus Christ; (2) that the Church in the power of the Holy Spirit might evangelize the world; and (3) that the Church will be a body of believers—the Bride of the coming Saviour—and that the Body may be built up in the most holy faith.

Now three things provided the incentive, the stimulus, the provocation, the impulse, the motivation for the New Testament Church. These were an event, an enablement, and an emotion.

An Event

The event was the crucifixion and the resurrection of Jesus Christ. Until Jesus was crucified and rose from the grave, His disciples did not understand what He meant when He said, "Freely ye have received, freely give." When He said to them, "Upon this rock I will build my church; and the gates of hell shall not prevail against it," they did not comprehend because they were thinking in terms of an earthly kingdom. Their concern and their interest appeared to be on who would be the greatest in the Kingdom. "What will we get out of following Thee? How do we figure in this program?" But after they saw Jesus die and rise from the grave, there does not appear to be a great deal of interest as to what they would get in the Kingdom. But they, because of their love for Christ, were constrained to serve Him.

The enemies of Christ endeavored to destroy the New Testament Church. They first of all crucified the Leader; but when they stopped one voice, thousands of voices took up the message of the Christ of God. When they nailed one pair of feet to the cross, thousands of feet began to tread the trails of the world and tell men of the saving grace of God through Jesus Christ, His Son.

They put them in jail, but angels turned them loose. They brought them before authorities, and these voices testified of the power of the Lord Jesus Christ and caused men to tremble on their thrones and cry out, "Almost thou persuadest me to be a Christian."

Let your imagination go to that huddled company of Christians who gathered in the Upper Room in Jerusalem after the crucifixion of Jesus. Jesus was gone! He had been crucified and buried, and it had been reported by several that He had arisen from the grave. Those disciples, behind locked doors and bolted windows, looked back; and when they did, they saw Calvary. The shock and the shame of it revived within them their Messiah. They thought His kingdom had been narrowed to the dimensions of a grave, that His only throne had been six hours on a bloody cross between two thieves. But now it is reported that He is up and out of the grave and alive forevermore. They were confused.

And then as they looked within themselves, they saw inadequacies, fears, and jealousies. Impotence hung about their necks like millstones. But despite their fumbling thought and despite their unsteady moves, two things helped them in that critical hour. One was an event, and the other was a promise.

The event was that their Messiah had conquered death, hell, and the grave, and He had said, "Because I live, ye shall live also." There had been, of course, many infallible proofs that He was indeed alive forevermore.

The other thing that helped them was the promise: "Ye shall receive power, after that the Holy Ghost is come upon you: and ye shall be witnesses unto me both in Jerusalem, and in all Judea, and in Samaria, and unto the uttermost part of the earth."

An Enablement

When Jesus came to the disciples, gathered behind those closed doors in the Upper Room, the Scripture says, "They were assembled for fear of the Jews." He greeted them, "Peace be unto you." And then "he showed unto them his hands and his side." It was at that time that Jesus said, "As my Father hath sent me, even so send I you." And John adds so very significantly, "And when he had said this, he breathed on them, and saith unto them, Receive ye the Holy Ghost." That was the commission and the enablement; that was the calling and the empowerment; that was the task and, thank God, the equipment; that was the command and the authority to carry through that command.

Immediately upon receiving the Holy Spirit the disciples began witnessing. You cannot read the story of the New Testament Church and the Acts of the Apostles without thrilling at the accomplishments made in the power and the force of the Holy Spirit. In Acts 2, in Acts 3, in Acts 4, and right on through we see again and again, when they had prayed, the Holy Ghost came upon them, and they gave witness with boldness.

In the Old Testament there are few exhortations to the believers to tell others about God. God did tell Ezekiel that if he failed to warn Israel, their blood would be upon his hands; but Ezekiel had the Holy Spirit upon him. In his day there was no widespread evangelistic fervor, no commission, no passion for souls, no love that loved unto death, no fire that burned to bring others to a knowledge of God.

Even among the disciples of Jesus before Pentecost there was no all-out effort to win the lost. Jesus sent out the seventy disciples, and they came back a great deal more enthused about the fact that devils were subject to them in the name of Jesus than the fact that souls were saved.

It seems that all the work of the Kingdom was centered in the person and the personal ministry of Jesus Christ. It may be significant at this point to remember that from the time of the baptizing of Jesus until the time of His resurrection, the Holy Spirit seemed to be concerned exclusively with the Lord Jesus Christ. But now at Pentecost the Holy Spirit no longer is exclusively occupied with Jesus and His ministry. When performing miracles, Jesus said to the disciples, ". . . the works that I do shall he do also; and greater works than these shall he do; because I go unto my Father." "And I will pray the Father, and he shall give you another Comforter, that he may abide with you for ever." In other words, He was saying, "Your ministry, your miracles, your works, will not be confined to a small geographical area, but all the world will hear the gospel because I go to My Father and will send you the power of the Holy Spirit."

In the Old Testament, of course, the Holy Spirit came upon prophets, upon priests, upon kings, and upon a few people who were called to a special work, a special task, and a special ministry. But on the Day of Pentecost Peter stood up and said, "This Holy Spirit, this enablement, this power to witness is for all those who believe and repent—your sons and daughters, your old men, your young men, young maidens, your children, your grandchildren, this generation, the next generation, the generation after that, for Jews and for Gentiles, those who are near and those that are far off, those who are present at Pentecost and those who will come later. This is for you, your children, and all those that are afar off, even as many as our Lord, our God shall call."

And with this glorious experience would come the responsibility of witnessing. "And ye shall be witnesses unto me." Jesus said that upon receiving the promise of the Father, the Holy Spirit, that repentance and remission of sins should be preached in His name among all nations.

The story of the New Testament Church after receiving the enablement—that tremendous motivation—is that they went everywhere preaching; they spoke the Word of God with boldness; they said, "We cannot but speak the things which we have seen and heard." For the most part the disciples were ordinary men; fishermen and tax collectors, they had never made a great impact upon the villages and towns in which they lived. They were not well known except to a small circle of relatives. They were not prominent; in fact, they were unknown until they met Jesus. But when they met Jesus and were filled with the Holy Spirit, that made the difference. He filled their hearts and hurled them into the streets and byways, and their voices began to tell the glorious story of Jesus.

Rome lifted her fist and said, "You cannot preach." But they said, "We must preach what we have seen and heard."

The ecclesiastical powers of that day said, "You cannot preach any more in His name." But they said, "We must preach what we have seen and heard."

They defied kings; they preached sermons; they went to prison; they died as martyrs; they shouted the message across the world; they shook the Roman Empire from center to circumference. They turned the world upside down. They had the motivation. They had the glory. They had the determination. They had the "go ye."

Now the remarkable part of this story is not just the fact that they accomplished so much in such a short period of time without radio. How did they do it without television? without the printed page? The remarkable thing is not that they were able to accomplish so much but that those common, ordinary people even *tried* to do it! They tried to do it because they had met the Master and had been filled with the Spirit and had been set on fire. They had the enablement; they had the motivation; they had the power.

One of the outstanding characteristics of the fullness of the Spirit is the desire and the ability and the power to witness for Christ. And we might measure our fullness of the Spirit by our desire to witness for the Lord. The fullness of the Spirit gives us the motivation, the dynamics, the effectiveness, the vitality which will enable us to attempt great things for God.

An Emotion

A third motivation was an emotion. You must become emotionally involved if you are to win souls. You do not win souls by cold calculation. You do not win souls by good organization. You do not win souls with computers. All of those things might add something to your program in soul winning; but before you become a soul winner, you must become emotionally involved with those with whom you deal. You must have a love for souls. It is a spiritual work and spiritual work involves the whole man—spirit, soul, and body.

We can never fulfill the Great Commission without a passion for souls, without a fire that burns. We must be motivated by the same spirit that led the Master to pause when He heard blind Bartimaeus, or when He saw the sorrow of the widow of Nain, or when He looked in pity upon the affliction of the man born blind.

We must feel some of the compassion that Jesus felt when He saw the needy, confused, hard-driven multitudes that were overcome with the mystery of life's meaning. The Scriptures tell us that "he was moved with compassion." This expression reveals a kind of sympathy that does not exhaust itself in sentiment but issues in action. Jesus did something about it.

Only shallow souls and shallow minds can look upon sinning humanity without concern and with a kind of detachment and aloofness. A Spirit-filled Christian must be moved by the situation that prevails in our world today with wars and lawlessness and immorality and hypocrisy all around us. How can we be complacent? How can we sing and shout and dance about and do nothing about a world that is perishing all around us?

Love is not only an attitude; love is a concept. But it is more than that. It is more than a theory. It is more than even a gospel. It is more than an emotion. It is a program. It is an action. "For God so loved the world, that he gave his only begotten Son."

There are three approaches to Christianity—all three necessary and essential as a whole but unsatisfactory only as a part.

There is the *intellectual approach* to Christianity. Now there must be a reason given for the hope we have. We must be rational and logical; we must be proper, correct, sophisticated, and even cautious. And it would not hurt to be careful.

Then there is the *emotional approach.* Our Christianity must be emotional. I don't believe there is any such thing as an encounter with Jesus Christ without some kind of emotion. Now I did not say hysteria, but I said emotion. There is nothing wrong with emotional sermons. There is nothing wrong with emotional songs. There is nothing wrong with emotional worship. It is not even wrong to give emotionally on occasions. The harm is done when we live by our emotions and are controlled by our emotions, when we have passion with no program, when we have feelings but no plans, when we have heart but a little head.

The third approach is *action.* It is the will of God that the intellectual approach and the emotional approach be reflected in our expressed action, that our will be brought into subjection to the will of God. Not a passive will, but an active will to get on with doing the work of God and fulfilling the Great Commission.

When Jesus said to Peter, "Lovest thou me?" three times, Peter said, "Thou knowest that I love thee." And to paraphrase what Jesus really meant, "If you love Me, get on with the work you are supposed to be doing. You don't need to express to Me your love in platitudes and in sermons and in songs, but feed My sheep; get some action into your expression of love."

There is a healthy emotion attached to the doctrine of the cross of Christ. We are told that when Luther stood looking at the painting of Christ, he cried out with the deepest emotion, "My God, my God, for me." Macaulay was so upset upon seeing the slaves of Africa that he was unable to sleep for days and nights. William Booth, when he saw the drunks in the gutters of London, was unable to eat or sleep for a week or two. These men felt deep emotion and then they shook the world.

The movements of the world are heart movements to a great degree. Out of the heart are the issues of life. The movements of the world in most cases have been launched and carried through by men who felt keenly.

God grant that we shall feel a genuine love for a perishing world. God grant that we shall avail ourselves of the enablement and the power of the Holy Spirit.

May our purpose and our program be to fulfill the will of God on earth and to carry out the commission to preach and to teach Christ the world over. May we dedicate ourselves to provide a means that men may learn to know God in a personal experience. May we determine under God to evangelize this world through the power of the Holy Ghost.

May we in truth and in fact become the body of Christ worshiping God in truth and in spirit. May this be a dynamic church at work in winning the lost to Christ and in ministering to the distressed and the discouraged and offering strength to the weak.

May this dynamic church send out its young men and women to preach Christ at home and abroad.

May this Spirit-filled church lead all other denominations into the fullness and glorious baptism of the Holy Ghost. May this be a New Testament church, not in theory only, but in fact and in experience.

May our purpose be to evangelize the world. May we be a lighthouse to those in darkness, a gateway to heaven, a bulwark of the faith of our fathers, an anchor that holds in days of apostasy, a haven for the distressed and the discouraged, a source of bread for the hungry, living water for those that are athirst, an oasis for those in dry places.

May our church be the fear of hell, and the wonder of heaven, the open enemy of decay, the salt of the earth, the light of the world, a friend to the friendless, a shelter from the storms of life.

May our church be "the house of God to the crowds that throng the city streets or jostle in the marketplace; to the carefree youth who with joyous feet dance through the world that Thou hast made; to the masters in the realm of thought, and toilers all 'neath the rod; to the lonely hearts by men forgotten, may the Assemblies of God be the house of God.

MORNING MESSAGES

THE PLACE OF THE WORD IN REVIVAL

A Message Given Tuesday Morning, August 27, 1968

DONALD F. JOHNS

THE TEXTS SELECTED FOR OUR STUDY are 2 Chronicles 36:15-21 and Ezra 1:1-5. Although these may be found on the same page of your Bible, a lapse of seventy years occurs between them. The Chronicles text precedes the seventy-year captivity in Babylon; the Ezra text terminates it.

Why were these texts selected for an exposition of a Biblical revival? To answer this question, we must determine the meaning of the term *revival.*

Today we often use the term *revival* rather loosely. Sometimes, for example, we say that the church is holding revival meetings when what we mean is that the church is holding *evangelistic* meetings. Now although *revival* and *evangelism* may be related terms, they are by no means synonymous. *Revival* is something that happens to the people of God. *Evangelism* is something that the people of God do.

David understood the relationship between revival and evangelism. In Psalm 51:12, 13 he said, "Restore unto me the joy of thy salvation; and uphold me with thy free Spirit. Then will I teach transgressors thy ways; and sinners shall be converted unto thee."

Confusion of revival with evangelism usually results from failure to distinguish between cause and effect. When the people of God are revived, then they evangelize. The cause, being revived, has as its effect evangelism.

What is revival? Consult any standard dictionary of the English language and you will find that *revival* means "a bringing back to life of consciousness, a renewal, a restoration."

Why then were these texts chosen as representative of revival? The answer is obvious: the Chronicles text reveals the spiritual, moral, and physical declension of the people of God; the Ezra text (paralleled closely by the last three verses in 2 Chronicles) reveals the renewal and restoration of the people of God—in short, their revival.

Recall, however, that our topic is not simply *Revival,* but *The Place of the Word in Revival.* Do these verses emphasize the place of the Word in revival? Definitely! In some cases the emphasis is implicit. In 2 Chronicles 36:15 notice the word *messengers;* in verse 16, the words *messengers* and *prophets.*

However, we need not content ourselves with these implicit references. In some cases references to the Word of God are explicit and emphatic, fairly shouting for our attention. Notice 2 Chronicles 36:16, "His words." Observe also the phrase that occurs both in 2 Chronicles 36:21 and in Ezra 1:1, "The word of the Lord by the mouth of Jeremiah."

Closely related, but not actually part of our assigned text, is 2 Chronicles 36:12: "Jeremiah the prophet speaking from the mouth of the

Lord," and also 36:22, "The word of the Lord spoken by the mouth of Jeremiah."

Ezra 1:1-5 clearly presents revival or renewal as promised in the Word of God. Cyrus made his proclamation, the offerings were taken, the chief of the fathers and the priests and the Levites and other interested parties went to Jerusalem "that the word of the Lord by the mouth of Jeremiah might be fulfilled" (Ezra 1:1). Thus we arrive at our first major insight: *the Word of God promises revival.*

Surely Daniel, a prophet of the captivity, was aware that the Word of God promises revival. (See Daniel 9:2, 17, 18.)

Notice that Daniel refers not merely to the words of Jeremiah, but to the Word of the Lord which came to Jeremiah the prophet. Daniel invests these words with the same kind of authority as does Ezra in 1:1 when Ezra views it as "the word of the Lord by the mouth of Jeremiah." This view of the authority of the Word is almost identical with that of the unknown Chronicler (believed by many Bible scholars to have been Ezra himself) who not only views it as "the word of the Lord by the mouth of Jeremiah" (36:21, 22), but also as "Jeremiah the prophet speaking from the mouth of the Lord" (36:12).

It should be noted, however, that the Chronicles text and the Ezra text stress the oral transmission of the Word of God. In Ezra 1:1 and in 2 Chronicles 36:12, 21, 22, there is an emphasis upon the mouth as the organ of communication. However, we must remember that Jeremiah himself never entered into the Babylonian captivity. Jeremiah 40 tells us that Jeremiah was given a choice to remain in Judah or go to Babylon with the captives. Jeremiah elected to remain behind in Judah. However, fearful Jews soon forced him to go with them to Egypt where probably he lived out his remaining years. This brings into focus the fact Daniel did not have access to the spoken words of Jeremiah but to the writings of Jeremiah only.

We know that more than once Jeremiah wrote down the Word of the Lord which came to him (Jeremiah 30:2; 36:2, 28; 51:60). It was undoubtedly to the writings of Jeremiah that Daniel referred when he said, "I Daniel understood by books the number of the years, whereof the word of the Lord came to Jeremiah the prophet, that he would accomplish seventy years in the desolations of Jerusalem" (Daniel 9:2).

The promise of seventy years of desolation was made orally (2 Chronicles 36:21), recorded in writing (compare Jeremiah 30:2; 25:11, 12; 29:10), and read by the prophet Daniel.

Similarly, a renewal or revival was promised the people of God to end its period of desolation. It was made orally (Ezra 1:1), recorded in written form (compare Jeremiah 23:8; 29:14; 30:19; 32:15), and when read by Daniel, formed the basis for his prayerful appeal for the restoration of the temple, the city of Jerusalem, and the nation. If Daniel believed that the Word of God promises revival, can we afford to believe less?

The second insight to be derived from a study of our text is: *the Word of God promotes revival.* Now from logic we know that if a proposition is true, its obverse is also true. The obverse of the proposition, "Regard for the Word of God contributes to revival," is simply this: Disregard of the Word of God contributes to nonrevival.

Surely the truth of the obverse is evident in our texts. Second Chronicles 36:12 tells us that King Zedekiah failed to humble himself "before Jeremiah the prophet speaking from the mouth of the Lord." Verses 14-16 tell us that the chief priests, the fathers, and the people "mocked the messengers of God, and despised his words, misused his prophets, until the wrath of the Lord arose against his people, till there was no remedy."

It took the desolation of the temple and of the city of Jerusalem and the captivity of the people of God to bring about a proper regard for the Word of God. Notice how the prophet Daniel viewed the chastisement as confirming the Word of God. "And he hath confirmed his words, which he spake against us, and against our judges that judged us, by bringing upon us a great evil: for under the whole heaven hath not been done as hath been done upon Jerusalem" (Daniel 9:12). "To fulfill the word of the Lord" (2 Chronicles 36:21) is to confirm it (Daniel 9:12) and to establish a regard for it. This in turn prepares for and promotes the revival itself.

Notice how the confirmation of the Word of God as recorded by Jeremiah directs Daniel's attention elsewhere in the Word of God. He says, "Therefore the curse is poured upon us, and the oath that is written in the law of Moses the servant of God, because we have sinned against him. . . . As it is written in the law of Moses, all this evil is come upon us" (Daniel 9:11, 13). Daniel's respect for the Law has been confirmed by God's discipline of His people.

But notice further, Daniel's respect is not for the Law only, but also for the prophets. He says,

"Neither have we hearkened unto thy servants the prophets, which spake in thy name. . . . Neither have we obeyed the voice of the Lord our God, to walk in his laws, which he set before us by his servants the prophets" (Daniel 9:6, 10). There is no doubt that God's disciplining of His people promoted Daniel's respect for the Word of God.

Surely knowledge of the Word of God teaches us that God will not allow His people to disregard His Word with impunity. All of God's people at all levels are subject to the judgment of His Word. King, chief of the priests, the people (2 Chronicles 36:11-14), great men, young men, maidens, old men, the stooped with age (2 Chronicles 36:17), princes (Daniel 9:8), even Daniel himself (Daniel 9:5, 20)—all are subject to the judgment of God's Word. An understanding of this will promote revival.

God's Word not only promises revival and promotes revival, but *the Word of the Lord provides the bases for revival.*

First, *the Word of the Lord reveals the holiness of God.* Why was Israel's sin so offensive to God? The answer is obvious. It was a transgression of God's holiness. God's presence is so holy that it hallows that within which He dwells. Verses 15 and 14 refer to the temple in Jerusalem as "his dwelling place" and "the house of the Lord which he had hallowed in Jerusalem."

We are further informed that by their transgressions, the Israelites had polluted the house of the Lord. Now why should an offense against the temple be considered an offense against the holiness of God? Psalm 26:8 contains the answer. In it David refers to God's habitation as "the place where thine honor dwelleth." When God's people defile the hallowed temple of God, they insult His honor.

Daniel in his prayer is even more explicit in his recognition of God's holiness. He says, "O Lord, righteousness belongeth unto thee" (Daniel 9:7) and, "The Lord our God is righteous in all his works which he doeth" (Daniel 9:14). Notice how Daniel sets the holiness of God in opposition to the sinfulness of God's people and to the punishment which resulted from that sin. "O Lord, righteousness belongeth unto thee, but unto us confusion of faces . . . because of their trespass that they have trespassed against thee" (Daniel 9:7).

The Chronicles text similarly associates Israel's punishment with Israel's disregard for the demands of God's holiness. "But they mocked the messengers of God, and despised his words, and misused his prophets, until the wrath of the Lord arose against his people, till there was no remedy" (2 Chronicles 36:16).

Second, *the Word of the Lord reveals the compassion of God.* Second Chronicles 36:15 tells us that God sent His word to His people "because he had compassion on his people, and on his dwelling place." God is concerned about the welfare of His people.

The Lord, speaking through the prophet Jeremiah, beautifully portrays His compassion for His people. "When I would comfort myself against sorrow, my heart is faint in me" (8:18). "For the hurt of the daughter of my people am I hurt. . . . Is there no balm in Gilead? is there no physician there? why then is not the health of the daughter of my people recovered?" (8:21, 22). Here God presents Himself as the compassionate physician of Gilead wishing to bind and heal the spiritual wounds of His people.

In Jeremiah 9:1 the Lord, through Jeremiah, again pictures His compassionate emotional involvement with the welfare of His people. "Oh that my head were waters, and mine eyes a fountain of tears, that I might weep day and night for the slain of the daughters of my people!" Just as a parent suffers with a child who is ill, so God is involved in the spiritual suffering of His people. "Woe is me for my hurt! my wound is grievous: but I said, Truly this is a grief, and I must bear it" (Jeremiah 10:19).

Jeremiah is often referred to as the weeping prophet, but it is not Jeremiah who weeps. It is God who weeps through Jeremiah. God is compassionate. He is concerned about the welfare of His people.

Third, *the Word of the Lord reveals the faithfulness of God.* Our Chronicles text tells us that it was because of God's compassion on His people that He "sent to them by his messengers, rising up betimes, and sending" (36:15). The phrase *rising up betimes* is sometimes translated "rising up early." The entire phrase, *rising up betimes, and sending* is rendered in the Amplified "sent to them persistently." Certainly the word *persistently* speaks to us of the faithfulness of God.

Surely the author of Chronicles must have had in mind the prophecies of Jeremiah when he spoke of the persistence and faithfulness of God in sending messengers to His people. The phrases *rising up betimes* or *rising up early* is used at least seven times in Jeremiah.

Notice how God through Jeremiah uses the phrase *rising up early* to emphasize His persistent faithfulness. (See Jeremiah 7:25; 11:7; 26:5; 35:15; 44:4; 25:4.)

Observe now, in 25:3 Jeremiah includes himself among those faithful prophets who have been persistent voices for God to His erring people: "And I have spoken to you, rising early and speaking; but ye have not hearkened." Jeremiah could affirm that God was faithful because he himself had been one of God's faithful and persistent prophets.

Fourth, *the Word of the Lord reveals the mercy of God*. God sent His prophets in order that His people might repent. But how were the prophets received?

The king did not repent. Second Chronicles 36:12, 13 informs us that Zedekiah "did that which was evil in the sight of the Lord his God, and humbled not himself before Jeremiah the prophet speaking from the mouth of the Lord. . . . He stiffened his neck, and hardened his heart from turning unto the Lord God of Israel."

The religious leadership did not repent. Priests, pastors, and false prophets refused to hearken to the call to repentance. According to Jeremiah 2:8, "The priests said not, Where is the Lord? and they that handle the law knew me not: the pastors also transgressed against me, and the prophets prophesied by Baal."

The Lord also attempted to direct His mercy to the poor and the humble of His people. They also rejected His appeal. Of these the Lord testifies in Jeremiah 5:4, "Therefore I said, Surely these are poor; they are foolish: for they know not the way of the Lord, nor the judgment of their God."

Then the Lord appealed to the great (Jeremiah 5:5). "I will get me unto the great men, and will speak unto them; for they have known the way of the Lord, and the judgment of their God." But the great also rejected the mercies which God extended toward them.

All of this is summarized by the Chronicler in verse 16, "They mocked the messengers of God, and despised his words, and misused his prophets." Nehemiah, looking back upon these times, said, "Nevertheless they were disobedient, and rebelled against thee, and cast thy law behind their backs, and slew thy prophets which testified against them to turn them to thee, and they wrought great provocations" (Nehemiah 9: 26). Notice how Nehemiah stresses the intent of God in sending the prophets "to turn them to thee." When the prophets testified against the people, the purpose was to turn them to God.

Here again the Word of the Lord reveals God's mercy.

Fifth, *the Word of the Lord reveals God's desire*. God speaks again and again because He desires to save, not to punish. In verse 16 the Chronicler tells us that "the wrath of the Lord arose against his people, till there was no remedy" because the people rejected the compassionate, faithful, persistent attempts of God to turn them to Himself.

God's desire is to save, not to punish. Hear His plea in Jeremiah 4:14, "O Jerusalem, wash thine heart from wickedness, that thou mayest be saved. How long shall thy vain thoughts lodge within thee?"

God is so desirous of pardoning that in Jeremiah 5:1 He ordered the prophet, "Run ye to and fro through the streets of Jerusalem, and see now, and know, and seek in the broad places thereof, if you can find a man, if there be any that executeth judgment, that seeketh the truth; and I will pardon it." Did Jeremiah find such a man? Apparently not, for Jeremiah 8:6 says, "I hearkened and heard, but they spake not aright: no man repented him of his wickedness." In their resolute determination to fulfill their own desires, men ignore the desire of God to forgive their sin and their iniquity.

The Word of the Lord, then, provides the bases for revival by revealing the holiness of God, the compassion of God, the faithfulness of God, the mercy of God, and the desire of God.

Our last major insight is that the Word of the Lord produces revival. It was the Word of the Lord which moved Daniel to pray for the temple, the city, and the nation. It was "that the word of the Lord by the mouth of Jeremiah might be fulfilled, the Lord stirred up the spirit of Cyrus king of Persia" (Ezra 1:1) so that he made his proclamation which resulted in the restoration.

Notice that Cyrus says "he hath charged me to build him an house at Jerusalem, which is in Judah" (Ezra 1:2). In some way the Word of the Lord came to Cyrus. Perhaps it was the prophecy in Isaiah 44:28 to which Cyrus referred: "That saith of Cyrus, He is my shepherd, and shall perform all my pleasure: even saying to Jerusalem, Thou shalt be built; and to the temple, Thy foundation shall be laid."

Restoration is more than a matter of rebuilding temples, cities, and nations. In its most pertinent sense, it is a rebuilding of the spirit. To accomplish His ends the Lord not only stirred up the spirit of Cyrus (Ezra 1:1); He also stirred up the people. Observe how it is phrased in Ezra 1:5, "Whose spirit God had raised." Without the renewal of spirit, the building of temples, cities, and nations is meaningless.

Jeremiah was aware that what God's people needed was a renewal of spirit and of heart. It is a theme which runs throughout the whole book.

For example, in Jeremiah 29:13 we find God saying, "And ye shall seek me, and find me, when ye shall search for me with all your heart."

In Jeremiah 31:31, "Behold, the days come, saith the Lord, that I will make a new covenant with the house of Israel, and with the house of Judah."

In Jeremiah 31:33 He tells us the implications of that new covenant! "I will put my law in their inward parts, and write it in their hearts; and will be their God, and they shall be my people."

In Jeremiah 32:40 He continues, "I will put my fear in their hearts."

In Jeremiah 33:8 we find, "And I will cleanse them from all their iniquity, whereby they have sinned against me; and I will pardon all their iniquities, whereby they have sinned, and whereby they have transgressed against me."

Surely these passages convince us that God is interested in more than physical restoration. He is interested in spiritual renewal, in revival. This revival comes when the Word of God is written in the heart and on the spirit. When the Law is written in the heart and on the spirit of God's

people, then they turn to God with the prayer of Daniel 9:19, "O Lord, hear; O Lord, forgive; O Lord, hearken and do; defer not, for thine own sake, O my God: for thy city and thy people are called by thy name."

What is the place of the Word in revival? The Word of the Lord promises revival; the Word of the Lord promotes revival; the Word of the Lord reveals the bases for revival, informing us of the holiness of God, the compassion of God, the faithfulness of God, the mercy of God, and the desire of God; and the Word of the Lord produces revival when we allow it to be written in our hearts and on our spirits.

We Pentecostals, of all people, ought to be epistles of Christ, "Written not with ink, but with the Spirit of the living God; not in tables of stone, but in fleshy tables of the heart" (2 Corinthians 3:3). If we are such epistles of Christ, we will be "able ministers of the new testament" (2 Corinthians 3:6). When we are revived, we will be able to minister to others what God has ministered to us.

In a very real sense, revival provides the basis for evangelism, and revival is impossible without our allowing the Word of God to do its work in our midst. Let us commit ourselves to renewed respect for the Word of God. Let us feed on the Word of God. Let us allow the Word to work in our hearts. Let us minister the Word to others. This is the divine order.

THE PLACE OF THE WORD IN REVIVAL

A Message Given Tuesday Morning, August 27, 1968

H. W. STEINBERG

IN 1789 A MUTINY DEVELOPED ON THE Bounty, a British ship sailing for the Pacific Islands. Fletcher Christian, the leader of the mutineers, put Captain William Bligh and 18 crew members in a small boat and set them adrift.

The six mutineers together with ten women and a fifteen-year-old girl then landed on Pitcairn Island which was less than three miles square. After the *Bounty* had been unloaded, it was set afire so none could leave the island.

In a short time the mutineers were distilling alcohol, and the attendant evils of drunkenness followed. As a result of the debauchery five of the mutineers died.

As the one remaining mutineer was looking through a chest taken from the ship, he discovered a Bible. His life was transformed, and he began faithfully to teach the women and children who were with him. In time the entire population of the island became God-fearing, living according to the Word of God.

When the Word so effectively transforms the lives of unbelievers, it is understandable that the Word is also a very important agent in the revival of believers who are not living as close to God as they should. A study of 2 Chronicles 36:11-23 emphasizes the importance God attaches to the Word when spiritual declension exists. It has important lessons for believers today.

In the years prior to the Babylonian Exile, Judah again drifted from God. "Moreover all the chief of the priests, and the people, transgressed very much after all the abominations of the heathen; and polluted the house of the Lord which he had hallowed in Jerusalem" (2 Chronicles 36:14).

Of all the things God might have done about this tragic condition, it is interesting to note that His first manifestation of love and concern was the preaching of the Word. "And the Lord God of their fathers sent to them by his messengers, rising up betimes, and sending; because he had compassion on his people, and on his dwelling place" (2 Chronicles 36:15). Four of the writing prophets whose ministries were prominent during this time were Jeremiah, Ezekiel, Habakkuk, and Zephaniah.

God sent His Word because acceptance of the Word always results in revival and spiritual vigor. The Scriptures were an important factor in all Old Testament revivals.

Just as it was the Word which was effective in Old Testament revivals, so the Word has been prominent in revivals in church history. A report in a Chicago religious paper concerning the Welsh revival of 1904 observed that the leader of this revival was primarily a man of the Word. The report indicated: "He is no orator; he is not widely read. The only book he knows from cover to cover is the Bible." Evan Roberts was a coal miner who completely devoted available time to the study of the Word. It is not without significance that God chose this 26-year-old man to become the human instrument to lead the Welsh Revival.

When the Bible becomes the controlling force in every phase of life, man will be what he ought to be. This is why God sent the Word to Israel. This is why there must be an honoring of Scripture today.

A further consideration of the condition of Israel prior to the Exile indicates that people of all levels rejected God's Word rather than conform to it. The attitude of the people is dramatized in their treatment of Jeremiah. When the scroll containing God's message to His people was read to King Jehoiakim, he took a knife, cut the scroll in pieces, and threw it in the fire. Later Jeremiah was taken by the princes of Judah with the consent of Zedekiah and thrown into a pit filled with mire.

While Judah's rejection of the Word was manifested in drastic ways, it should be kept in mind that the Bible can be just as effectively rejected today through neglect and indifference as through insult and hostility. The neglect of the Word in personal devotions, in the family altar, in the the auxiliary agencies of the church, and in preaching is rejection of the Word. When people compartmentalize life in such a way that God's Word does not have a vital control over every aspect of life, they have rejected the Word.

A very encouraging truth which emerges from Israel's dark situation is that God does not give up just as soon as His people backslide. In His great love He chastened Judah to encourage restoration. The nation which God had intended to be a world leader fell under the control of heathen nations.

Today God still deals with His people in the same way. When they wander from the Word, He does not cast them away at the first indication of failure. He lovingly chastens them.

The third lesson which can be learned from Judah's experience concerns itself with their ultimate acceptance of the Word. The people of Judah could have taken any one of three attitudes mentioned in Hebrews toward the divine chastening. They could have despised it (Hebrews 12:5), they could have fainted under it (Hebrews 12:5), or they could have chosen to be exercised by it (Hebrews 12:11).

When Judah responded to divine chastening and gave priority to God's Word, things began to happen. Cyrus issued a decree permitting the people to return to Jerusalem. The financial needs of the people were supplied, and sacred vessels were also provided for the temple of the Lord. Volunteers rose to return to Jerusalem to rebuild the temple.

It is helpful to observe that God's people were not free from opposition as they determined to put God first. They suffered opposition and ridicule, but the temple was rebuilt in spite of opposition and hardship. When God's people seek His face for spiritual renewal, it can be expected that Satan will do all within his power to hinder. But as they give priority to His Word, there will always be revival.

When the Word is embraced and applied to every facet of life, there cannot help but be revival. Believers must make the Word prominent in personal devotions. Parents must make the Word prominent at the family altars. Sunday school teachers and other leaders in the church must concentrate on teaching the Word. Pastors, evangelists, and missionaries must declare the whole counsel of God. The greatest revival is just ahead for people who delight themselves in the Word of God.

If God's people today want to exalt the Lord whom they love, they will give top priority to the Word. Scripture produces Christ-honoring people; and when Christ is given His rightful place in every life, revival can fulfill its mission.

Many have enjoyed Billy Sunday's tribute to the Bible:

"Twenty-nine years ago, with the Holy Spirit as my guide, I entered in the portico of Genesis, walked down the corridor of the Old Testament art galleries, where pictures of Noah, Abraham, Moses, Joseph, Isaac, Jacob, and Daniel hang on the wall. I passed into the music room of the Psalms where the Spirit sweeps the keyboard of nature until it seems that every reed and pipe in God's great organ responds to the harp of David, the sweet singer of Israel.

"I entered the chamber of Ecclesiastes where the voice of the preacher is heard, and into the conservatory of Sharon and the Lily of the Valley where sweet spices filled and perfumed my life.

"I entered the business office of Proverbs and on to the observatory of the prophets where I saw telescopes of various sizes pointing to far-off events, concentrating on the bright and morning Star which was to rise above the moonlit hills of Judea for our salvation and redemption.

"I entered the audience-room of the King of kings, catching a vision written by Matthew,

Mark, Luke, and John. Thence into the correspondence-room with Paul, Peter, James, and John writing their epistles.

"I stepped into the throne-room of Revelation where tower the glittering peaks, where sits the King of kings upon His throne of glory with the healing of the nations in His hand, and I cried out:

'All hail the power of Jesus' Name,
Let angels prostrate fall;
Bring forth the royal diadem,
And crown Him Lord of all.'"

THE PLACE OF LEADERSHIP IN REVIVAL

A Message Given Wednesday Morning, August 28, 1968

ARTHUR H. GRAVES

In the Lord's work there is no greater blessing than a good leader—and no greater problem than a bad one.

In the organization of Israel after the death of Joshua, the spiritual leader was the priest. This was natural because the priest was the custodian of the Law and the minister of salvation through the sacrifices and ritual of the tabernacle. So Israel was not left without designated official leadership.

Since the priest's office was hereditary, there was always the possibility that the one to whom the office belonged might not be faithful to the ministry of that office. Failure in the priesthood could create a barrier between God and His people.

Such a condition existed with Eli and his sons. The sons were demanding a share of the sacrifices that was more than what belonged to them (1 Samuel 2:12-17). They were morally corrupt in taking advantage of members of the congregation (1 Samuel 2:22). They were rebellious in refusing correction.

Without removing Eli from office, God bypassed him by raising up Samuel as a prophet to meet the need for revival. Samuel was literally born for the revival, and even his childhood and youth were dedicated to preparation for that ministry (1 Samuel 2:26; 3:19-21).

The first thing that must be true of all revival leaders is that they are in living communication with God. It was the loss of this living communication with God by the people and their officers which produced the great need of revival (1 Samuel 3:1). The restoration of communication in Samuel's ministry opened the way for revival. His prophetic ministry attained an authority as Samuel judged the people (1 Samuel 3:20; 7:15) and was God's instrument in selecting and anointing of kings.

The study of three great revivals in Scripture —the one under Samuel, the revival in which John the Baptist ministered, and the revival under the apostles in the beginning of the Church —indicates that God takes the initiative in revival. The special birth and childhood of John, preceded by the prophecies in the Old Testament, clearly indicate that God prepared for the day when "the word of God came unto John the son of Zechariah in the wilderness" (Luke 3:2). As for the revival under the apostles which eventually became worldwide, it was prepared for by God's sending both His Son and His Spirit.

One purpose of revival was to prepare God's people for important changes in their program. In Samuel's case the transition was to the setting up of a king. In John the Baptist's case it was to the introduction of the gospel. In the case of the apostles it was to the worldwide mission of the Church.

While the initiative and power of revival came

from God, the human leaders were given a decisive role. As Samuel and John the Baptist were born for revival, so leaders like Paul were born *out of* revival and extended it beyond the limits of its beginning.

The purpose of revival in the Old Testament was to improve and correct the spiritual lives and obedience of God's people. The evangelistic objective was not really the going of Israel to other peoples with a message so much as it was to exhibit before other nations the joys and blessings which a right relationship with God could bring. Revival in the Old Testament was something to *show* more than something to *tell*.

This was expressed in the words of Moses recorded in Deuteronomy 4:6-8: "This is your wisdom and your understanding in the sight of the nations, which shall hear all these statutes, and say, Surely this great nation is a wise and understanding people. For what nation is there so great, who hath God so nigh unto them, as the Lord our God is in all things that we call upon him for? And what nation is there so great, that hath statutes and judgments so righteous as all this law, which I set before you this day?"

The ministry of John the Baptist marked the end of the Old Testament type of revival in which the children could return to the experiences of their fathers and the blessings of the fathers would be visited again on their sons.

The revival which began on Pentecost brought a completely new experience to all. The apostles were caught up in a work of the Spirit which they had never seen and so were moving from moment to moment by faith. Not only this, they were expected to give instant explanation and must be able to defend and interpret the revival in response to the questions and misconceptions of the crowd. Here was revival leadership at its busiest. Add to this the fact that this was a group operation, and they had no group organization. They had been a group of disciples as they walked with Jesus, but He so dominated each situation that nothing like Pentecost had ever confronted them before.

In those early days in Jerusalem it seemed that the place of leadership in revival was everywhere. All their knowledge of the Old Testament and their remembrance of what Jesus had told them was needed now. The apostles learned that leaders who have the joy of a Spirit-anointed ministry may become the targets of persecution. It was not the new converts who were set upon by the authorities, but the leaders in the revival. How they met this early test speaks well for their devotion and faith.

We learn from the Book of Acts that a revival may need basic and far-reaching corrections, even in the midst of great results. The leaders must be the instruments through whom God could make the needed changes.

The revival which began at Pentecost continued for years and swept multitudes of converts into the Church while its leaders, as yet, showed no comprehensive understanding of God's full plan for the revival. Peter's word in his first sermon was, "Let all the house of Israel know" (Acts 2:36), and no one in the revival had had a message for anyone farther away than Samaria since that day.

God took the initiative in presenting the Gentile problem to Peter. This required action by the revival leadership. And it was as complicated a situation as any national or racial problem is today. How careful and flexible and faithful Peter was in his response to the Lord. When he stood up in Cornelius' house and announced, "Of a truth I perceive that God is no respecter of persons" (Acts 10:34), he was functioning perfectly as a leadership-channel from the Head of the Church for needed correction.

With great freedom the apostles ministered and with great concern they counseled together about their ministries. Their concern for the truth was greater than their consideration of individuals, and every man's ministry was put to the test of the Word of God (Acts 11:2, 3). The brethren at Jerusalem showed a remarkable freedom from personal prejudice as they were willing to give up lifelong ideas when challenged by accounts of the Holy Spirit's working in harmony with the Scriptures.

Only a few illustrations of procedure are recounted and referred to in the New Testament, but what is given is very instructive. Whether it involved the leading spokesman, Peter, or that "new" apostle Paul (Acts 15:12), the Jerusalem brethren were intent on protecting the work of God.

When it was first recognized that the Gentiles were included in God's program of revival, it could not be foreseen what problems might arise in applying this to particular cases. The questions concerning circumcision and the Law were not raised in the privacy of a rooftop where an apostle had gone to pray. They were discovered in ministry on the field as revival preachers presented contradictory ideas.

Again the group leadership came into function as a council at Jerusalem was arranged (Acts 15:1-32). Considering the difficulties of time and travel, this meeting between the field ministry and the apostles and elders in Jerusalem was a tremendous exercise on behalf of the unity of the Early Church. The efforts made to retain unity in the Early Church were born of the interest in keeping the whole Church, at home and abroad, moving together in the advance of the great revival and the establishment of the truth.

The letters written to particular churches as well as the narrative of the Book of Acts are important in understanding the place of leadership in revival.

While generations come and go, the present church has the same Lord and the same Spirit as well as the same commission. Let us avail ourselves of these resources.

THE PLACE OF LEADERSHIP IN REVIVAL

A Message Given Wednesday Morning, August 28, 1968

MARCUS GASTON

Both the Scriptures and church history attest that God works through chosen leaders; and when He discovers men who conform to His spiritual requirements, He uses them to the limit despite their human weaknesses. Such men were Moses, Gideon, Nehemiah, Peter, Paul, Luther, Wesley, Calvin, Knox, Judson, Carey, Whitefield, Finney, and a host of others.

All great revival movements begin with the appearance of the man destined of God to be a leader. The burden of the times becomes to him an intolerable load; he feels the hand of the Lord upon him; the voice of God speaks to him; the Spirit of God possesses him; and he goes forth to be God's agent in leading men into newness of life.

Samuel was this kind of leader. He was God's man whom God used to bring about spiritual revival in Israel. From his life we can learn much about the place of leadership in revival.

I. The Need for Leadership

Samuel was the last of the judges. When he came on the scene, the political, spiritual, and moral conditions in Israel were at low ebb. The priesthood was corrupt. Eli's sons, who ministered at the tabernacle, were guilty of irreverence, selfishness, and immorality. Idolatry and vice abounded on every hand.

There was need of a man sent from God, and Samuel was that man. He was God's chosen vessel to wrestle in prayer for Israel, to announce God's will to the people, and to lead the nation back to God by way of repentance and rededication.

We see a parallel to the times of Samuel in the conditions of our day. A Christian editor asks: "What has happened to our national morals? An educator speaks out in favor of free love. A minister condones sexual excursions by unmarried adults. A high court labels yesterday's smut as today's literature. TV programs pour out a flood of sick, sadistic, suggestive situations."

While our standards have lowered, our crime levels and social problems have increased. Today we have a higher percentage of youth in jails and reformatories than ever before. The figures on school dropouts, sex deviation, dope addiction, high school marriages, broken marriages, and crimes of passion are the highest ever.

On the religious scene, the gospel message has been trimmed and compromised to fit what men want to hear. To a large extent the church has become merged with the world. It has adopted so many of the world's ideals, customs, and habits that it is fast losing its spiritual influence. It was not surprising to read this report not long ago in *Christianity Today*: "A recent scientific sampling by Lou Harris and Associates of the view of two thousand Americans shows that clergymen are down in public esteem and confidence to a rating below that of doctors, bankers, scientists, military leaders, educators, corporation heads, psychiatrists, and even local retailers. Their rating suggests disturbing things about the direction in which Americans are turning for a solution to human problems."

Conditions on every hand in our day call for spiritual leadership, even as in the days of Samuel. The times are ripe for God to raise up spiritual leaders through whom He can bring revival to His Church and a harvest of souls among the unconverted.

When the fortunes of the chosen race were at their lowest, God gave the spiritual leadership needed to bring the people back to Himself. He can do it in America today! He is looking for those whom He can use as leaders, men after His own heart who can provide that authoritative, spiritual, sacrificial leadership needed for revival in our generation.

II. Features of Leadership

A. God's Leader Must Have a Life Above Reproach

One of the important aspects of Samuel's great spiritual influence was his righteous life. His character was such that he didn't leave himself open to censure.

Actions do speak louder than words. As one minister put it, "The preacher must *be* a good sermon before he can preach as he ought."

Former President Woodrow Wilson spoke some weighty words about preachers (and this goes for spiritual leadership in any capacity) when he said: "You do not have to *be* anything in particular to be a lawyer. You do not have to *be* anything in particular, except a kindhearted man perhaps, to be a physician. You do not have to *be* anything, nor undergo any spiritual change, to be a merchant. The only profession which consists of *being* something is the ministry of our Lord and Saviour."

B. God's Leader Must Be a Man of Prayer

A key to Samuel's life of power with God and with man was his life of prayer. Frequently we read of his earnest intercessions on behalf of the nation. The Psalmist recorded in Psalm 99:6: "Moses and Aaron among his priests, and Samuel among them that call upon his name; they called upon the Lord, and he answered them."

There is absolutely no substitute for prayer. Great preaching will not take its place, nor will a few degrees after our names, nor a winsome personality, nor a well-planned and executed program, nor anything else.

It is one thing to give mental assent to prayer and quite another thing to consistently put it into practice. Men are difficult objects to move, and it is much easier to pray for temporal needs than for situations which involve the intricacies and stubbornness of the human heart. But it is in just these situations that the man of God must prove the power of prayer to move human hearts in the direction in which he believes the will of God lies.

Dr. A. C. Dixon beautifully summarizes the matter of the importance of prayer: "When we depend upon our money, our teaching, our education, our preaching, we get what these can do. But when we depend upon prayer, we get what God can do—and what all of us need is what God can do!"

What is it that we want to see in our various ministries? Is it not a "demonstration of the Spirit and of power" resulting in the edifying of believers, the winning of the lost, and the exalting of our Lord Jesus Christ? We want and must have the supernatural in our ministries. And that is exactly what God promises will result from intercessory prayer. He guarantees in Jeremiah 33:3: "Call unto me, and I will answer thee, and show thee great and mighty things which thou knowest not."

C. God's Leader Must Be a Faithful Witness of God's Message

In the opening verse of the third chapter of First Samuel we are told that "the word of the Lord was precious [rare] in those days." Then in the closing verse of that chapter we read that "the Lord revealed himself to Samuel in Shiloh by the word of the Lord." It is thrilling to watch Samuel from that time onward speaking not that which pleased himself, but speaking the whole counsel of God and hiding nothing that God revealed.

In 1 Samuel 7:3, we see Samuel speaking to all the house of Israel and saying, "If ye do return unto the Lord with all your hearts, then put away the strange gods and Ashtaroth from among you, and prepare your hearts unto the Lord, and serve him only." Here Samuel gives a courageous, clear call to repentance, although the message of repentance is never popular and never easy to preach.

First Samuel 8 gives the picture of Israel clamoring for a king. God tells Samuel to protest solemnly unto them and show them the manner of the king that shall reign over them—to tell them of the disappointments and heartaches that are ahead if they get the king they want. Now this wasn't an easy message to deliver when all the nation was putting on a noisy demonstration for a king, but in verse 10 we read, "And Samuel told all the words of the Lord unto the people that asked of him a king."

These are just two samples of something we see over and over again in the ministry of this man Samuel. Always when the word of the Lord came to Samuel, he proclaimed it faithfully and fully, regardless of the consequences to himself. No man can be a leader in revival apart from this faithfulness to the Word of the Lord.

Not "Safety First" but "God First" is the watchword of God's spokesman—the man whom God can use to lead the people to spiritual renewal.

D. God's Leader Must Have the Anointing of the Spirit

First Samuel 3:19, 20 declares: "And Samuel grew, and the Lord was with him, and did let none of his words fall to the ground. And all Israel from Dan even to Beer-sheba knew that Samuel was established to be a prophet of the Lord." This is to say that the Spirit of the Lord was upon Samuel. It was through the anointing of the Spirit that Samuel spoke to Israel those words that brought them back to God. It was through the anointing of the Spirit that Samuel prayed those prayers that turned the hearts of the people to repentance and obedience. It was through the anointing of the Spirit that Samuel exercised the spiritual leadership that directed Israel into those paths that finally culminated in the glory of the kingdom under David and Solomon.

Spiritual leadership can only be exercised by Spirit-filled, Spirit-anointed men. Other qualifications for leadership are desirable. This is indispensable.

Leadership is often viewed as a matter of natural endowments and personality traits—intellectual capacity, administrative ability, force of will, enthusiasm. But these are not the factors of paramount importance in the area of spiritual leadership. There is no such thing as a self-made spiritual leader.

Spiritual leaders are not made by election or appointment. True spiritual leadership is a thing of the Spirit and is conferred by God alone. It comes by the anointing of the Holy Spirit to those who have met God's qualifications—to those who are filled with the Spirit and who walk daily in the Spirit, so that their intellect and emotions and will all become available to God for the achieving of His purposes. Under the Holy Spirit's control, natural gifts of leadership are sanctified and lifted to their highest power. The spiritual leader influences others, not by the power of his own personality alone, but by that personality irradiated and interpenetrated and empowered by the Holy Spirit.

III. The Cost of Leadership

A. Self-sacrifice

Hannah took her son, Samuel, to the house of the Lord at Shiloh, so far as we know, she never took the child home again.

We can recognize Hannah's sacrifice in giving up the child so dear to her heart. But let us not forget there was a cost to Samuel also. It cost him the joys of homelife. It cost him the happy fellowship that would have been his with the three sons and two daughters who were later born to Hannah.

A cross stands in the way of spiritual leadership, a cross upon which the leader must consent to be impaled. If we are walking with Jesus, there is one hill around which there is no detour—Golgotha! We cannot pick out the triumphal entries and leave the crosses, anymore than we can pick out the sunshine and leave the rain. The degree in which we allow the cross of Christ to work in us will be the measure in which the resurrection life of Christ can be manifested through us in dynamic leadership in the things of God.

B. Loneliness

William Sanford LaSor writes: "The greatness of Samuel has to be measured against the times in which he lived. It was a chaotic period in Israel's history. . . . At the head of Israel stood Saul, beset with a terrible melancholia that at times seemed madness; no man's life was safe in his household or his court. Division in the state, insanity at court: in the midst of this stood Samuel, a lonely figure of tremendous stature, a man whose job it was to start the organization of a kingdom."

From its very nature, the lot of the leader must be a lonely one. He must always be ahead of his followers.

Moses paid this price for leadership. He knew the crushing loneliness of misunderstanding and misconstrued motives.

Paul was a lonely man. "This thou knowest,

47

that all they which are in Asia be turned away from me" (2 Timothy 1:15).

The leader must be a man who, while welcoming the friendship and support of all who can offer it, has sufficient inner resources to stand alone, even in the face of fierce opposition, in discharging his responsibilities.

C. CRITICISM

In 1 Samuel 8:4, 5 we view Samuel suffering criticism and rejection by the people. How will he stand in adversity? Once again we see the greatness of the spiritual stature of this man. When he left his public post, he said, "As for me, God forbid that I should sin against the Lord in ceasing to pray for you."

No spiritual leader is exempt from criticism, and his humility will nowhere be seen more clearly than in the manner in which he reacts to it.

Samuel Logan Brengle was one of the great leaders of The Salvation Army. Once when Brengle was subjected to caustic criticism, he replied: "From my heart I thank you for your rebuke. Will you, my friend, remember me in prayer?" On another occasion he answered: "I thank you for your criticism. It set me to self-examination and heart-searching and prayer. This always leads me into a deeper sense of my utter dependence on Jesus . . . and into sweeter fellowship with Him."

When the harsh words are flying thick and fast, don't forget the statement of one veteran in the work of the Lord: "Often the crowd does not recognize a leader until he has gone, and then they build a monument for him with the stones they threw at him in life."

IV. The Rewards of Leadership

A. THE PRESENCE OF GOD

The load that Samuel carried as God's appointed leader in Israel was heavy, but God supported him and cheered him with His divine presence. God revealed Himself to Samuel in ways that others knew nothing about. God spoke to him, encouraged him, led him, comforted him. Though it was necessary for him to walk a lonely path, he was not alone. God's presence was with Samuel in a marvelous way all his days.

B. THE PURE JOY OF SEEING FRUIT FROM ONE'S LABORS

Samuel labored in difficult days, but he saw a great change in Israel. His preaching and praying were used of God to bring a great spiritual revitalization—so much so that Ewald, in his *History of Israel*, says, "There can be no doubt that all the greatness which the following century boasts goes back to Samuel as its real author."

Whether or not it is in the purpose of God to send a worldwide revival to change the course of history, there need be no hesitation in predicting the coming of revival to any local church when the scriptural conditions are met. When leaders long for a spiritual awakening and quickening and lead the people in the way of desire and faith and obedience, God will give results.

C. THE PROMISE OF HEAVENLY REWARDS

Samuel didn't have the revelation from God on this that we have. We have the inspired teaching of the apostle Paul: "If any man's work abide . . . he shall receive a reward." We are also privileged to have the words of the Lord Jesus. To those who minister faithfully He will say one day, "Well done, thou good and faithful servant: thou hast been faithful over a few things, I will make thee ruler over many things: enter thou into the joy of thy lord."

THE PLACE OF OBEDIENCE IN REVIVAL

A Message Given Thursday Morning, August 29, 1968

ERNEST S. WILLIAMS

UNFORTUNATELY much of the professing church has turned from the true gospel to another gospel. Having lost sight of salvation from sin through repentance and faith, they have turned to a humanized religion based on human betterment—better housing, better jobs, better education, and better social uplift for the poor and those who have been denied what they call social justice. Pointing to the usual church, they say it has outlived its usefulness, has deteriorated into a sort of religious social club.

Jonah was called to go to Nineveh and cry out a warning message. "Yet forty days and Nineveh shall be overthrown." It was a startling message. How could he deliver it?

Jonah was a man of God but got terribly tangled up as he considered the message. A devout Jew, he suffered, as many others of his race, from prejudice. God had called Israel to separation, to avoid contamination with evil such as was common among the Gentiles. But like many Christians of our day, he misread the divine meaning of separation.

"Be separate" does not mean to withdraw from all contact with those who know not the Lord. It means, Be not contaminated with evil.

Morally we are to be separate. "Come out from among them, and be ye separate." "Touch not, taste not, handle not" that which would corrupt holiness of soul. Even the appearance of evil is to be avoided, and there is to be "no fellowship with the unfruitful works of darkness."

But this does not mean we should live secluded lives. We are to be witnesses, carriers of the gospel, warning against sin, inviting sinners to change their ways, to accept the Lord Jesus that they might live for Him now and be prepared for the life which is to come. Jonah was to be pure in principles and habits, but free to reach needy men, a freedom which he came near throwing away.

Although Jonah was a prophet, the Book of Jonah is not a prophecy. It is the story of a man of God and some of his struggles.

Let us think of some possible reflections of Jonah. What would his people think were he to defile his Jewish separation, as he understood it, by taking God's message to a heathen city? Then he feared that God, so tender of heart, might after all refuse to destroy the city. What would this mean to his reputation as a prophet? How distorted one's thoughts may become! What confusion wrongly directed thoughts may bring. Jonah so yielded to confusing thoughts that his soul sank into despair.

Jonah's message was a message of doom which God used to awaken the people of Nineveh to their need and peril. And when it was finally delivered, God was in it. It is not only what we preach, but how full of love and the Spirit we are. We have a message and a commission, "Go ye." If we have not been going, let us go.

Across the street from one of our older and well-attended churches lived a man. The church called a new pastor, and this pastor dropped in on this man, inviting him to the church, telling him about Jesus. The man said, "For twenty years I have lived in this home, and you are the first person who has spoken to me about church or Christ."

I wonder how many there are, right in our neighborhood, to whom we have shown no interest? We let opportunity after opportunity slip from our grasp.

Who can estimate the value of the personal touch? So much of the ministry of Jesus was personal. He touched the leper; He gave sight to the blind; He comforted a distressed woman. Over and over it was the personal touch. Let Him be our example.

When I was a lad, I was a sinner. I often attended Sunday evening services at a small church in the neighborhood. Thinking back, the minister was not a great preacher, but the warmth of his welcome endeared him to me. And in that church was an elderly man who sat on a side bench next to the wall. I do not recall ever hearing him testify, but there was something about him that impressed me as to his godliness. Later I worked with him for a time. He did not say much. From time to time he would speak a few words to me, telling me of Jesus and how I ought to give my life to Him.

He may not have known it, yet his every word made its mark in my heart. We are to sow beside all waters.

Some years ago I met a minister in Iowa— an ordinary man who did not impress me in any unusual way. Then I was told that he pastored a rural church, visited among the people, looking on all the territory round about as his parish. And I was told that he had the most far-reaching ministry of any in the district. He loved and showed his love in the interest he showed for all. They called on him to pray for their sick, to bury their dead, and many gave their hearts to the Lord. He did not preach denomination, he preached Jesus.

We need a courage of faith. Jonah shrank—and when he shrank, he failed. It was when he obeyed the divine command that his message had success.

The world needs spiritual help. The Church needs fresh revival, a revival of divine power, of heart compassion, of unselfish zeal. Without this, men may be ever so learned, ever so naturally gifted, yet fail. We must remember the admonition of Jesus, "Without me ye can do nothing."

May God set our souls on fire and help us that we come not short in these days in which we live!

THE PLACE OF OBEDIENCE IN REVIVAL

A Message Given Thursday Morning, August 29, 1968

HAL C. NOAH

DURING THE DISPENSATION OF ISRAEL the Jews were both custodians of the Word of God and responsible for its proclamation. The fact that the Jews failed to carry out God's purpose for the Gentiles is discussed in Romans 9:30-33.

However, there were some exceptions. Jonah is one, although he must be classified as an unwilling missionary. Nevertheless, Nineveh was evangelized in spite of Jonah's negative attitude.

Jonah was a prophet in Israel during the reign of Rehoboam. His name means "dove," and he occupies a unique place as the first foreign missionary.

Jonah was instructed by the Lord to "arise, go to Nineveh, that great city, and cry against it; for their wickedness is come up before me" (Jonah 1:2). God was concerned about that great city.

Today we are concerned about the wickedness of our great cities! Their drunkenness, murder, dope, riots, and racial difficulties are the great problems of our day.

Nineveh was the capital of the Assyrian Empire with a population of from 600,000 to 1,000,000. There were 120,000 children who had not reached accountability in Nineveh. It was probably the largest city in the world at that time!

Instead of obeying God, Jonah consulted "with the flesh"—his own will—and rose up to flee to Tarshish, a city in the opposite direction.

During Jonah's runaway voyage a severe storm arose, so terrible that even the heathen sailors were terrified. They went so far as to call a prayer meeting and asked Jonah to attend!

Jonah pled guilty to being the troublemaker but did not request passage to Nineveh. The sailors on board began to question him instead of immediately tossing him in the water. These heathen sailors were more concerned for *one* life than was Jonah for the hundreds of thousands of people who lived in Nineveh!

The Bible says God prepared a great fish. There were three purposes for it. The first was *preservation*—it kept Jonah from drowning. The second was *correction*—it made him face up to his responsibility as a prophet and the awfulness of living out of God's will. The third was *restoration*—Jonah came out of the sea as one coming forth from the grave.

Chapter two deals with a change in Jonah. God used that fish to teach us the gospel of the second chance for saints who see their condition of self-will and disobedience and repent of it.

The Word of the Lord came unto Jonah the second time, and the Bible says the people of Nineveh believed the preaching of Jonah and repented. They did this because he was a prophet with a testimony of deliverance from certain death. He had experienced God's resurrection power—and this was a sign to them. We too must experience this same power of resurrection and deliverance through Jesus Christ our living Lord.

It seems unbelievable, but after the whole city had been saved, Jonah was very displeased and exceedingly angry.

Jonah then built himself a booth and sat in its shadow. He was angry, pouting, and sitting in self-pity because God had saved the city. "And the Lord God prepared a gourd, and made it to come up over Jonah." For this the prophet was glad because the gourd provided comfort for him. We cannot criticize Jonah too much here when we consider the Christians who are happier with the comforts of life than the promotion of revival.

God next dealt with Jonah by preparing a worm. It was prepared to destroy the gourd—and no bird, man, or beast could destroy that worm. God said He would take a worm to thresh a mountain. There were mountains of selfishness and wrong attitudes in Jonah. The worm caused the gourd to wither.

Then God prepared an east wind, and Jonah prayed that he might die. God said to Jonah, "Doest thou well to be angry . . . thou hast not labored, neither madest it grow; which came up in a night, and perished in a night" (Jonah 4:9, 10).

We who are Christians in this hour are God's representatives. We not only have one city, but cities by the hundreds that we are commissioned to evangelize. I fear that we, like Jonah, are calloused and indifferent, filled with self-pity. We are too occupied with the gourds. Let us be careful that a mere worm does not destroy the thing in our lives that we care about, as it did in Jonah's.

Do we have something in our lives that takes the place of the love of lost souls? If we have lost this love for souls, God will restore it. "The love of God is shed abroad in our hearts by the Holy Ghost which is given unto us" (Romans 5:5). God help us to ever be filled with the love of our Lord Jesus Christ for a world that is lost.

AFTERNOON MESSAGES

THE MINISTRY OF THE CHURCH TO THE LORD

A Message Given Tuesday Afternoon, August 27, 1968

G. RAYMOND CARLSON

"Worthy is the Lamb . . . to receive" (Revelation 5:12).

"As they ministered to the Lord" (Acts 13:2).

THE EXPRESSION *ministry to the Lord*, as used in this message, does not refer to ministry as being done unto the Lord. It is, rather, an expression synonymous with the word *worship*.

All of God's purposes center in Himself. His purpose preceded His creation. He declares that all things are made for Himself. "For of him, and through him, and to him, are all things: to whom be the glory forever" (Romans 11:36). "For by him were all things created, that are in heaven, and that are in earth, visible and invisible, whether they be thrones, or dominions, or principalities, or powers: all things were created by him, and for him: and he is before all things, and by him all things consist" (Colossians 1:16, 17).

All divine actions find birth in God's will and are according to His purpose. "Thou art worthy, O Lord, to receive glory and honor and power: for thou hast created all things, and for thy pleasure they are and were created" (Revelation 4:11; compare Ephesians 1:5, 6, 9).

God's purposes and acts are for His own glory. "Even every one that is called by my name: for I have created him for my glory" (Isaiah 43:7; compare Isaiah 60:21; 61:3). Little wonder that in the prayer Jesus taught His dis-

ciples to pray (Luke 11:1-4) so much of the prayer is given to worship—and that as a priority.

God the Father never had a thought from eternity to eternity that did not center in God the Son. To the Father, Christ is everything, and He loves Him so much that He wants to people the universe with those who are formed in His image. "For whom he did foreknow, he also did predestinate to be conformed to the image of his Son, that he might be the firstborn among many brethren" (Romans 8:29).

In the sacred scene of John 17 we are given a glimpse of the holy of holies. We stand with bowed heads and hearts and with shoes removed as God the Son holds conversation with God the Father. Listen as Jesus "lifted up his eyes to heaven, and said, Father, the hour is come; glorify thy Son, that thy Son also may glorify thee" (John 17:1).

The Greek word for glory is *doxa*. At one time the word meant "opinion." If one's opinion agreed with others, he was orthodox; if it differed he was heterodox. The two opinions formed a paradox. Gradually the word *doxa* came to mean "one's opinion of God," and finally to mean "glory." Thus we have the Doxology, which is the science of glory.

Perhaps nowhere more than in John's Gospel is the glory of Jesus Christ revealed more wonderfully. The special characteristic of John's message is his testimony to the *doxa*, the glory that

54

shines through the Person, life, and work of Christ. He witnesses to the glory of the Word become flesh. Even though Jesus was not yet glorified, John sees the entire life of Jesus illuminated by brilliant shafts of glory. These luminous shafts were not mere reflections of future glory. Even in His humiliation Jesus manifested glory.

John said, "We beheld his glory." Such an insight demanded a special perception. The Jews saw Jesus without seeing His glory and they were angered and offended. In the midst of the dark tragedies and unspeakable sufferings of the Saviour, John saw an unquenchable light shining through that awful darkness as a glory that radiates through the humiliation of the Saviour.

Jesus Christ is all in all. This is the testimony of Scripture. Moses, by whom came the Law, testified that grace and truth would come by Christ. Portrayed in Genesis as the Promised Seed, the Isaac who was not spared, the Joseph sold by His brethren and exalted as Saviour and Prince, He is the sacrificial Lamb of Exodus, the Perfect Offering of Leviticus, the Sin-Bearer of Numbers, and all-sufficient Guide of Deuteronomy.

Listen to the testimony of the sweet singer of Israel, to Isaiah, Jeremiah, Ezekiel, Daniel, Micah, and all the prophets. Each one declares Him to be all in all.

Throughout the four Gospels, the Acts, and the Epistles, Christ is all in all. All bear testimony to the words of the Father, "This is my beloved Son, in whom I am well pleased" (Matthew 3:17).

Little wonder that the millions of the glory world join with loud voices in proclaiming, "Worthy is the Lamb that was slain to receive power, and riches, and wisdom, and strength, and honor, and glory, and blessing" (Revelation 5:12).

I. What Is Ministry to the Lord?

The Revelation states, "Worthy is the Lamb . . . to receive." Do we not place the emphasis here all too seldom? Again and again we come to our Lord that we might receive from Him. And when we do come to Him with an expression of grateful praise, is it not for what He does for us? This is well and good. But how much time do we spend in adoration of Him for who He is rather than for what He has done. This latter should not be left undone, but do you not think He craves expression of our love for who He is?

The "Lord did not set his love upon" us or choose us because of who we were, but because He loved us (Deuteronomy 7:7, 8). Why do we love Him? It is reasonable to love God because He has been good to us. The love which we express to Him because of His kindness to us is acceptable to Him. It is, however, a lower degree of love and less selfless than that love which arises from an understanding and an appreciation of what God is in Himself, aside from His gifts.

I love my wife. I love her even more dearly today than I did at the marriage altar. I am grateful that she is a wonderful homemaker and an excellent housekeeper. But I love her not foremost for this; I love her because I love her.

"Worthy is the Lamb . . . to receive." For the most part our communication with Him is so we may receive something from Him. But does He not yearn to receive something which none other than His children can give Him? It is true that in a sense we can give Him nothing, but it is also true that He desires nothing more than our love expressed in worship to Him for His total worthiness.

Christ must have preeminence (Colossians 1: 18). At Jordan's banks the Father called the attention of the world to the Son in whom He was well pleased. Again He gave preeminence to the Son at the Transfiguration where He said, "Hear ye him." The Holy Spirit gives preeminence to the Son (John 16:14), and the heavenly hosts magnify Him (Revelation 5:8-14).

Jesus is the Word of God (John 1:1), the fullness of God (John 1:14), and the full revelation or explanation of God (John 1:18). In this latter verse— ". . . the only begotten Son . . . hath declared him"—the word translated "declared" in its original meaning is the word from which we get our word *exegesis*, meaning "to reveal or to make known." It is in the aorist tense which denotes a once-for-all action. Jesus is the full revelation of God.

The Christian revelation tells us that One is God the Father Almighty, Maker of heaven and earth, who is to be worshiped in the Spirit, in the name of Jesus Christ our Lord.

II. How Do We Minister to the Lord?

The term translated "ministered to the Lord" in Acts 13:2 is rendered "worshiped the Lord" by some translators. True ministry to the Lord is true worship.

The word *worship* comes to us from the Anglo-Saxon word *weorth-scipe,* which, in the development of the language, became *worth-ship* and then *worship*. It means "to ascribe worth." When we worship, we are acknowledging worth. The words, "Thou art worthy, O Lord, to receive glory and honor and power" (Revelation 4:11), and similar expressions, get to the central meaning of worship as indicated by the word itself.

An excellent description of worship is given by Dr. P. F. Bresee. He states:

"Worship rises high above all forms. If it attempts to find utterance through them, it will set them on fire, and glow and burn in their consuming flame and rise as an incense to God. If it starts with the impartation and receiving of the great thought of God; if it waits to hear His infinite will and eternal love, it spreads its pinion to fly to His bosom, there to breathe out its unutterable devotion. . . .

"It is not the learning of some new thing; not a new shading of some thought which is a matter of interest; it is not the repeating, parrot-like, of some written form. But it is the cry of the soul, deep, earnest, intense, loud, the farthest removed from what might be regarded as cathedral service, with the intoning of prayer and praise, and where the light falls but dimly, the muffled music and sentiment rolling back upon the mind in subdued sensibility. I suppose this is about the best earth-born, man-made form of worship one can find. But that which is here described is something altogether different . . . different from a gathering of people who wait to be sung at, prayed and preached at until they can decently leave. Worship seen here rises from the soul . . . outbursting passion of . . . heart . . . breaks forth like a pent-up storm . . . rolls forth like a mighty tornado" (*The Preacher's Magazine,* March, 1960).

The word *worship* is first found in Genesis 22:5. Abraham is on his way to offer up Isaac to God and he calls it worship. This setting provides a clue to worship. It denotes giving God something. (See 1 Chronicles 16:29 and Matthew 2:2, 11 as other illustrations of what worship is.)

Ministry to the Lord is different from ministry to the church and to the lost. The former is that which goes up to God, something which is given to God by man. As such, it is worship. The other two are that which comes from God to man. In other words, they are something received from God.

Abraham, in worshiping God, was not only giving God something but he was giving God something he had received from God.

Abraham offered Isaac who is a type of Christ. Aaron and his sons took the ram of consecration in their hands and waved it before the Lord for a wave offering (Leviticus 8:25-27). In like manner we, with hearts full of Christ, worship the Father in spirit and in truth. That is why the great hymns of the Church are so full of Christ. They exalt His Person and His work, His glory and His grace. We should occupy our thoughts with Him rather than with His blessings. We worship the Giver and not His gifts.

Abraham told the servants, "Abide ye here . . . I and the lad will go yonder and worship." Abraham could only worship in the place "of which God had told him," the "place afar off."

Our place of worship, of ministry to the Lord, is yonder. We must go from here to yonder. That place is within the veil—in the inner court.

God presents some of the requisites for ministry to Him in Ezekiel 44. In verse 5 He instructs us to "mark well," to observe, to pay attention to His words. The passage points out the difference between ministering to human need and to the Lord Himself. The former is not enough; the latter must have priority.

In Luke 17:7-10 the Lord presents this same concept. He speaks of the servant who has been plowing or feeding cattle. Coming from the field the servant, instead of sitting down to eat, girds himself to first serve the master. We are so prone to talk about plowing and feeding instead of ministering to the Master. More of our conversation and thoughts relate to the results of our labor than to worship and ministry to the Lord of the harvest. There are far more Marthas than Marys. But Mary had done the "one thing needful" and had "chosen that good part."

III. The Importance of Ministry to the Lord

The pressure is on us for ministry in the outer court where all can see. God desires that we shall come alone in the inner court to offer sacrifices on the altar of incense. He places priority on ministry to Himself.

The Arabian Desert experience of three years was an important part of Paul's life. Elijah dwelt at Cherith. God performed a miracle there just as He did when fire came down from heaven. Human desire is for the ministry in a Corinth or Ephesus without an Arabian desert, for a fire experience at Carmel without the aloneness of a Cherith. Response seems better, offerings are better, the soulish thrill is better in Ephesus or

Carmel; but spiritual growth comes by the desert and Cherith.

Note the expressions in Ezekiel: "They shall come near to me to minister unto me"; "they shall stand before me to offer unto me." Involved is drawing near, standing before, waiting. The goose hollers to get back to the crowd. The eagle soars alone to the heavens and gains perspective. "They that wait upon the Lord shall renew their strength; they shall mount up with wings as eagles; they shall run, and not be weary; and they shall walk, and not faint" (Isaiah 40:31).

When God's saints gather in some secret place, behind an iron or bamboo curtain at the risk of their lives, they do so not to hear some noted speaker or singer, but rather to worship the Master through the Spirit. Sadly and tragically many of us are too prone to praise human ability and personality. True worship, true ministry to the Lord, centers in Him. There is only one thing that will bring us into the inner-court relationship—from out there doing to the inside standing and waiting—and that is love for Him.

God's greats of old were altar builders. Noah is the first recorded builder of an altar. He was followed by Abraham, Isaac, Jacob, and Moses.

Noah's first act on coming out of the ark following the Flood was to build an altar (Genesis 8:20). Later he lost his perspective and planted a vineyard (Genesis 9:20). The results of his sacrifices on the altar caused the Lord to "smell a sweet savor" (Genesis 8:21). When he planted a vineyard, he became the first recorded drunkard of history (Genesis 9:21). Each of us must decide where our priorities will be.

Picture Abraham as he offers to God on the altar. The unclean birds of the air swoop in to steal from the sacrifice. Abraham takes a stick and drives them away. Always the enemy strikes to rob us and God of our sacrifice of worship. Eternal vigilance is necessary. Abraham pitched his tent and built an altar. Today altogether too many have pitched out the altar and spend their time building "tents."

Twice as much effort is required for worship as for work. Isaiah saw the seraphims above the throne of the Lord. "Each one had six wings; with twain he covered his face, and with twain he covered his feet, and with twain he did fly" (6:2). As Isaiah saw the Lord, he recognized his own inadequacy.

IV. Results of Ministry to the Lord

Ministry to the Lord will bring delight to Him and blessing and power to us. New insights and strengths will come to the worshiper. Worship and ministry within the inner court will open new vistas of God's glory and grace to us. The worshiper will find a new source of strength through his rich personal fellowship with the Lord. There will be the offering of incense which is pleasing to God. The gifts of the Holy Spirit will operate. The worshiper will find a depth in the Holy Spirit which will be therapeutic to his whole being. "He that speaketh in an unknown tongue speaketh not unto men, but unto God" (1 Corinthians 14:2). I am of the conviction that this type of worship cleanses the subconscious and edifies—builds up—the one who ministers unto God. And the Holy Spirit will make "intercession for us with groanings which cannot be uttered" (Romans 8:26).

Ministry to the Lord involves love, admiration, wonder, and adoration. No doubt the most serious charge that can be brought against Christians today is that we are not sufficiently in love with Jesus. Paul writes, "For whether we be beside ourselves, it is God: or whether we be sober, it is for your cause. For the love of Christ constraineth us" (2 Corinthians 5:13, 14). In Weymouth's translation the passage reads, "For the love of Christ overmasters us."

Overmastered by Christ's love, Paul went to ungodly, iniquitous Ephesus where the Lord helped him to establish a great church (Acts 19) and where he labored night and day for three years (Acts 20:31).

Just a few years later Paul wrote a letter to these former raw heathen (Ephesians 2:1, 2) and addressed them as those who are "blessed with all spiritual blessings in heavenly places in Christ" (1:3).

In less than forty years the beloved John in Revelation 2:1-7 was given a message for that very church. The church was still doctrinally sound, orthodox, hating evil. They were known for their works, labor, and patience. But the three cardinal graces (1 Thessalonians 1:3) were gone. It was no longer the work of faith, the labor of love, and patience of hope; faith, love, and hope were gone. God's indictment was that they had left their first love.

If we are to survive the present world upheaval, we shall need to recapture the spirit of ministry to the Lord in worship. We need a new revelation of the greatness of God and the beauty of Jesus. It seems that we have trained a generation occupied in finding things for which to thank God. There is a vast difference as to where we focus our attention. Is our need the object of our worship and ministry? Or is God the object of our worship and ministry?

The late A. W. Tozer wrote: "And the church, the poor church! We have banquets, we have conferences, we have Sunday schools, we have morning worship and evening gospel services— we have everything. We're the busiest crowd of little eager beavers that ever tramped over the North American soil. But we are not worshipers. There is scarcely a church service where we can feel the spirit of worship . . . the churches are too busy promoting people and things to cultivate the presence of God."

Does this mean that we shall not minister to the church and to the world? No! A thousand times, no! In Acts 13 the brethren *first* "ministered to the Lord and fasted." Then under the Spirit's direction Paul and Barnabas were sent out to minister to human need. This is balance. Ministry to the Lord will bring a burden for human need.

As the Father sent the Son into the world, even so the Son sends us (John 17:18; 20:21). To have a fruitful outer-court ministry, it is imperative that we make inner-court ministry a priority.

THE MINISTRY OF THE CHURCH TO THE SAINTS

A Message Given Wednesday Afternoon, August 28, 1968

D. V. HURST

Text: Ephesians 4:8-16.

THE CHURCH HAS A GREAT PRIVILEGE and solemn responsibility to minister to the saints—its own. The church has a mission to itself—the responsibility to build itself up.

In fulfilling this responsibility, it must minister to the whole man: body, soul, and spirit. The precedent was set in the Early Church. But primarily it is to the inner man that the church ministers, for this is the essential being of man. Although the outer man breaks, ages, and dies, the inner man can be renewed day by day.

"Bodily exercise profiteth little: but godliness is profitable unto all things, having promise of the life that now is, and of that which is to come" (1 Timothy 4:8). Can we paraphrase this? "Ministering to the body profits a little; ministering to the spirit profits unto all things in this life and in the life to come."

The church has been given the means and the message with which to minister to itself. In fact, the means is in the message. In the words of Peter to the man at the gate, "Such as I have give I thee," is found the ministry of the church. Freely it was received; freely it must give. Such as it has, it gives.

To discuss this theme, let's look at four basic questions: (1) Why is the church responsible to thus minister? (2) Who shall minister? (3) What is to be ministered? or, What is the content of ministry? (4) According to what pattern is this ministry to be performed?

First, to work on common ground, let us define two terms.

1. *Saints* are the individual believers, the church itself. The view in which some are seen as especially holy and self-sacrificing and therefore worthy of veneration or canonization after death is hardly in keeping with Paul's epistles addressed to the living—the "saints" of Rome, Ephesus, or Colossae. Repeatedly in his epistles he writes to all the saints, to the whole church. One does not have to die to be called a saint; but he is one here and now if he believes in the Lord Jesus Christ.

2. *Ministry* has "service" as its root idea. The words for *minister* mean "table waiter, under-rower in a large ship, or servant." In their Biblical context, however, they take on added connotation. This is best seen in some of the persons assigned to minister—apostles, prophets, evangelists, and pastor-teachers.

There is a spiritual quality attached to the word *ministry* in the New Testament. Hence, in essence, the term means "spiritual service." It is spiritual in content, means, motive, and purpose. Indeed, we are talking about spiritual service when we talk about ministry to the saints.

Ministry can be physical or material service, but with a spiritual motive and purpose which conveys a spiritual content. A cup of water in His name is a spiritual service! Two examples can be given:

1. Jesus ministered to the disciples with a towel and basin. He performed this service to

the disciples only. He apparently did not make a practice of it in general. He did not "stand at the city gate" to do so. Nor was He preoccupied with this kind of ministry even to the disciples or the "saints." He performed it to teach a great truth: the least in service can be the greatest in motive and purpose—a pure, nonselfseeking ministry. His purpose was more than to wash their feet; it was to teach truth through demonstration.

2. Paul told the Romans he was going to Jerusalem to "minister unto the saints" (15:25). He had gathered money for the poor saints there. He said, "It hath pleased them verily [at Macedonia and Achaia]; and their debtors they are. For if the Gentiles have been made partakers of their spiritual things, their duty is also to minister unto them in carnal things." He continued, "When ... I have performed this, and have sealed to them this fruit, I will come ... unto you ... in the fullness of the blessing of the gospel of Christ." However, he asked them to pray that his "service which I have for Jerusalem may be accepted of the saints" (Romans 15:27-31).

Now there is a spiritual tone to all of this deed. A spiritual response gave it. A spiritual concern and purpose took it. Prayer accompanied it. It was indeed a spiritual service, a true ministry. But again, it must be noted that Paul also was not preoccupied with this kind of ministry.

It is significant to note in passing that the social concern of the Early Church was toward the saints themselves and that only as dire need indicated. The Early Church was not a socialservice institution dealing in a physical ministry directed either inward or outward!

With this understanding, then, the meaning of the following texts can come into sharp focus: Ephesians 4:8-12; 1 Corinthians 4:1; 1 Peter 4: 10, 11; 1 Corinthians 14:26; 16:15; Hebrews 6: 10, 11; 2 Corinthians 3:6.

I. Why Is It So Vital that the Church Direct Much of Its Spiritual Service Inward?

1. It is the will of God. It is God's purpose to build up a body of believers in the image of His Son! Paul said, "For whom he did foreknow, he also did predestinate to be conformed to the image of his Son, that he might be the firstborn among many brethren" (Romans 8:29). Other texts supporting this are: Acts 14:14-17; Ephesians 5:27; John 17:21-23; Ephesians 2:10.

Jesus implied that the Father had a hand in building His Church as He said to Peter, "Flesh and blood hath not revealed it unto thee, but my Father which is in heaven" (Matthew 16:17).

Paul made it clear that the gifts of Christ—apostles, prophets, evangelists, and pastor-teachers—were given to the church to build it for the ministry.

2. The second reason becomes clear—God is using the church to build the Church, to minister to the saints. The church is an instrument, a channel of God's purpose to build the body of saints being perfected in the image of His Son.

Paul said, "God hath set some in the church, first apostles, secondarily prophets, thirdly teachers, after that miracles, then gifts of healings, helps, governments, diversities of tongues" (1 Corinthians 12:28). Concerning any who may be gifted for ministry, he said, "Seek that ye may excel to the edifying of the church" (1 Corinthians 14:12).

So God is using the church to build the Church, to minister to the saints. But the third reason adds dimension to this.

3. The ministry to the saints is so important that God sent the Holy Spirit to enable the Church to perform effectively and in full accomplishment—"Not by might, nor by power, but by my Spirit, saith the Lord" (Zechariah 4:6).

In discussing the working of the Holy Spirit when He would come, Jesus made it clear that one of His purposes would be to minister to the saints. He was to teach them all things; guide them into all truth; receive of the things of Christ and show them to the saints; and glorify Christ and make Jesus real; communicate assurance of spiritual experience, knowledge, and understanding. These essentially are ministries to the Church, building it up in faith and knowledge and edifying the believers.

The Holy Spirit, then, was sent to enable the Church to minister to itself, to add broad and deep supernatural dimensions to this ministry and to provide all that was necessary for its perfection.

4. A fourth reason is this: The survival of the true Church is at stake as well as its fulfillment of its mission. These are "perilous times." The enemy has always attacked and will continue to attack the Church. It must be built in the faith and in the Spirit to withstand the attack. But the Church must do more than resist attack. It must be on the move, "about the Father's business," doing the "greater works" of which Christ spoke. "The gates of hell shall not prevail"; but only if the Church is mighty in the Word and

strong in the Spirit. It can prevail in the world only if the Spirit prevails in it!

II. Who, Then, Shall Minister?

We have answered this, in effect. We have talked about the ministry without distinguishing between the "cleric" and the "layman." However, some distinction can be made and should be made.

1. *There is a called and chosen ministry!* God has provided all that is necessary for a strong, viable, called, chosen, set-apart, endowed, and sent-out ministry. The record of Acts shows this. Christ gave the apostles, prophets, evangelists, and pastor-teachers to the Church. The purpose of these gifts and the cost of their provision underscores their worth! It sets them apart!

Paul himself is an example. He said he was "made a minister, according to the gift of the grace of God given unto me by the effectual working of his power" (Ephesians 3:7).

2. *However, there is a place of ministry for all believers.* Paul said, "Unto every one of us is given grace according to the measure of the gift of Christ" (Ephesians 4:7). He used the same word *grace* with which he referred to his own gift making him a minister by the effectual working of his power. This strongly suggests that no member of the Body is without some spiritual task and spiritual gift for it.

This same point is underscored later in the same passage. In Ephesians 4:12 three phrases set forth the purposes of the gifts of Christ—for the perfecting of the saints, for the work of the ministry, and for the edifying of the body of Christ.

The construction is such that the first phrase supports the second and third. Then the saints are perfected for the work of the ministry. (The King James Version inserts a comma and, in effect, modifies the meaning.) The saints are brought to a condition of fitness to discharge their functions in the Body. Thus they are fitted for the work of the ministry.

The next result is that the Body is edified. The third phrase depends upon the first two. Thus the perfecters of the saints edify the Body, and the saints themselves—in their ministry according to the gift of grace—edify the Body!

Paul seems to stress this same point in Romans 12:4-8. All are members of the one Body but vary in gifts according to the grace that is given. Each is to function according to that grace— whether prophecy, according to the proportion of faith; or ministry, waiting on ministering; or he that teacheth, on teaching, etc.

This is again implied in Paul's second letter to Timothy: "All scripture is given . . . that the man of God may be perfect, thoroughly furnished unto all good works" (2 Timothy 3: 16, 17). All Scripture is for all the saints that all might grow thereby and minister therewith.

This lesson with many implications is taught in two great pictures in the Word: The Church as the body of Christ and the Church as the Living Temple.

In the Body concept the principle is that every believer shall contribute. In our basic Ephesians passage, Paul said, "That which every joint [or member joined to] supplieth, according to the effectual working in the measure of every part" (Ephesians 4:16). Here there is an infinite variety in the Spirit but an inworking unity of the Spirit in this variety. Each member makes contribution as the Spirit works in him.

In the Living Temple concept believers are "living stones." Peter says they "are built up a spiritual house, a holy priesthood, to offer up spiritual sacrifices" (1 Peter 2:5). And he compares the saints as "lively stones" to Christ the living stone and says, "Ye also, as lively stones, are built. . . ." Each living stone shares in the living, spiritual ministry of the temple!

This is the ingenious source of strength and edification in the Church! Under the new covenant *all* participate in the spiritual life and work of the Church. None are spectators; all are living stones or living members, royal priests and kings. All can minister; all can approach the throne of God directly, communing with God and in behalf of others. All in turn can communicate with the saints and minister to them for God.

The Church is strong when this principle is in force and all minister one to the other. The Church is weak when it is ignored and the ministry is left to a select few—the called and chosen. Balance is needed between the ministry of the pastor-teachers and that of all believers. The pastor-teachers need to be held up in prayer that they might perform their ministry, and all believers need to "wait on their ministry" that with excellence they might edify the Church.

Early Church examples of believers who ministered in excellence are Stephen and Philip. They went on to further ministry and the Church was blessed. This is the pattern for today!

III. What and How Do We Minister?

If the Church is to be built up, with what is it to be built? What material will the spiritual mason, tinsmith, and carpenter use? What is the content of ministry? What is to be "served"?

Peter addressed the lame man (Acts 3) and said, "Such as I have give I thee." The Church that would minister must possess! It ministers best what it has been given by Christ! The Church needs to rediscover the provisions in Christ, the true contents of spiritual ministry, the true message and means of ministry.

We minister to the deep-seated spiritual needs of man. We minister to the heart of man—to the root of man's personality. The full gospel is the answer to all of man's need. In ministering to the saints, the Church seeks to apply the whole gospel to the whole man for then alone can he be made whole. Since man lives his life "out of the heart," it is primarily to the needs of the heart that the Church speaks.

The answer to the questions what and how is one and the same. The method is in the message!

1. *We minister the things of the Lord Jesus Christ*—the "things" freely given to us by the Father who "spared not his own Son, but delivered him up for us all" (Romans 8:32) that he might give us these things. We minister the provisions of His death, His resurrection, and His coming again.

a. Things of the past—repentance and forgiveness.

b. Things of the present—the indwelling life and intercessory work of our Priest.

c. Things of the future—His promises, the prophetic view of things to come, and the "powers of the age to come."

We minister Christ, the "Water of Life" and the "Bread of Life"; the "eternal Truth"; the integrating core of all knowledge, understanding, and learning; the beginning and the end; and the One by whom "all things consist" and for whom all things exist; the heavenly exalted, sovereign, way-preparing, interceding, omnipresent, and coming again Christ; the all in all; the answer to all man's needs.

2. *We minister the things of the work of God*, the "whole counsel of God," the living Word in the written Word, the "manna which thou knowest not," for "man shall not live by bread alone, but by every word that proceedeth out of the mouth of God" (Matthew 4:4). The commandments, the precepts, and the judgments of the Lord; the Lamp, the Light, and the Way; the words of Christ which are "spirit and life"

—these things we minister to build up the saints in the full assurance of faith.

3. *We minister the things of the Spirit*, the things "of the kingdom of God," not "meat and drink; but righteousness, and peace, and joy in the Holy Ghost. For he that in these things serveth Christ is acceptable to God, and approved of men" (Romans 14:17, 18).

a. We minister the baptism of the Holy Spirit (Acts 1:8) which brings a fullness and abundance, an enablement and enduement, a power for service.

b. We minister the fruit of the Spirit Galatians 5:22, 23): Love—no greater has ever been known than God's love "shed abroad in our hearts by the Holy Ghost" (Romans 5:5). Joy—Christ's joy which He promised when He left and which the Spirit brings. Peace—with God and the peace of Christ, a peace that "passeth knowledge." Longsuffering, gentleness, goodness, meekness, temperance—the gentle character traits of great living, universally admired. Faith—the foundation for all good living and without which no man can please God.

c. We minister the gifts of the Spirit, the equipment and enduement for true spiritual service: The word of wisdom, the word of knowledge, faith, gifts of healing, the working of miracles, prophecy, discerning of spirits, tongues, and interpretation (1 Corinthians 12:8-10). We minister prayer in the Holy Spirit and the "communion of the Holy Ghost."

d. We minister "songs and hymns and spiritual songs" building up the saints in the songs of the soul set free. We minister spiritual-mindedness and thanksgiving, sanctification and holiness born of the Spirit, without which no man shall see God.

We minister all of these things of the Spirit and more, seeking to bless the Body of Christ in the Spirit and by the Spirit "speaking the truth in love" and building it up.

4. *We minister the things of the sacraments*—water baptism and holy communion symbolizing the inward work and continuing work of Christ in our behalf and standing for the promises that build faith and hope. For this we are told to do until He returns!

5. *We minister things that abide*—"now abideth faith, hope, charity, these three; but the greatest of these is charity" (1 Corinthians 13:13). "God is love" and out of divine love flows love, faith, and hope.

a. We minister faith that abides, because with it life has meaning and promise, and they "that cometh to God must believe that he is, and that he is a rewarder of them that diligently seek him" (Hebrews 11:6).

b. We minister hope that abides because "we have been begotten unto a living hope," and "we are saved by hope." We know "the hope of his calling, . . . the riches of the glory of his inheritance in the saints; and what is the exceeding greatness of his power to us-ward" (Ephesians 1:18, 19) and hath planted us with Him in death and raised us with Him in resurrection. In faith and hope we patiently await its manifestation. And "when Christ, who is our life, shall appear, then . . . [we] also shall appear with him" and be like Him for we shall see Him as He is!

c. We minister love that abides, because man needs love above all else. His greatest need is to be loved, to know someone cares. We can lead man to experience this divine love and to love God in return.

When life is reduced to its minimum, void of all facade and the "abundance of things," these three remain! Although the heavens shake and the elements "melt with fervent heat," these three things abide! These, we minister!

6. *We minister the things of eternal life*, the life of Christ, abundant, full, and eternal. "For as the Father hath life in himself; so hath he given to the Son to have life in himself" (John 5:26). Therefore, he who receives the Son hath life.

Jesus said, "I live by the Father; so he that eateth me, even he shall live by me" (John 6: 57). Again, He said, "I am come that they might have life, and that they might have it more abundantly" (John 10:10). And again, "He that believeth on me hath everlasting life" (John 6:47).

IV. Finally, We Minister to Seek to Build Up the Saints According to the Divine Pattern Which Is Christ Jesus Himself

It is His image to which God ordained the saints should conform. His life and character are the pattern. This is the standard of excellence by which the Church measures all its work in the effort to build up the saints.

Conclusion

The church must minister to the saints in this day and thus fulfill the will of God as an instrument of His purpose. All saints must minister and seek to develop their ministry, seeking to excel for the good of the Body.

Who would choose a "mess of pottage" or an abundance of material things over and against an eternal birthright and an abundance of spiritual possessions? Who would choose to minister the material things as against the spiritual things? May the Church make its choice right and choose to "declare all the counsel of God," the new covenant in the Spirit, that men of God might be made perfect, throughly furnished unto all good works, and that they may be built up in the faith and edified, and that God may be glorified.

THE MINISTRY OF THE CHURCH TO THE WORLD

A Message Given Thursday Afternoon, August 29, 1968

CYRIL HOMER

Luke in his Gospel said, "For the Son of man is come to seek and to save that which was lost" (Luke 19:10). This is the whole meaning of the gospel as it relates to this world. This verse of Scripture is taken from the account of the conversion of Zacchaeus and is amplified by the Parable of the Pounds (Luke 19:11-26). In this one passage then is recorded the conversion of one person; the statement of the purpose of Christ in His redemptive work; the necessity for Christ to share His ministry with members of His kingdom, who, occupying until He comes, must make the most of their talent and time having the evident promise of fruitfulness for effort given.

This passage also gives us that grand statement that bewildered many religious leaders: "That he was gone to be guest with a man that is a sinner" (Luke 19:7). In derision they uttered words that actually and accurately described the mission of Christ. The central thrust of the gospel is that God is interested in the eternal welfare of humanity and has sent His Son to manifest His love and to die in redemptive action to provide forgiveness of sin. He has also enlisted the help of every citizen of His kingdom to take this message to "every creature."

We have become so taken up with the issues of this age that the church in many places has lost the keen awareness that men still have to go to hell if they die in their sins. The great danger of this church generation is that it can become so busy with the social and materialistic problems it neglects the one great work committed to it. A man's soul is infinitely more important than his body. It is a simple fact that once a man's soul is in right relationship with God, divine provision is made for body, soul, and spirit. The voice of God is speaking as clearly today as it was in the beginning of the Christian church: "Go ye into all the world, and preach the gospel to every creature" (Mark 16:15).

In the Parable of the Pounds we find that God provides a kingdom, gives the kingdom citizens their mission, provides the means of accomplishment, and promises to return someday for an accounting.

I. The Church Under Orders

John W. Stott has said, "Jesus is like a commanding officer who can deploy his forces as he chooses and send them wherever he likes." Christ has all authority to say, "*Go!*" Having commanded the Church thus, He has never cancelled His orders! In the light of the ever-expanding world population, it is imperative that we hear His voice calling us as soldiers of the Cross into the ranks of His royal army.

There are a number of prerequisites for a successful army. Included are absolute discipline, intensive training, adequate weapons, and clearly stated objectives. When each of these phases has been accomplished, there is produced a potentially victorious army living in a thoroughly disciplined manner and carrying out in detail its commander's orders.

As a chaplain in World War II I was sent to a unit in Hawaii. This unit had been well trained for several years; its equipment was the most modern of that war; it was at full strength in manpower. In spite of all of these factors a restlessness existed in its ranks because this unit had never been engaged in action with the enemy. The AWOL rate was high; morale was low.

One day the entire unit was assembled and told to get ready to leave the island; the equipment was boxed and sent to the port. Almost immediately the spirits of the men began to lift. The men were awakened very early one morning and in the gathering dawn were told to board trucks headed for Pearl Harbor where a ship was waiting.

Excitement was high. No one knew where we were going, but at least the purpose of our being a fighting unit was nearing realization. Once out to sea, we found ourselves a part of a great convoy plowing its way through the South Pacific. At last the day arrived when all the men were gathered on the deck of that great ship, and the announcement was made that we were a part of the Tenth Army on its way to Okinawa to meet the enemy in its home territory. A great shout lifted into the air, and from that moment an exhilarating spirit captured the men. We were finally *under orders* and were moving out to accomplish our objectives. Our training, discipline, and weapons had been welded together, and we were now about to engage in battle! We had our orders!

In this same way Christians must be trained and disciplined by the Word, by the Spirit, and by experience. We must know that our "weapons . . . are . . . mighty through God to the pulling down of strongholds" (2 Corinthians 10:4). The orders are explicit; enemy territory is vulnerable. The very gates of hell shall yield to the Church and to the gospel of Jesus Christ. Under His orders there is no frontier that is impenetrable; no enemy that is invincible; no power that can silence us. The Church has heard its Commander cry, "Move out!" One can hear the steady tramp of marching feet moving to the ends of the earth. The message will be carried! We are under divine orders!

II. The Church Under Authority

God knew that the commission to go with the gospel would not be sufficient unless He accompanied it with a promise of power and authority. After His death and resurrection, with the full flush of victory over Satan upon Him, Christ spoke to His Church and said, "As my Father hath sent me, even so send I you" (John 20:21).

The Word of God teaches that Christ came preaching the good news of the gospel, healing all manner of diseases, casting out demons, and taking complete charge of every situation that confronted Him. In like manner He has given us the same authority. According to Mark 16:15-18 these truths are evident: under the preaching of the gospel men who believe will be saved; the Church will have power over Satan; believers will be filled with the Holy Spirit, speaking with new tongues; believers will be protected by God from unseen attacks perpetrated by Satan; and the ministry of divine healing shall be exercised by the laying on of hands.

With this conferring of authority Christ made two great statements concerning power. First, in the postresurrection appearances He announced, "All power is given unto me in heaven and in earth. Go ye therefore, and teach all nations, baptizing them in the name of the Father, and of the Son, and of the Holy Ghost" (Matthew 28:18, 19). We are moving under the authority of an all-powerful Commander. How can we be defeated?

The other statement of Christ is found in Luke 24:47-49: "Repentance and remission of sins should be preached in his name among all nations, beginning at Jerusalem. And ye are witnesses of these things. And, behold, I send the promise of my Father upon you: but tarry ye in the city of Jerusalem, until ye be endued with power from on high."

This statement is amplified in Acts 1:8: "But ye shall receive power, after that the Holy Ghost is come upon you: and ye shall be witnesses unto me both in Jerusalem, and in all Judea, and in Samaria, and unto the uttermost part of the earth."

The baptism of the Holy Spirit was given primarily as an impetus to witnessing the gospel worldwide. The Early Church almost literally fulfilled its obligation to Christ's commission. They moved through the earth with apostolic authority over devils and over man-made persecution. Let us in like manner take up our authority and with power in the Holy Spirit make His message known in all of the world.

III. The Church Under Ordination

The Church is ordained by Christ to achievement. We read in John 15:16: "Ye have not chosen me, but I have chosen you, and ordained you, that ye should go and bring forth fruit, and that your fruit should remain. . . ." He who is the Alpha and the Omega and who sees the end from the beginning has told His Church that its message will be both effective and productive.

In the days of the Early Church even Caesar's household was invaded with the gospel, and it yielded converts. In modern times the most difficult nations and tribes have been reached and have responded. Now the Church flourishes in these areas. Communism once boasted that it would wipe out the church of the living God; but years have passed, and the Church still lives in communistic countries. We shall find fruit attending our efforts as we are endued with Holy Ghost power and are quick to move out on the mission that God has given us.

As we approach the end of this Church Age, we shall have to match the expanding population growth and consequent increasing opportunities of ministry with a stepped-up pace of gospel activity. God has plans for days like these. We must wait in His presence, find His plans, and then be quick to carry out His orders. With modern means of transportation and communication the Church should find itself in its greatest hour of achievement. Let us rise and take this gospel across the street, across the city, across the nation, and around the world.

"This gospel of the kingdom shall be preached in all the world for a witness unto all nations; and then shall the end come" (Matthew 24:14).

PAPERS

FULFILLING OUR MISSION

FIVE YEAR PLAN OF ADVANCE
FIRST YEAR PROJECTION—1969

"... For the time is at hand" (Revelation 22:10).

JESUS CHRIST IS COMING SOON. We believe that God has brought us to this crucial stage of world history because "the time is at hand." We have a mission to fulfill.

And we know that a spiritual mission can be fulfilled only through adequate spiritual preparation and deliberate commitment to God's will. We dare not let past blessings nor present victories lull us into a sense of false security. Neither can we let Satan destroy us through a sense of hopelessness because of abounding iniquity.

We do not spend time preparing for our mission because we are afraid to face our world; rather, we invest time in spiritual preparation because the crisis demands so much more than has ever been demanded of us. We dare not go our own way: we must have God's leading.

Believing that God has called us and empowered us to make an *impact* on our world, the Committee on Advance suggests the following emphases for the Year of Revival:

Identify the Mission of our Church

One task of the Committee on Advance and the Council on Evangelism is to define clearly our church's primary mission. We cannot succeed if we do not understand what God wants us to do. Therefore, this mission must be the the concern of every member.

Mobilize Our Resources for Revival

Mobilization is already underway. Departmental leadership seminars held just before the Council on Evangelism brought national and district leaders together to share in these plans. As a result, action will soon be reflected in departmental activities on national, district, sectional, and local levels.

Proclaim the Mission

As we understand what our mission is, we will earnestly prepare to fulfill it. Therefore, our mission needs to be proclaimed from every pulpit of our Fellowship. We must keep the implications of our mission clearly before us through all the means at our disposal. We must describe this mission clearly so that all our people, including our children, will catch this sense of destiny and share in fulfilling it.

Activate Revival Efforts

We believe revival is spiritual renewal for God's people. Our own hearts must be prepared before we can perform effective service. Our Movement was born in the fires of revival. Spiritual commitments are still made when hearts are aflame with the Holy Ghost. To increase hunger for spiritual renewal, we encourage revival efforts on a wide scale throughout our Movement—in local churches and sections, in districts, for ministers, at camp meetings, on our college campuses, and for headquarters personnel.

Call for Total Commitment

The 1968 watchnight services in our churches will provide the opportunity for a call to total commitment by each individual—commitment of our time, our resources, our abilities, and our lives to fulfill our mission in today's world. Special materials will be available to help each minister and congregation provide a memorable communion-commitment service—to begin to involve all our people in the Year of Revival.

Thrust Forth Laborers

The Plan of Advance is not an effort to tell God how He must work. It is not designed to set a time when each church should move from spiritual renewal to evangelistic outreach. These activities will continue to occur simultaneously, for spiritual preparation inevitably leads to outreach. As this occurs, personal witnessing will be intensified. Ministers and congregations with hearts aflame will move into new areas to spread the Pentecostal message. The banner of Christ will be lifted up in all the world. And when we pray the Lord of harvest to thrust forth laborers, we must be prepared to be the laborers He chooses to thrust forth.

❂ ❂ ❂

Truly, "the time is at hand." Now is the time for us to give ourselves unreservedly to fulfill our mission in today's world. We must move with God in the direction that He chooses so that we may effectively declare His message. The times demand our best. We dare not give any less.

MAINTAINING SPIRITUAL PRIORITIES

GUIDELINES FOR FIVE YEAR
PLAN OF ADVANCE 1969-1973

THE COMMITTEE ON ADVANCE, having prayerfully studied the role of our church in the light of God's Word, believes the fulfillment of our mission depends upon maintaining or, where necessary, restoring certain spiritual priorities. These basic priorities must be the guiding principle of our united effort to serve effectively in these crucial times.

The Priorities of Our Fellowship in Relation to God Are:

To worship Him in spirit and in truth.

"God is a Spirit: and they that worship him must worship him in spirit and in truth" (John 4:24). See also Psalm 29:1, 2; 1 Timothy 2:8.

To maintain unbroken communion.

"If we walk in the light, as he is in the light, we have fellowship one with another, and the blood of Jesus Christ his Son cleanseth us from all sin" (1 John 1:7). See also Luke 10:38-42; Ephesians 4:16.

To share in the ministry of intercession.

"For we know not what we should pray for as we ought: but the Spirit itself maketh intercession for us with groanings which cannot be uttered" (Romans 8:26). See also Ephesians 6:18.

To yield to the Holy Spirit for the full expression of His gifts and fruit.

"The manifestation of the Spirit is given to every man to profit withal" (1 Corinthians 12:7).

See also 1 Corinthians 12:14; Galatians 5:22-25; Colossians 3:12-15.

The Priorities of Our Fellowship in Relation to Believers Are:

To keep in focus our distinctive Pentecostal message and mission.

"And, behold, I send the promise of my Father upon you: but tarry ye in the city of Jerusalem, until ye be endued with power from on high" (Luke 24:49). See also John 7:37-39; Acts 1:4-8; 4:29-33.

To cultivate a sense of mutual responsibility as members of the body of Christ in fulfilling our mission.

"For as the body is one, and hath many members, and all the members of that one body, being many, are one body: so also is Christ" (1 Corinthians 12:12). See also 1 Corinthians 3: 9, 10; Ephesians 4:11-16; Philippians 1:3-5; 2 Thessalonians 3:1.

To use God's Word both in the church and in personal devotions.

"Let the word of Christ dwell in you richly in all wisdom" (Colossians 3:16). See also Matthew 4:4; 2 Timothy 3:14-17; 1 Peter 2:2.

To recognize the prophetic significance of our times.

"Be ye also patient; stablish your hearts: for the coming of the Lord draweth nigh" (James

70

5:8). See also Luke 21:24-33; 1 Thessalonians 4:16, 17; 2 Timothy 3:1-5.

To keep eternal values in view.

"For we must all appear before the judgment seat of Christ; that every one may receive the things done in his body, according to that he hath done, whether it be good or bad. Knowing therefore the terror of the Lord, we persuade men..." (2 Corinthians 5:10, 11). See also Ezekiel 3:17-19; Jude 23.

The Priorities of Our Fellowship in Relation to the Lost Are:

To base soul-winning efforts on the premise that man's primary need is regeneration, although social improvement will follow.

"Except a man be born again, he cannot see the kingdom of God" (John 3:3). See also Romans 3:20-25; 2 Corinthians 5:17; Titus 3:5.

To discern the value of human souls for whom Christ died.

"Forasmuch as ye know that ye were not redeemed with corruptible things, as silver and gold,...but with the precious blood of Christ, as of a lamb without blemish and without spot" (1 Peter 1:18, 19). See also Mark 8:35-37; John 3:16; Revelation 21:8.

To realize the eternal tragedy of souls meeting God unprepared.

"It is better for thee to enter into life maimed, than having two hands to go into hell, into the fire that never shall be quenched: where their worm dieth not, and the fire is not quenched" (Mark 9:43, 44). See also Luke 16:19-31; Revelation 20:11-15.

To expect the Holy Spirit's enablement for an effective witness to the lost.

"But ye shall receive power, after that the Holy Ghost is come upon you: and ye shall be witnesses unto me both in Jerusalem, and in all Judea, and in Samaria, and unto the uttermost part of the earth" (Acts 1:8). See also John 15:26, 27; Acts 2:1-41; 8:26-39.

o   o   o

What we are as a church depends upon what we are as individual members, for a church is the sum of its component parts. *All of us are the church.* By the guidelines we set for ourselves, we determine the direction our church will go.

Only as each of us personally adopts spiritual guidelines for his own life shall we be able to fulfill our mission as a body of Pentecostal believers in today's world.

MORNING SEMINARS

THE BIBLE BASIS FOR EVANGELISM

Speaker: **CORDAS BURNETT**
Moderator: **J. ROBERT ASHCROFT**
Panelists: **BLAKE FARMER, RON McCONNELL, WILLIAM MENZIES**
Recorder: **KENNETH GAMERDINGER**

WEBSTER's *Seventh Collegiate Dictionary* defines *evangelism* as "the winning . . . of personal commitments to Christ." What better definition can be found for this, the mission of the church? "To win personal commitments"—to win souls—to reach men for Jesus Christ.

True, men's ideas of this process have changed from time to time. Who among us does not remember the "protracted meeting," the "revival," the "campaign"? Perhaps all too often we remember these for they were times for men to *camp* and all of us suffered pains when they were gone.

We sometimes speak of revival as if this were evangelism. In the strictest sense of the word, this is not true. The word *revival* comes from the Latin *revivo* which means "to live again" and normally connotes a renewing or making to live again of drifting, discouraged, perhaps backslidden Christians—those who once had lived and now need to live again.

But in evangelism we are not dealing with cold, backslidden, discouraged saints who need to be revived. We are dealing with the total lostness of men, the fact that all men without Jesus Christ are hopelessly and eternally lost. Evangelism is the labor of rescuing men and women from the tragic and final destiny that awaits all men without Jesus Christ.

Once again, Webster says *evangelism* is "a militant, crusading zeal." Our task is to wage unrelenting war against the forces that bind men's souls, and like the crusaders of the past, knowing that if we fail, there is no hope; the world is lost.

Such a declaration that man is eternally lost and needs to be won to Jesus Christ is not a dictum rising out of the philosophical dissertations of ancient men or theological dogma contained within the traditions of our church. This whole, all-important, world-encompassing task—that of winning souls—finds it authority in the only place we can look with absolute certainty—in the Book that describes God's relationship to His creatures and the creatures' relationship to God. That authority is the eternal, infallible, and ever-precious Word of God. In this Book—not in Plato or Aristotle, in Augustine or even St. Thomas, in Kant or Schopenhauer, in Kierkegaard or Brunner, in Niebuhr or Tillich—in this Book is the answer to man's eternal quest, the picture of his lostness, and the truth of redemption. To God's Word we must, therefore, turn if we are to find a true basis for evangelism.

With this in mind, and at the risk of an almost puerile oversimplification, may I suggest a simple outline from God's Word that will set forth this pattern for evangelism: (1) Man is lost; (2) God did something about it; (3) man has no excuse; and (4) we have an obligation.

Man is lost—hopelessly, tragically, everlastingly lost. God's Word has made this abundantly clear. Romans 5:12 reads: "Wherefore, as by one

74

man sin entered into the world, and death by sin; and so death passed upon all men, for all have sinned." In the same epistle Paul declares that "all have sinned, and come short of the glory of God" (Romans 3:23); and again: "The wages of sin is death; but the gift of God is eternal life" (Romans 6:23). He made it clear that whether man was or was not under the jurisdiction of the Law, the result of sin was and is the same: "For as many as have sinned without law shall also perish without law; and as many as have sinned in the law shall be judged by the law" (Romans 2:12).

The Old Testament prophet Ezekiel cited God saying: "Behold all souls are mine; as the soul of the father, so also the soul of the son is mine: the soul that sinneth, it shall die" (Ezekiel 18:4). And James 1:15 says; "Then when lust hath conceived, it bringeth forth sin; and sin, when it is finished, bringeth forth death."

Will anyone be bold enough to declare that Jesus did not know and understand the eternal nature of and the ultimate destruction of sin? Consider His warning to those who brought Him news of the murdered Galileans: "I tell you, Nay, but, except ye repent, ye shall all likewise perish" (Luke 13:3). Or when He compares those men standing before Him to the eighteen who had perished at the Tower of Siloam: "Think ye that they were sinners above all men that dwelt in Jerusalem? I tell you, Nay: but, except ye repent, ye shall also perish" (Luke 13:4, 5).

The apostle Paul, once again echoed this lostness of man without God when he wrote to the church in Thessalonica: "And to you who are troubled rest with us, when the Lord Jesus shall be revealed from heaven with his mighty angels, in flaming fire taking vengeance on them that know not God, and that obey not the gospel of our Lord Jesus Christ" (2 Thessalonians 1:7, 8). To Paul there was no in between—there would be vengeance and eternal punishment on two classes of people: those who did not know God and those who knew Him but had not obeyed Him. Surely this encompasses the whole wide world. His Word is clear: all men are sinners, all sinners are lost—therefore, all men are lost.

Secondly, let me show you that God set out from the beginning to do something about the lostness of sinful man. From His seat in the eternities He could see that there was and could be no redemption for the sinner apart from a propitiation for sin by One "who knew no sin" (2 Corinthians 5:21). There was no one in all the universe worthy of such an assignment ex-

cept the only begotten Son of God, the very Creator of men. There was no other way—so at the Jordan's edge we hear the Baptist declaring, "Behold the Lamb of God, which taketh away the sin of the world" (John 1:29).

From the very beginning God ordained that Jesus Christ should die on Calvary's cruel, skull-like brow—a propitiation for man's sin. One must note, however, that He did not offer His Son in some cruel, judicially, conscious manner just so He could absolve Himself of guilt for, or indifference to, the plight of this hell-bound world. The Bible says, "For God *so loved* the world, that he gave his only begotten Son, that whosoever believeth in him should not perish, but have everlasting life" (John 3:16). God really did not want man to perish; He wanted him to be saved. Paul declared it again when he wrote to Timothy about the Lord "who will have all men to be saved, and to come unto the knowledge of the truth" (1 Timothy 2:4). And again he wrote of Jesus "who is the Saviour of all men, specially of those that believe" (1 Timothy 4:10).

Peter declares: "The Lord is not slack concerning his promise, as some men count slackness; but is longsuffering to us-ward, not willing that any should perish, but that all should come to repentance" (2 Peter 3:9).

One cannot read the story of a suffering and loving Saviour and not become aware of several truths of tremendous importance in this day of conflicting theologies concerning the extent of the Atonement and the final destiny of the lost. First, Jesus died for *all* men—not just a few. His was not some kind of Calvinian limitation by election. He did not die for a few—and send the rest to an ever-burning hell. First Timothy 2:4 declares: "Who will have *all* men to be saved, and to come unto the knowledge of the truth." John 3:16 declares that He *so loved* the world that He died for all. Rich and poor, bond and free, Gentile and Jew, red and yellow, black and white; there is no limited atonement in Christ. He paid the price for all—for every man.

Again it must be abundantly clear that if God felt sufficiently strong there was no other way to redeem lost man but to give His Son, there can be no salvation apart from Jesus Christ. Just as sure as the death of Jesus was required by His own Father as punishment for sin, just so sure will unpropitiated sin bring eternal death to the sinner. Jesus Himself said, "I am the way, the truth, and the life: no man cometh unto the Father, but by me" (John 14:6).

The philosophies and the religions of this world are myriad that offer a Christless way. Muhammad's sword and his battle cry, "There is but one God, and Allah is his prophet"; Buddha with his never-ending fruitless quest for nirvana; Shintoism with its reverence and devotion to deities enshrined in the memory of one's ancestral relations—all speak of a way. But God has said: "There is a way which seemeth right unto a man; but the end thereof are the ways of death" (Proverbs 14:12).

We have seen a revival of the philosophy of universalism which would have us believe that ultimately all men—perhaps even the devil—will be restored; that judgment against sin is temporal, not eternal. Scholars and theologians in almost every church have embraced this nefarious bit of untruth which could have been born in no place but the pits of hell.

There was, is, and shall be, no salvation apart from Jesus Christ. Peter preached "no other name...whereby we must be saved" (Acts 4:12). Jesus Himself made it abundantly clear when He said: "He that believeth on him is not condemned: but he that believeth not is condemned already, because he hath not believed" (John 3:18).

Paul declares: "When the Lord Jesus shall be revealed from heaven with his mighty angels, in flaming fire taking vengeance on them that know not God, and that obey not the gospel of our Lord Jesus Christ" (2 Thessalonians 1:7, 8).

There is no second chance. There is no restitution of all things. There is no redemption of Satan nor mitigation of Satanic power in this world or in the world to come.

There is no redemption apart from Jesus Christ. This is the Biblical basis for evangelism. This is the Biblical imperative for evangelism.

As we look at this Biblical base, we cannot but recognize that it does away with a soft sentimentalism that would have at least some men be saved without suffering the burning flames of eternal damnation. But the Bible has no room for an "unlost population" because of men having not heard. In addition to God's Word itself, all men have at least two "bibles" from which they can arrive at truth—a word written in nature roundabout, and a burning conscience within. Psalm 19:1-4 puts it so beautifully: "The heavens declare the glory of God; and the firmament showeth his handiwork. Day unto day uttereth speech, and night unto night showeth knowledge. There is no speech nor language, where their voice is not heard. Their line is gone

out through all the earth, and their words to the end of the world."

Paul declared in Romans 1 that man is without excuse: "The wrath of God is revealed from heaven against all ungodliness and unrighteousness of men, who hold the truth in unrighteousness; because that which may be known of God is manifest in them; for God hath shown it unto them. For the invisible things of him from the creation of the world are clearly seen, being understood by the things that are made, even his eternal power and Godhead; so that they are without excuse" (Romans 1:18-20).

Listen also to Paul at Iconia: "Unto the living God, which made heaven, and earth, and the sea, and all the things that are therein: who in times past suffered all nations to walk in their own ways. Nevertheless he left not himself without witness, in that he did good, and gave us rain from heaven, and fruitful seasons, filling our hearts with food and gladness" (Acts 14:15-17).

The second of these noncanonical "bibles" that declares man a sinner in need of a Saviour is man's own heart. "For when the Gentiles, which have not the law, do by nature the things contained in the law, these, having not the law, are a law unto themselves: which show the work of the law written in their hearts, their conscience also bearing witness, and their thoughts the meanwhile accusing or else excusing one another" (Romans 2:14, 15). Man's heart has always been quick to condemn him. Jeremiah recognized that when he cried: "The heart is deceitful above all things, and desperately wicked: who can know it?" (Jeremiah 17:9).

The Biblical basis for evangelism is abundantly clear. All men are sinners; all sinners are lost; therefore, all men are lost. Even the heathen in some far country, far from the luxuries and niceties of our civilization, who has not heard about this salvation—he, too, is lost without Christ and without hope. This is the Biblical basis for evangelism.

There remains one more facet, however, of this imperative. If all men are lost, if God did something about this lostness, if God wants all men—not just a few—to be saved, then what can we do—no, what *must* we do?

Once again, we are not left to find answers midst the philosophies of this world. The Lord Jesus Himself pointed the way when he declared to His disciples: "Go ye into all the world, and preach the gospel to every creature" (Mark 16:15). Matthew has almost the same command: "Go ye therefore, and teach all nations, baptizing them in the name of the Father, and of the Son, and of the Holy Ghost" (Matthew 28:19).

Jesus told his waiting disciples: "Ye shall be witnesses unto me both in Jerusalem, and in all Judea, and in Samaria, and unto the uttermost part of the earth" (Acts 1:8).

It is written of the Early Church: "Scattered abroad throughout the regions of Judea and Samaria . . . they . . . went every where preaching the word" (Acts 8:1-4). This was the Master's plan—and still is today. The Biblical basis for evangelism demands that we preach His Word in order that we may win souls to Jesus Christ. He did not and does not expect us to do it alone. To the disciples who were to witness in Jerusalem, Judea, and Samaria, He first of all declared, "Ye shall receive power, after that the Holy Ghost is come upon you" (Acts 1:8). To those same disciples at an earlier hour, He had made abundantly clear the relationship of the Holy Spirit to evangelism—not only as an anointing for the evangelist in order that he might preach, but as a convicting, redeeming Person of the Godhead toward lost men.

In John 16:8-11 Jesus declared: "When he [the Holy Ghost] is come, he will reprove the world of sin, and of righteousness, and of judgment: of sin, because they believe not on me; of righteousness, because I go to my Father, and ye see me no more; of judgment, because the prince of this world is judged." It is our business to preach and to tell; it is His business to convict and redeem. No man can come unto the Father except the Holy Spirit draw him. No man can be born again except it be by the Spirit.

With this burning command aflame in our hearts and conscious of the all-powerful spiritual Personage promised to accompany us, can we do less than fulfill our responsibility?

"Thus it is written, and thus it behooved Christ to suffer, and to rise from the dead the third day: and that repentance and remission of sins should be preached in his name among all nations, beginning at Jerusalem. And ye are witnesses of these things" (Luke 24:46, 48). It "behooved Christ to suffer"—and it must needs behoove us to offer ourselves as did He. Let not the curse of Meroz be ours: "Because [we] came not to the help of the Lord, to the help of the Lord against the mighty" (Judges 5:23).

The Biblical basis for evangelism offers us an awesome responsibility. Through the years many have asked—some in innocence and some in defiance—what happens to the heathen, and to all the lost, if they do not hear the Word? Will they be eternally damned? God's Word is clear: they already are judged; they will be lost; they are in the hands of a merciful but also a just God.

The question is not what will happen to them, but what will happen to us if they do not hear? To this all-important, burning question, God sends an answer ringing down the corridors of time to every earnest soul: "When I say to the wicked, Thou shalt surely die; and thou givest him not warning, nor speakest to warn the wicked from his wicked way, to save his life; the same wicked man shall die in his iniquity; but his blood will I require at thine hand" (Ezekiel 3:18).

This, then is the Biblical basis for evangelism. The world is hopelessly lost, but God loved the world and gave His Son to redeem that world. Ours is to tell men about this Christ and to snatch their souls "as brands from the burning." Someone, I think it was Fred Jarvis, has put it bluntly and succinctly when he wrote, "Failure to tell sends millions to hell."

Panel Discussion and Open Forum

Question: How can we account for the apparent slow down in Assemblies of God growth?

There was hearty agreement that the evangelistic work of the church can be accomplished only by revived hearts. It was noted that revivals are born only in times of intense and personal prayer, and certainly our own Movement's history testifies to that fact. The times of our greatest evangelistic outreach were also the times of soul-searching before God which resulted in the total involvement of the entire church. There is a need for a renewed emphasis on personal prayer for individual purifying and revival.

Several hindrances to the implementation of evangelism were discussed at length. The first hindrance to a united effort for evangelism is the confusion over the meanings of the terms we use to discuss it. Terms like *revival, evangelism,* and other related words need distinctive and commonly accepted definitions.

Another problem is the communication of spiritual truth to lost men in this generation. It was stated that the continued use of old English terminology created some misunderstandings. It was felt that this problem would persist as long as the most commonly used version of the Bible in our Movement is the King James Version. It was pointed out that it is possible to communicate using symbols as old as man by giving them new and clarifying explanations. The proclamation of the gospel must be phrased in contemporary language in order to be understood. This was qualified by the thought that it is not necessary to use vulgar or even casual terms to explain spiritual truths. Plain, acceptable, common English is desirable for maximum effectiveness. This practice would be endorsed by the fact that the Holy Spirit communicated His truths to the writers of Scripture in the common language, and not in a vocabulary out of common usage.

Question: Does our responsibility for proclaiming the gospel end when we contact people with that good news, or are we also obligated to win them?

It was agreed that we are responsible for teaching men, and that it must be done in the power of the Holy Spirit. Simply informing men by verbalizing the gospel is not enough—it must be "not by might, nor by power, but by my Spirit" which is the implicit command of God. However, it was recognized that it is the Holy Spirit who convicts and draws men, and we must be careful not to try to take His place.

Question: What are some of the hindrances to effective evangelism?

Evangelism, which is the legitimate assignment of the people of God, often becomes confined to the church building. Evangelism is more than a function of the building.

Another hindrance highlighted was the fact that many Assemblies' church services have become stereotyped. In many churches the Sunday evening service has traditionally been designated as an "evangelistic" service. But changes in church attendance habits have turned Sunday nights into a time when only the saints usually attend; and if an unsaved person attends at all, he would probably attend on Sunday morning, which is usually a service geared toward those who are already Christians. This was pinpointed as a possible reason why conversions in evangelistic services are apparently on the wane.

Another problem area investigated was the fact that we have unintentionally propagated "revivalism evangelism" which seems to have the same people "reclaimed" or "saved" over and over again. We have never developed an approach to evangelism which would assist new Christians to mature spiritually. Such an approach, stressing the need for development, would prevent many of those backsliders from needing to be reclaimed.

Question: Does the fact that these problems exist indicate that we have been wasting time during all these years of growth and development?

There was agreement that we have not been wasting time, but using the means that were most successful for the time. It is not now just a question of replacing old methods with new ones; it is a question of finding ways to supplement our ministry to the world with effective means of accomplishing the new challenges that confront the Church in this generation. It was also noted that we should make full use of the tools we already have as well as developing those supplementary means.

It was apparent that the delegates present felt that in order to fulfill our mission to the lost world in our generation, we must adopt a multilevel approach to evangelism. We must expand our vision to include new methods and new language to communicate the timeless gospel of Jesus Christ. We must carefully study our methods and approach to evangelism and supplement wherever necessary and retain and take advantage of the best of what we are already using.

COOPERATING IN MASS EVANGELISM

Speaker: **U. S. GRANT**
Moderator: **G. W. HARDCASTLE II**
Panelists: **MELVIN BREWER, HAL HERMAN, FRANK McALLISTER**
Recorder: **MAYNARD KETCHAM**

HAVING BEEN PRIVILEGED TO PARTICIPATE in some large mass evangelism efforts, I have been often blessed and convinced that the medium certainly has been used of God all through the Church Age.

Mass evangelism was born on the same day as the Church. The masses were in Jerusalem that day. The gospel was preached in the power of the Spirit. Three thousand decisions for Christ were recorded.

There were other great meetings. Philip must have shaken Samaria with his preaching. Many turned to the Lord, and there was great joy in the city. Another great meeting, perhaps often overlooked, was conducted by Peter in what I note was a "twin-city" crusade. In Acts 9 he wrought a miracle of faith on a man in Lydda. The result was that "all that dwelt in Lydda and Sharon saw him, and turned to the Lord."

These New Testament crusades do not evidence a lot of preplanning by men but certainly were in the program of God. They were accompanied by prayer and dedication. And preeminence was given to the preaching of the Word. Specifically, they preached Christ.

Though the Church has had an almost continuous parade of great men, a comparative few can be classified as crusaders in mass evangelism. Those who stand out are men like Jonathan Edwards, John Wesley, George Whitefield, Charles Finney, D. L. Moody, Billy Sunday, and Billy Graham.

Some rare qualities seem characteristic of the great evangelists. Dr. Robert Ferm, in his book, *Cooperative Evangelism*, calls them "inclusivists" as contrasted with "separatists." He describes the separatists as those very orthodox people who hold quite scripturally to fundamentalism and quite scripturally to a separated life. They also often carry their separatism to the extreme of withdrawing from all others who do not hold their doctrinal views. They have a history of having opposed men caught up in great moves of God because of the very nature of their inclusiveness.

A careful study of the several evangelists will disclose that they too believed in separation from sin, but not from people. They, very scripturally, became "all things to all men, that they might by all means save some" (1 Corinthians 9:22). Their inclusiveness has dictated that no one be excluded in their efforts to reach all men for Christ. At the same time they preach an uncompromising message that changes lives and communities. This is a rare quality and is not always understood or accepted by the separatists.

A deeper look into the success of men leading in mass evangelism will reveal they have been men of prayer. This stands out as the foundation of their strength. They have also had a unique ability to encourage cooperation from the churches and communities where they labored, despite the always-present opposition of the separatists groups.

Without a doubt the man doing the greatest work in mass evangelism today is Dr. Billy Graham. Since it was given to me to set the wheels in motion to bring this man to our city and to serve on the executive committee as one of the vice-chairmen, I have had an excellent chance to observe both the man and his method, as well as the results.

The Graham crusades are conducted on a simple format which he calls the "three P's": (1) preparation, (2) penetration, and (3) preservation. This format is likened to an hourglass with large areas at either end, connected by a small neck. The two larger parts of the hourglass speak of preparation and preservation. The crusade services are the "neck."

In our case the total preparation lasted almost a decade, from the first contact with the team until the crusade began. Many miscellaneous happenings caused discouraging delays. But in the end everyone felt the crusade timing was in the will of God.

From the time our local committee received a firm commitment from Dr. Graham, our actual feverish preparation consumed a year. The group which originally extended the invitation (The Graham Crusade Invitational Committee) was incorporated into a larger committee. Actually there were two main committees: (1) the executive committee with some fifty members; and (2) the general committee of about 150 members.

Six months before the crusade offices were established, two members of the Graham organization came to live in the city to bring the preparation to its final stages. The executive committee met regularly with these men, and the general committee was called in as needed.

Three months before the crusade, prayer meetings were organized in homes, offices, and industries. Regular prayer-time broadcasts went out from several radio stations at prayer-time each day. It was estimated that eight thousand prayer meetings were being conducted daily throughout the area. This alone was enough to bring revival. Some of the prayer meetings are continuing in business areas.

Better than twenty-five hundred counselors were trained in Christian life and witness classes. These people committed to memory much of the Scripture, and their lives were enriched long before the meetings started. The choir consisted of five thousand voices and met in segments for rehearsals prior to the meetings. Some fifteen hundred ushers were functioning during the crusade. Add to this list scores of clerical helpers,

and the crusade was guaranteed good attendances if only the workers came. The preparation was so thorough and so saturated with the Word and prayer that most of us conceded that even if Billy Graham could not come, there would be a great revival in Kansas City.

All of the above mentioned groups flowed right into the "neck" of the hourglass and became part of the penetration. It lasted only ten days. But our municipal ball park witnessed its greatest crowds ever with a peak attendance of fifty-five thousand people.

The total attendance for the ten days was 364,000. There were 11,380 decision cards signed. The large budget was met early in the crusade without any dramatics or pressures. The finances were handled by a committee of able local businessmen, and an audit was made and published. We were able to invest some excess funds elsewhere in the kingdom of God.

Preservation is an important part of such a crusade. All those making decisions were assigned to a local church, and most of them were contacted in their homes within forty-eight hours. This follow-up was pursued just as far as possible to get them established in the faith and in a Bible-believing church. This type of thorough nurturing of the young Christian necessitated maintaining an office for almost a year.

It should be evident that in such a cooperative crusade as this, the more a church contributes, the more handsome will be the returns. I have long since determined not to ask, "What is there in it for me?" I sincerely ask myself, "What can I contribute that will bless my city and enhance the kingdom of God?" If my church should not see immediate visible returns but if we have given aid in securing souls for the church of Jesus Christ, this should be reward enough. But we were not left barren.

In such endeavors try not to wait until the project is already launched. The church everywhere is looking for Spirit-filled leaders. I believe our Pentecostal brethren can and should provide that leadership in their areas. You have nothing to apologize for, and you will be accepted if you will make yourself available.

Today we need the deepest social concern—the concern for men's redemption. None will seek to save the lost except those who are saved. To us has been given the burden of a dying age.

Let us not only proclaim redemption in the face of impending judgment but also preach, saying, "The kingdom of heaven is at hand."

Never was evangelism—all types of evangelism—more needed than in this age.

Panel Discussion and Open Forum

Of all the "isms" in the world of today, "evangelism" is the only one outlined in the Word of God. True revival can come only when the hearts of all participants are ready. No city can be stirred through a mass campaign until the pastors are right with God, until they have a genuine burden, until they are willing to pay the price.

One panelist cited his own background, having been raised in a liberal church. After he was filled with the Spirit and entered the Pentecostal ministry, he became a "separatist." He now has moved to the center of the road and can cooperate with all who are genuinely saved and who will preach the unadulterated gospel of Jesus Christ.

An evangelist stated he is keenly aware that the ministry of the evangelist is only a portion (and possibly only a small portion) in the great ministry of building up the kingdom of Christ. If the converts won in campaigns are not carefully shepherded and fed and nurtured by the pastors in organized churches, then the results of evangelism will be largely dissipated. Thus mass evangelism itself is futile without the preparation of pastors and the establishment of churches.

No campaign can be effective unless there is an atmosphere of deep spirituality. The message must be given in truth, clarity, and love.

The speaker then emphasized two things: (1) We need to love the souls of men; (2) men must realize that we love them. There is no such thing as mass evangelism. It is individual evangelism —man to man—which eventually will move multitudes and nations toward Christ.

A missionary, commenting on the revival sweeping Korea, stated that it was born out of desperation! When the work was at a low tide and all missionaries and nationals involved were so deeply burdened that they were willing to fast regularly, systematically and effectively, and to pray constantly, then God brought a unity and defeated the powers of darkness. Today one of the greatest Pentecostal churches in the world has been established in Seoul. Thirteen other churches have been established in the city, and the denominational churches in Korea have been shaken with the Pentecostal message. Government officials have acknowledged that the Assemblies of God has been responsible for a revitalization in the nation.

Practically every speaker attested that mass evangelism begins with individual revival, individual witness, and individual ministry—and with a love and compassion for the hearts of men (not in the mass but as individuals).

EVANGELISM IN A CHANGING SOCIETY

Speaker: **FLOYD THOMAS**
Moderator: **RICHARD DOBBINS**
Panelists: **GAYLE ERWIN, GUNNAR JACOBSEN, ROBERT SITES**
Recorder: **CURTIS RINGNESS**

HE WAS A TEEN-AGER just turned 18 and a part of our congregation. Upon meeting him in the church foyer, I commented that he had been absent for several weeks. He remarked, "Yes, I guess so, and I have my reasons. I like to be where there's a little action you know—like where it's for real."

Later he was filled with the Holy Spirit and came to me very excited and said, "Wow! This is where it's happening!"

How many of our generation think we're not for real or there just isn't anything happening?

Have we evangelicals been too interested in saving our institutional necks to do much that was brave and risky?

The accelerating trend toward a total urban culture has become so great that we are faced with the greatest problems that have ever come our way. The government is confronting difficulties such as traffic, air pollution, congestion, juvenile gangs, racial conflict.

Americans are desperately afraid. Thousands change their daily routines for fear of crime. School integration is seen as a main way to mend a split city. Many Negroes feel that their children get thin educations, that classes are merely custodial in central-city schools. Many blacks now see riots as a legitimate maneuver.

Cities are not understood by middle-class, suburban Americans. To them, cities are rude, abrasive places, made up of such things as cheap lodgings and topless nightclubs—places in which the hippies, the homosexuals, the derelicts thrive.

We are confronting a change in culture that lies below the level of technology. We can educate, pour money into festered areas, create solutions on paper; but the basic concern that confronts us is one of compassion.

Our motives must be examined, and we must ask ourselves if we are interested in building churches only in those areas where adequate resources may be found and where people are responsive to our programs.

Our first reaction to all this may be as Jonah's was when God called him to Nineveh; we may want to flee to another field. But the Holy Spirit urges us on and gives us added insight. The true Christian understands sin. He knows that the utopian plans of government will never heal the sores of our modern Babylons. The Christian knows that Christ has provided redemption.

The Assemblies of God must enter the population centers of the world with a positive sense of responsibility and faith. We will not be content to escape into a warm corner, away from pain and suffering. Discipleship calls us to enter the world as Christ entered it.

God's Word is still true and speaks to this day. Micah was well acquainted with the sin and the corruption of his day, the hatred of one class for another, the rejection of God's Word, and the scramble for wealth at any cost. Yet

Micah had a positive faith in God's will being accomplished. His words were, "He has showed thee, O man, what is good; and what doth the Lord require of thee, but to do justly, and to love mercy, and to walk humbly with thy God?" (Micah 6:8).

We must take steps toward removing un-Christian prejudices. Modern denominations cannot expect to minister effectively if antiurban prejudices are maintained and if rural folkways determine the channels of communication.

The church must recognize that Americans by and large have become an urban people and that the church must minister to an urban world. According to the 1960 census, 69.9 percent of the population was urban.

While there should be no neglect of rural and small town churches, our denomination will need a careful plan for church extension. Churches must be established at an accelerated rate, and we must not be guided by past criteria. Those criteria were based on discovering the location where the highest concentration of people who were considered "good prospects" lived and on the speculation of how soon the new church could become self-supporting. We must now give attention to the unchurched slums. The need must determine our future thrust. To ignore blighted areas is to encourage poverty, crime, and spiritual ignorance to increase.

As we go to our sin-sick and blighted cities, let us recall that it was in a great city that Jesus carried His cross.

In some circles it is assumed that the population explosion will assure church growth. Not so. The church that experiences growth will be the one that keeps abreast of change and makes the necessary changes in methodology. The urban church will not grow simply because there are more people. The people are there in greater numbers, but the composition of the population has changed.

Not only is the urban population growing, but it is on the move. Cities are taking on a different age, racial, and cultural composition. Many families are changing houses as often as they change cars. In a recent year more than 34 million persons changed residences in the United States. Of this number, more than six million moved to another state, and more than five million others moved to a different county. Can our churches continue to avoid changing methods so as to be effective in a state of transition where membership and leadership are concerned?

The city is made up of neighborhoods where

stress and tension is cause for church concern. Shippey, in *Protestantism in Suburban Life,* writes there are five areas of tension and conflict, and most of them can be traced to the wide varieties of people who live in close proximity. He includes conflicts between newcomer and old-timer, white-color and blue-collar, Jew and Christian, Catholic and Protestant, Negro and white.

Is it Christian to remark, "I go to a church that has a good class of people"—and with a smugness that reveals the lack of mission on the part of God's people?

What is a church going to do? In some cases, success has been seen through witnessing out of the usual or traditional mold! Programs and schedules must be made to fit the new day. The Catholics' success in participation lies in the fact that they provide many opportunities for people to attend services throughout Sunday and during the week, rather than insisting that everyone come on Sunday morning at eleven and Sunday night at eight.

Senior citizen centers have been very helpful to elderly reclusive persons who so often hide away in dingy apartments or single rooms in the slum areas. Am Assemblies of God church in San Francisco canvassed a Negro slum area for people over 60 who might be interested in a program which included counseling, handcrafts, reading, a fellowship hour, and a luncheon served for a nominal charge. The ladies of the Women's Missionary Council made this a ministry for their group. Over three years, more than two hundred different people were drawn to the center. Many were brought into an experience of salvation. In addition, they were brought out of loneliness and fear.

In this day, especially in our urban areas, we must take a different approach to Christian education. In some instances great success has been realized through a Bible club program. This is usually conducted in homes during the week immediately after the children are out of school. In one metropolitan area this program was initiated by the Assemblies of God church. It is considered an extension of their Sunday school on a weekday basis. They are contacting Muhammadans, Buddhists, and many other faiths who would be prejudiced against entering a Christian church building.

Some urban churches are having Bible studies and prayer meetings in homes. There are problems that certain pastors have reported; but, in my analysis, most of the problems have arisen through a lack of good planning. Denomination-al leaders have reported that many churches have increased in attendance through this method. The host of a particular meeting is urged to invite unsaved couples. A simple format should be followed that can be taught in several training sessions.

Apartment-house evangelism faces some unique problems. Apartment residents possess characteristics that set them apart as a distinct urban public. People with common domicile needs are attracted to this type of housing.

There is a great rate of mobility with apartment-house dwellers. Effective religious work with transient apartment residents may not result in building a given minister's church attendance, but it should be the object of each pastor and church to pursue vigorously a ministry to these neglected people.

In a convention held in Denver, Colorado, in the interest of apartment-house evangelism, one representative concluded that there is only one effective way to "get in"—through an infiltration method. He suggested that church members who live in apartments should be urged to open their homes for "coffee clubs" at which time the minister could be present and become acquainted with the residents.

A type of ministry not often used by evangelicals may be part of the total answer. We will truly obey Jesus' command to "lose our life" as a church when we seek to give ourselves to those in need. Have you thought of yourself in the role of one helping to supply rat poison or climbing slum steps to intervene with a rent-gouging landlord, or appearing in court for someone caught in a crossfire of justice and injustice? At a given moment these may be the only valid means to reach downtrodden people.

Royal Rangers may have to take a different turn in the city. A youth who has a way with broken-down autos may be enlisted to attract others to the youth center. Get involved with your Teen Challenge program and use the converts to begin rehabilitating the youth in your area. Or start your own program to help these youngsters whom God loves.

People have been attracted to our churches by our paying for spot announcements on radio. This type of announcement can follow a *Revivaltime* broadcast. All the other news and broadcast media have a good ministry in large urban areas.

Our society is changing; but our God is unchanging. He still effectively works as we evan-gelize in the power of the Spirit. We will continue to find an effective way to evangelize because this is the task that our God called us to do!

Our God must not be relegated to a past society. He is the God of Abraham, Isaac, and Jacob, and the God who used Moses and Joshua to lead the children of Israel. Here was a God who was in touch; a God who moved; a God who identified Himself with the movements of history.

To evangelize this changing society we must do three things God has given us to do:

1. We must proclaim the good news. The story is simple. Christ died for sinners. This truth has the power to save.

2. There is the task of reconciliation. This is begun for us in Jesus Christ. "God was in Christ, reconciling the world to himself" (2 Corinthians 5:19). The task of reconciliation travels out to every broken fragment of our common life.

3. There is the task of demonstration. The Early Church had no buildings in which to gather, except homes. The preachers didn't depend upon enticing words of man's wisdom, but words in demonstration of the Spirit and of power.

I think God wants a different breed of men and women who are as radical as any in our day, who will risk new methods in evangelizing our changing society with the always contemporary and changeless gospel.

Panel Discussion and Open Forum

One panelist observed we all agree ours is a changing society. However, he said, he does not agree with change for change's sake. Rather, we should change only when there is a better approach. He observed there is a definite need for new spiritual life in our churches. Then the Holy Spirit will motivate Christians to get out where the people are and become involved in soul-winning ministries.

Another panelist commented on the importance of relating to the needs, circumstances, and conditions of the people. Once again we are getting outside the prison of our buildings, out to where the people are—getting into the homes and neglected areas. He said if we filled all the Pentecostal and other evangelical churches, we would still fall far short of what we should do. The church must not withdraw, but must infiltrate. It is essential that we follow the New Testament pattern and give emphasis to smaller units, the participation of families in prayer services in homes, etc.

Another panelist commented on the problems and challenges of the inner-city. He raised the question, *What is the city?* Not just buildings, pavements, traffic, noise, confusion, bright lights, etc., but people. He said we must reach the people with the gospel of Jesus Christ. We need a change of heart and attitude. There is an unwillingness on the part of many to work among the people of the inner-city. We must reach into the ghettos where the poor live, as well as into the high-rise apartments where the middle class and more affluent live. With whitened harvest fields under our noses, we are moving away.

Question: What can we do to motivate our Assemblies of God people to move into the inner-city?

It was pointed out that national and district leadership cannot do this by themselves. The pastor must lead his people to witness.

Question: Should a church stay in a transitional neighborhood or move when many in the congregation favor relocating?

If members of the congregation resent the idea of an integrated church, let them move. But the denomination should seek to retain the church property if it is strategically located. There will be problems in every transitional neighborhood, but we must meet these problems in a Christian spirit.

Question: Are Negro ministers included in the membership of the Assemblies of God?

The General Superintendent replied in the affirmative. He stated our districts have every right to grant credentials to Negro ministers. At the present time we have 25 Negro ministers, and it is hoped this number will increase. He then referred to the General Presbytery's statement on social concern adopted August 21, 1968, which included the following pledge: "We further pledge to give ourselves in the Biblical way to meet today's challenge by a renewed dedication to proclaim the fullness of the universal gospel of Jesus Christ, both at home and abroad, without respect to color, national origin, or social status."

The moderator summarized: Techniques alone are not enough. We must have hearts touched with divine concern. Conscience money is not enough—that is, paying other people to do what we ought to do. The work demands the involvement of ministers and laity alike. We must teach urban sociology as it really is—not as what we would like it to be. The gospel of Jesus Christ is a broad message and has the answers to the issues and problems of today. The Pentecostal message *is* relevant to the needs of all men.

EVANGELISM THROUGH PASTORAL COUNSELING

Speaker: **SETH BALMER**
Moderator: **MARION GROFF**
Panelists: **KENNETH BARNEY, EARL BOOK, LLOYD CHRISTIANSEN**
Recorder: **EDWARD CALDWELL**

IN THESE DAYS of all kinds of counseling being given, it is high time the minister assumes his God-given role as a servant of Jesus Christ sharing the wonderful truths of the gospel.

The problems of humanity have not changed basically since the beginning of time. The answers can still be found in the greatest of books —the Bible.

The goal of a counseling minister is met if he can help one couple find their moorings and work through misunderstandings to acceptance of themselves under God. For the minister as a counselor is not just another listener to people's problems; he is a symbol of religion, representing life's central values to those who seek his help.

The Bible is the pastor's counseling handbook, and it is his privilege as a leader of the church to help each member of his congregation think through vital issues in their lives before they reach a breaking point.

We need to be reminded as clergymen that counseling of all kinds requires a willingness to grow, a willingness to try new approaches, a willingness to learn by mistakes, and a willingness to let the humblest parishioner teach a lesson about life.

Marriage is in flux; we are moving from a work-centered, paternalistic, inner-directed pattern to a leisure-centered, companionate, outer-directed pattern. By realizing this change, the minister, without surrendering the truth of the gospel, can emphasize what needs to be conserved while recognizing what needs to be changed in the light of an emerging new social system.

Consider some of the current changes in the American couple and family:

1. *The family is mobile both socially and geographically.* An industrially oriented society makes for ambition and wanting the best for one's family; but it also makes for a sense of "rootlessness and insecurity."

2. *Men and women are striving to live on equal terms,* their respective roles in a fluid state.

3. *A new leisure is offering families opportunity to be together.* However, too often this time is misused for poor pursuits, rather than building healthier marriages.

4. *The loss of parental authority has led to a feeling of uncertainty* in dealing with children, and makes it difficult for youth to find adequate standards of conduct.

In his role as a counselor the pastor has certain advantages:

1. *The minister can prepare couples for marriage.* This preparation for marriage is an absolute necessity.

2. *The minister has access to his families' homes,* and the parishioners have access to him.

3. *People look to the minister as a model*

Christian and to his house as an example of Christian family living.

The minister also has disadvantages:

1. *His lack of training.* The problems are there, but many ministers are untrained to handle them.

2. *The untrained minister's tendency is to judge or assure.* Because he preaches from the pulpit, he may try to function the same way face-to-face.

3. *The parishioner may be afraid to shock the minister* by the recital of his misdeeds.

4. *The minister also works with couples and families other than as a counselor.* After the Sunday morning service the couple in counseling greets the preacher with embarrassment because he now knows certain things about them.

In the final analysis, no marriage is any better than the two people involved. The basic need of every person is a new nature which comes with a born-again experience. If the parties can be brought to an acceptance of Jesus Christ as their personal Saviour, they will have taken the first and most important step in solving their marital problems. This is the pastor's golden opportunity.

Whenever two persons are engaged in a socio-legal relationship called marriage, certain attitudes, values, and behaviors are generated in the relationship. These come into focus in the counseling room.

The couple or individual marriage partners come to the counselor when difficulties are too large for them to solve alone, and they seek through a third party some adjustment of their problem and a restoration of harmony in their relationship. We are following those who regard marriage counseling as a "helping operation" among comparatively normal people whose problems can be dealt with on an adjustment level. It must be remembered there is such a malady as a "neurotic marriage." The pastor has a responsibility to appraise these and to refer them for psychological treatment.

The goal of marriage counseling is to help the couple involved work out solutions to their problems to their mutual advantage. The overall goal of the pastoral counselor is to help individuals to wholeness. By wholeness we mean that integration of individual character which enables the individual to realize himself at all levels of relationship—with nature, society, and God. The minister takes Jesus' scripture against divorce quite literally. For him this means holding the line against the rising divorce rate, par-

ticularly keeping this one couple together.

The novice pastor often asks, "Now that the couple has come, how should I set up counseling?"

Several possibilities exist:

See both marriage partners at separate times.

See both marriage partners together at the same time.

See one partner and refer the other to another counselor.

See only one partner, the other partner being inaccessible for counseling.

My experience is to work first with both partners separately, then together if at all possible. By all means seek to reach the couple spiritually. The greatest deterrent to marital problems is a right relationship with God. Remember "the nearer you keep to God, the nearer you will be to one another."

These things are worth remembering:

1. Marriage is a holy and desirable estate.

2. Development of future generations of spiritually, physically, mentally, and emotionally sound persons depends upon the health and soundness of marriage and the family.

3. God's power is greater than man's.

Alcoholism, dope addiction, financial, and mental difficulties are each very real problems to the counseling pastor.

I believe the statistics show that the most successful program to help the alcoholic is the old-fashioned gospel presentation used by gospel missions. More recovery has come from this than all of the others put together, including Alcoholics Anonymous.

As for drug addiction, I can be safe in saying that under the Teen Challenge ministry, started by David Wilkerson, the most successful rehabilitation has come from those who have surrendered their lives and been filled with the precious Holy Spirit. It appears this has been more successful than all other methods of treatment.

In relation to financial difficulties there are specific procedures in counseling including a presentation of literature with items on budgeting and money management.

I believe there is a need and a place for pastoral counseling in the ministry. Training in the behavioral sciences is helpful, yet let us never underestimate the power of the Word of God. The best way to change the behavior of a person is to lead him to the Lord Jesus Christ.

Inevitably, every pastor comes to grips with a counseling task too great for his knowledge.

It then becomes necessary to call in someone more qualified.

In referring to a specialist, be sure you know to whom you are referring the person.

Basically, it is time to refer a client to a specialist when any of the following is experienced:

1. When you feel unequal to the task;
2. When you feel you have done all you can do;
3. When rapport is lost;
4. When danger signals appear—overdependency or overinvolvement;
5. When you feel this is out of your field;
6. When you feel the need of other professional help.

In referring remember to protect the feelings of your counselee. Secure his permission and prepare him for the experience of meeting his new counselor. Above all, assure your counselee that referral is not abandonment.

But let me stress again that referral is the last resort in counseling. Human behavior is too complicated to make one statement to cover every case; however, the basic problem in many cases can be solved by sharing the wonderful love of God.

To be able to share the love of God with those you try to help is the key to success in pastoral counseling.

Panel Discussion and Open Forum

The pastor-counselor should avoid becoming an "expert" in all fields. He should avoid specific solutions, speaking instead of spiritual principles.

There is also a danger of the pastor-counselor becoming too involved emotionally. He should seek to be a counselor, not a complaint department.

The minister's preaching ministry can be "family oriented," establishing Christian principles and values. This can solve many potential problems.

In some situations it is wise for the pastor-counselor to be somewhat severe, seeking to bring people to repentance in prayer. While a pastor should maintain a spirit of love, there is a danger of being too indulgent. He must bring people face-to-face with the sinfulness of their sins—then point to the forgiveness available in Christ.

Since many emotional problems have immorality at their roots, it is vital to establish a relationship in which the counselee trusts the counselor to keep all confidences. The pastor must explain to the counselee that his pulpit ministry will warn against pitfalls and sins, but that the pastor will never use the counselee as a pulpit illustration.

When a counselee comes to leaning on the pastor-counselor too heavily, sometimes the pastor should find a friend to assist the counselee.

Pastors are sometimes challenged by boards who do not understand value of time spent in counseling. It is important to explain that counseling can lead to soul winning, and that this too is a part of the Great Commission. However, the pastor would do well to announce a time schedule when he is available for counseling.

One way to develop the ministry of counseling is to practice "therapeutic preaching"—counseling from the pulpit. People will then seek the pastor out, and he can move from informal to structured counseling when it is needed. It is seldom wise for a minister to advertise himself as a counselor. Remember, not all problems require complex answers. Sometimes confronting people with the Person and claims of Christ will solve so-called "complex problems."

Subjects recommended to be included in premarital counseling: Finances, intimate married life, family altar, church attendance, fellowship, communication, and inlaws.

One pastor said that his church sets aside one Sunday each year as "Wedding Bells Sunday" when the married couples are asked to "renew" their vows.

Those using tranquilizers sometimes come to a pastor to ask about the rightness of using these medications. The pastor-counselor should emphasize he is not a physician. He should, however, probe further to see if a spiritual problem is the root of the emotional symptom. He should also remember that divine healing includes mental as well as physical disorders.

When it is necessary for a pastor to refer cases of serious mental disorders to professional help, it is not recommended that a Freudian psychologist be obtained. It is suggested that pastor contact a good medical doctor for his recommendations of professional counselor.

It is our privilege as servants of the Lord to ask wisdom of God, no matter how difficult problems may be.

THE EVANGELISTIC CAMPAIGN IN THE LOCAL CHURCH

Speaker: **OTIS M. KEENER**
Moderator: **LLOYD SHOEMAKER**
Panelists: **ERNEST ESKELIN, JOHN THOMPSON,
W. GLENN WEST**
Recorder: **PAUL FELLER**

EVANGELISM IS NOT THE WORK OF THE CHURCH— it is the work of God. It was essential to spiritual and numerical growth in the first-century Church. Evangelism has been the secret of rapid expansion in the Assemblies of God. The flame of evangelism must burn brightly among us. Today's darkness can be countered by the light of love kindled afresh in our churches.

This kind of crusade doesn't just happen. It is promised by God but must be planned and prayed for by man.

I. The Pastor's Place

A. SCRIPTURALLY, HE IS THE SPIRITUAL LEADER

His shepherd-heart must be sensitive to God and man. Jesus wept because His own did not discern their day of visitation. The Bible teaches there is a season for all things—a time to sow; a time to grow! A time to weep; a time to reap! How blessed is the congregation whose pastor's ear is sensitive to the still small voice of the Spirit of God. For him, revival campaigns are not just scheduled by habit. They are spiritual seasons, planned prayerfully in the providence of God.

Pastors need heaven's help in deciding when, what, and whom. They should know when the Holy Spirit is moving and what He desires to do. The needs of the flock vary. Shepherds can detect these specific hungers. Campaigns can then be prayerfully planned with definite spiritual objectives.

In our statistic-conscious society, false evaluations often arise. Evangelism is not a spiritual game of "can-you-top-this?" We are linked with our Lord in an eternal effort of redemption. This involves spiritual birth, growth, and maturity.

The pastor must determine his planned campaign's specific objective: healing, salvation, prophecy, baptism in the Holy Spirit, prayer and deeper life, youth, dedication, or some other goal. Once he is settled on the when and what —the who will come into focus.

No one knows the needs of a congregation better than the Spirit-led pastor. He must plan to put an evangelist in the pulpit whose message will meet the present need. Men have varied ministries, given by the same Spirit. (In a personal survey, I discovered eight out of ten pastors never engage a man they have not heard.)

B. SPIRITUALLY, THE PASTOR IS LARGELY RESPONSIBLE FOR THE CRUSADE'S SUCCESS

Promotionally, he is the director. He may assign the mechanics of planning to others, but he alone can generate the spiritual enthusiasm that rallies hearts in a common cause. This necessitates clear communication both to the evangelist and the congregation. The burden born of the Holy Spirit in his heart must be shared. The pastor and evangelist then became a team —planning, praying, and pulling together.

Communication to congregations well in advance will pay dividends in attendance and interest. The fast pace of Americans demands ample notice to keep personal plans from conflicting with church outreaches. Many crusades suffer due to poor promotion.

The pastor should inform the staff, board, and church leaders as early as possible. Nothing discourages evangelists more than church-sponsored activities which conflict with the campaign. This is defeating in two ways. First, it brings doubt to the heart of the evangelist—he questions if they really expect revival. Second, it is a strong suggestion to the congregation that other things are more important.

It is not the sinfulness of sinners that defeats revival today as much as it is the satisfaction of the saints. Self-denial, discipline, and death to our desires are still the spiritual path to victory.

A visitation from God begins with a deep sense of need. This must first press the pastor down before God. He then shares these longings with the flock. A scriptural pattern evolves, and the church is called together to prayerfully seek the Lord. Then heaven hears and answers.

II. The People's Place

The apostle Paul establishes our relationship as believers: we are one Body. The energy and attention of every member is essential to revival. Victory or defeat often hinges on how many become involved. Ways must be worked out to spread the desire and burden for revival over the entire congregation. The Holy Spirit will then ignite a divine enthusiasm in all.

Some pastors prepare the people through a series of sermons. Preparatory messages may deal with the reasons for revival, the road to revival, and the results of revival. Those weeks prior to a crusade afford the pastor an opportunity to unite the church in singleness of vision and action. It is not unspiritual to plan ahead. God drew the redemptive blueprints of Calvary before the foundations of the world were laid.

Our objective is every member involved in evangelism. This is no hour for sleeping saints. Pastors, like the apostle Paul, must awaken believers from spiritual slumber. Every campaign is an opportunity to be bought up. The prophetic picture of these last days reveals time is running out.

The church must look upon special meetings like the farmer views the harvest season. Golden grain must be gathered before the storms break.

The leadership of the assembly must feel this urgency to enlist every hand.

Ushers should be assigned to come early and welcome the worshipers. This simple procedure shows you are expecting visitors to attend. Faith is contagious.

The music department should be enlisted too. Using people develops a sense of responsibility. If talented evangelists do everything, visitors may be attracted to these guests instead of the local church.

Sunday school workers, departments, families, and children can be involved by simple assignments which highlight their presence in services.

Public recognition of those who put forth special effort is always an incentive for others to work.

However, this involvement does not just happen. Casual announcements do not create much enthusiasm. Involvement will result from prayerful, careful planning. Some suggest a minimum of eight weeks for this period of preparation.

There is a vast gulf between the man on the street and the man in the pulpit. Consecrated Christians can bridge this chasm. Sinners are not told to attend church. The church is commanded to go to them.

III. The Evangelist's Place

The meaning of evangelist is "a bringer of glad tidings." God has given evangelists to the Church (Ephesians 4:11). Philip was recognized as an evangelist in the Early Church (Acts 21: 8). Paul exhorted Timothy to "endure afflictions, do the work of an evangelist, make full proof of thy ministry" (2 Timothy 4:5).

This is a high and holy calling. It is primarily a preaching ministry; man speaking for God. Powerful, persuasive preaching is a result of much study and prayer. Both of these are work —the assigned work of evangelists. No man will edify the church or evangelize the lost who neglects personal preparation.

Evangelists must move among churches as men who have heard from heaven. Shallow sermons will produce shallow saints. Sensational subjects will create confusion.

Conditions today demand evangelists. The Holy Spirit must set them in the church. *Revivaltime* Speaker C. M. Ward says an evangelist must "get his authority from Christ, his message from the Word of God, and his power from the Holy Spirit." Our confused civilization needs this kind of man. Preachers must return to those closets of prayer and then inform the people what God says.

Waiting upon God is the work of the ministry. Congregations can tell if the man behind the pulpit has been with Jesus. Men will take note of those who have been listening to the Lord. Men's talents may vary, their ministries will differ, but one Spirit must enable and enlighten them in divine love.

Our churches want and need evangelists with this positive gospel of glad tidings. There is plenty of demand today for men with a message that exalts Christ, exhorts to unity, edifies believers, and links people to their pastor.

The church today must confront some alarming trends. Pastors seem concerned about the scarcity of true evangelists. Evangelists are bewildered by the de-emphasis of revival campaigns, both in number held and in the length of meetings.

Undoubtedly America is changing its patterns of living. Economic advancement is providing comforts, conveniences, and luxuries. However, these things have not resolved man's basic problems of sin and self. Sorrow, suffering, and shame stalk our streets.

The hope of America rests in revival. This must begin in the house of the Lord. The church must not concede to the false philosophy that days of revival are over. We must claim the historic promise of the outpouring of God's Spirit upon all flesh.

When the Holy Spirit possesses pastors, people, and evangelists, love will flow through our churches.

There is a power to counteract the contrary currents of today. Has not God promised, "When the enemy comes in like a flood, the Spirit of the Lord will raise a standard against him"?

After looking honestly at the problems, let us examine the divine promises. They are still "yea . . . and amen" to them that believe. Revival will result when pastors, people, and evangelists are in one accord under the direction of one Spirit.

Panel Discussion and Open Forum

In our quest for security we tend to program ourselves to the extent that God is unable to do what He wants to do. Thus the need for pastors and evangelists to be sensitive to the leading of the Holy Spirit presented itself repeatedly throughout the seminar.

The discussion period was a time of presenting problems and giving possible and/or partial answers to the problems.

Several pastors pointed up the problem of not being able to secure an evangelist when the church is ready for a revival because the evangelists are booked for one or two years ahead. But the evangelist, faced with the need "to keep busy" in order to meet his living obligations, feels he must book well in advance.

The consensus was that the length of the evangelistic meeting needs to be more flexible. Let the meeting continue as long as the Holy Spirit leads.

An evangelist averages forty weeks of pay a year. Sunday night offerings are not always sufficient.

The pastor and evangelist should have a complete understanding about finances before the meeting starts. This understanding should be based upon the evangelist's needs and the church's ability to give. Suggested amounts varied from one-third more to four times the pastor's salary.

The church could include in its budget an adequate compensation for evangelists. The church could give special envelopes to the congregation two weeks before the meeting. The people could then give their love offering any time during the meetings.

The district, section, or larger church could "mother" (pay all expenses of) a revival for a smaller church.

A love offering for the evangelist should be for the evangelist; part of it should not be used for paying other expenses of the meeting.

The speaker reported a personal survey in which he sent questionnaires to fifty evangelists and fifty pastors. Five concerns of the evangelists are: financial problems; untrained altar workers; little or no evidence of plans for follow up; poor promotion; calendars crowded with other church-sponsored activities during the revival meeting.

Three concerns of pastors are: too much professionalism among evangelists and a lack of spiritual preparation; evangelists who do not work around the altar; side programs, such as foreign evangelistic campaigns, the evangelist consciously or subconsciously promoted.

Most evangelists present expressed a desire for a training seminar for evangelists conducted by qualified evangelists.

THE FOCUS OF CHRISTIAN EDUCATION

Speaker: **RICHARD DRESSELHAUS**
Moderator: **WILLIAM KIRSCHKE**
Panelists: **TROY BOGGS, DALE MAW, EDGAR PALSER**
Recorder: **HAROLD CROSBY**

THE APPROACH TO OUR TOPIC will be directed into five areas: (1) a reexamination of our history; (2) a redefinition of our terms; (3) a reassessment of our mission; (4) a reevaluation of our methods; and (5) a realignment of our purpose.

I. A Reexamination of Our History

The Assemblies of God has arrived at a point in its history when it must ask penetrating questions. Church historians are gambling on denominational parallelism— expecting the transition from a revival movement to a solidified institution to be complete within the foreseeable future. Such affirmations lead us backward, to explore foundations; inward, to discover motives; forward, to positive purpose. Our task is to explore the broad scope of Christian education as it relates to the overall task of church evangelism.

Christian education has played an important role in the development of our Movement. When early believers saw the necessity for Bible instruction and participating in evangelism, the Sunday school was organized. Massive Sunday school conventions, catchy slogans, and every-member-bring-a-member methodology resulted in a rapidly growing Sunday school that won the admiration of many. The Sunday school, during the formative years of our Movement, served as the basic structure of the church.

As went the Sunday school, so went the church.

A possible change in emphases is seen today. Recently someone commented: "The churches aren't emphasizing Sunday school so much anymore." Statistics would indicate that this is a true appraisal. Attendance boards have come down; the slogans have lost their appeal; the great Sunday school conventions of a decade ago have largely disappeared. Perhaps the emphasis has shifted to a kind of "whole church" concept; that is, we tend to place more emphasis on the involvement of the whole church in the task of evangelism.

At this point the mind fills with questions: Is there really sufficient evidence to indicate a trend away from the historical emphasis on the Sunday school? To this question we must give a qualified affirmative answer. Then have we now moved closer to a broader and more workable definition of Christian education? While it is true that Christian education must involve the many agencies of the church which have to do with instruction and evangelization, yet this can hardly justify a diminishing of the historical emphasis on the Sunday school.

If revitalization is necessary, what can be done to give the Sunday school a more dominant and vital role in the educational ministry of the church? And how can the Sunday school contribute more effectively to the evangelistic outreach of the church?

II. A Redefinition of Our Terms

Two terms call for definition. What do we mean by *evangelism?* And what do we mean by the general designation, *Christian education?*

Evangelicals are searching for a philosophy of education that is both Christian and Biblical. The distinction may seem like trivia; yet in light of modernistic appraisals of the Bible it becomes imperative to insist on a Biblical basis for curriculum, method, and application that is unquestionably Christocentric.

In the past we have thought of Christian education in a rather narrow sense as referring primarily to the Sunday school. The local church, however, must think of its educational responsibilities as reaching into many areas: home Bible study groups, weekday activity groups, day school programs, camping programs, college ministries, etc. While Sunday school is the largest of these groups and will occupy the bulk of our thinking, we must not think of it as the only agency in the spectrum of Christian education.

Next we come to the term *evangelism.* What precisely do we mean by evangelism? The word *evangelism* is not found in the Bible. However, the word *euaggelistes* from which we get the word *evangelist* is a close equivalent. *Eu* means "good," and *aggelos* means "messenger." Evangelism then means the going forth of a messenger with a good message.

This leads us to a threefold understanding of the term. Evangelism is a *passion.* The Early Church was gripped with an awareness of the intrinsic worth of the gospel. Motivated by this passion, it went forth to win men to Christ.

Second, evangelism is a *proclamation.* The Early Church spoke with words of inspiration and illumination. Men could not shun these words. Their hearts were pierced, their consciences stirred, and their wills changed.

Third, evangelism is a *program.* Second Timothy 2:2 says, "And the things that thou hast heard of me among many witnesses, the same commit thou to faithful men, who shall be able to teach others also." This was the program of the Early Church as it moved under the direction of the Holy Spirit.

Here again we are prompted to ask several questions. Is our program of Christian education both Biblical and Christ-centered? Does classtime revolve around a discussion of God's Word? Are people confronted directly with the claims of Christ on their lives?

We must guard against a secularization of our endeavors which seeks to interpret God's Word in the light of man's world, instead of man's world in the light of God's Word. Any program of evangelization through Christian education must be built upon Christ, the living Word, and upon the Bible, the written Word.

III. A Reassessment of Our Mission

The challenge of the Great Commission has been our motivation from the beginning. The words *go, preach, baptize,* and *teach* have triggered the deepest consecration to do God's work at home and abroad. The Great Commission, however, is churchwide as well as worldwide; individualistic as well as all-inclusive; immediate as well as futuristic. The point is this: What are we doing in Christian education to evangelize every person that is ours to reach? What about the preschooler—the one still too small? Or what about the elder citizens—those now too old? Doesn't our mission include them? Too often we bring a kind of priority-for-profits approach to bear on our program of Christian education—win those who can fit best into the machinery of a given program.

Much is being said about "moving outside the sanctuary" and into the world. Its advocates remind us of the immediacy of the Great Commission—the fact that our neighbor needs to hear even if he doesn't take time to come to our church.

In the Book of Acts we see a small church in a big world—a world of paganism and witchcraft. The sequence seems clear. It began in the Upper Room, the place of power; it moved to homes, the place of worship and fellowship; and finally it was thrust into the world to evangelize and to educate. This was the sequence at the beginning of our movement—the Upper Room, then the place of worship, and then the witness of the gospel to neighbors and friends.

One caution is needed, however. We dare not speak of worship or evangelism until we know well the intrinsic worth of the Upper Room. Perhaps this is where we have gone far afield. We have tried to motivate people to do the work of evangelism who haven't first been motivated by the Spirit. The people are awkward and unsuccessful. They work like a metric wrench on an American bolt.

So we ask: What are the dimensions of our mission and what is the power by which we hope to fulfill this mission? What are we doing to make each church an Upper Room and each department of education the framework within which Spirit-motivated people can do the work of evangelism?

IV. A Reevaluation of Our Methods

Since method must follow the awareness of mission, we return now to a discussion on methodology. In Robert E. Coleman's book, *The Master Plan of Evangelism*, the reader is asked to consider Christ's method of evangelizing the world. Mr. Coleman has adopted eight terms to describe this method:

1. *Selection.* Jesus called twelve men to follow Him. This reveals the heart of His strategy —a small, intimate group with which He could personally work.

2. *Association.* Jesus not only called these men, but He associated with them. The essence of His training program was just letting His disciples follow Him.

3. *Consecration.* Jesus expected and required absolute obedience. The disciples were consecrated to following the directives of their Master.

4. *Impartation.* Jesus gave His very Spirit to His disciples. Having thus received, they would possess and know the love of God for a lost world.

5. *Demonstration.* Jesus taught not by precept alone but more often by demonstration. His disciples knew because they saw.

6. *Delegation.* Jesus assigned work to the disciples. Since the time would soon come when they would have to carry on alone, Jesus patiently and gradually shifted the responsibility of the Kingdom to them.

7. *Supervision.* Jesus not only assigned a work load, but He supervised the assignment to be sure it was carried out successfully. When the disciples came back asking, "Why couldn't we?" Jesus was there with an answer.

8. *Reproduction.* Jesus expected His disciples to bear fruit for the Kingdom. In this way the Master's ministry would be expanded widely.

This must be our methodology of evangelism through Christian education. While the Sunday school seems to provide this framework most adequately, the other related agencies may certainly profit from it as well.

V. A Realignment of Our Purpose

The Assemblies of God is a revival movement. It must remain a movement and it must be motivated by spiritual renewal. How can we focus Christian education to help fulfill this central purpose?

1. *Biblical perspective.* The Bible is not a ref-

erence book, nor even just a blueprint. It stands over all that we do, either with a spirit of sanction or a voice of correction. To the extent that we are Biblical, we will succeed as Christian educators.

2. *Linear inspiration.* True spiritual motivation demands the example of leadership. From the top position in the structure of any program of Christian education to the most insignificant worker, the current of spiritual motivation must flow freely.

3. *Growth directive.* Reevaluation is an unpopular concept. Yet herein lies the key. We can move too fast and too far with programming and leave people—unsaved and saved alike— without spiritual moorings. Numerically Christ failed, but the men He won He secured well. The masses will be reached when the core of the church is strong.

4. *Centralized effort.* Every program must relate directly to the central purpose of spiritual decision and application. Each church must have a clearly defined philosophy of program and endeavor that will be compatible with this basic purpose. Unless men's lives are changed by a confrontation with Christ, unless men's lives are brought into conformity with God's Word, and unless these men are motivated to reproduce, we have failed in the basic purpose of Christian education.

Our world is a strange world, but a challenging world. It is so unpredictable that it can begin a decade intent on building a society of magnificence and end the same decade wondering how it can hold the pieces of its culture together.

Never has the gospel been such a live option to the ills of our world. When things are falling apart, the gospel declares, "All things are held together in Him" (Colossians 1:17, NEB). When breaches in rational thinking are apparent, the Cross becomes the linchpin to keep men together. If ever the gospel has had relevance, it is now. If ever the church has had a message, it is now. If ever the world has needed the light of God, it is now.

Against this backdrop of strangeness and challenge, we direct our efforts to the task of evangelism through a clear focus of Christian education. Motivated by the Spirit, guided by the Word, and challenged by the needs of this world, we find Christian education opens a door of glorious opportunity and becomes a means whereby we can participate more fully in the task of evangelism.

Panel Discussion and Open Forum

Christian education is: (1) communicating the truth of God's Word; (2) teaching Christ; (3) bringing a person to a confrontation with Christ, then leading him on to maturity; (4) the process of guiding the student through an experience of truth into a life of service to the glory of God.

Christian education is the Holy Spirit using a teacher, the Scriptures, and related curriculum materials to bring the student to the knowledge of Jesus Christ and spiritual maturity, according to the will of God.

Historically, the Sunday school has been the broad base upon which our entire Christian education has been built. The unit of the Sunday school is the classroom where the learning experience is created for the pupil; namely, a teacher, a pupil, and a lesson. This classroom situation must be kept in focus at all times when we discuss Christian education.

Question: Other related agencies have developed within the church to give a broader scope to Christian education. Do they provide the factors necessary for a genuine learning experience?

These related agencies have the potential of enhancing the total program, for the Great Commission is twofold: to win men and to make disciples. We must keep in mind that the teacher is the heart of the Christian education program. Replace the teacher with other leaders, activities, etc., in these related agencies, but it is not necessarily Christian education.

The role of the Christian day school is growing to add to the broader reach of Christian education. However, generally the Assemblies of God tends to separate academic training from spiritual training. Hence the existence of both the Sunday School Department and the Department of Education. Some felt that the time must come when all church-related education should come under the heading of Christian Education.

One hour per week in Sunday school is insufficient. The teacher must not be the sole repository of spiritual training. The Sunday school was never intended to replace home training. Family altar and spiritual training in the home are woefully lacking, and we must institute this base as fundamental to a sound program of Christian education.

Question: Why are so many Sunday school attendance boards disappearing?

Attendance is not emphasized as it once was, and the board is removed. We accomplish what we emphasize. With declining attendance the classroom loses its importance.

We must hold to Bible patterns and establish in our schools the methods Jesus used. A harvest of souls is possible only as we abide in the Word of God.

"Building a Wall of Faith" is an excellent theme for our Sunday school curriculum, but all curriculum materials should come under this theme. Materials now being produced by other related church agencies have little correlation and a great deal of overlapping with the Sunday school curriculum. All curricular materials should be correlated. This would include children's church materials. They should not be just another fifty-two lessons or programs, but an extension of the Sunday school lesson, week by week.

Complete indoctrination courses (catechisms) should be available for all ages. Pastors who have used "Foundations for Faith" report an excellent response. But this fine series is not being used as widely as it should.

For 180 years the Sunday school has been chiefly an institution of evangelism. This makes the Sunday school much more than just a place for education. More than eighty percent of all of our church members come directly from the Sunday school.

Occasionally the Sunday school gets "kicked around." It is criticized for its shortcomings, ridiculed for its pupils' ignorance, challenged by other agencies within and without the church, and de-emphasized by church leaders. Yet with all of this it has been and still is the greatest community outreach we have and is responsible for winning more souls than all other agencies combined.

A church becomes a solidified institution when it becomes so occupied with running the program of the agencies within the church that it forgets outreach. This is usually the sign that revival fires have dimmed and a burden to reach the lost is all but gone. All related church agencies should be carefully examined and carefully identified to determine the direction of their programs. The agencies should complement the Christian education program, not conflict or overlap.

Through the years these related church agencies have been developed to give a much broader scope to the total Christian education program in the local church. This is good. But herein lies a grave danger. The average Assemblies of God Sunday school has an enrollment of

113 and an average attendance of eighty-three with an average of eleven workers. Often other adults within the framework of the average Sunday school are either unwilling or unable to accept the responsibility of leadership in the "total church" program.

Hence the eleven workers, already filling positions of responsibility in the Sunday school, are called upon to staff the organization and give leadership to all of these related agencies. This overburdens the worker and greatly reduces his efficiency. What is even worse, the worker often arrives at a point of complete frustration just from trying to keep up with the program. Thus he finds himself so busy with the program that he fails to pray, study God's Word, visit the people, and win souls. The priorities are forgotten.

Both on a district level and on the local level these related agencies have come into direct competition and conflict. They compete for time on the calendar, for staff workers, for finances, for exposure. This causes a great deal of misunderstanding.

The Sunday school is still the broad base upon which the total Christian education program rests. Therefore the Sunday school should be emphasized. Smaller churches need guidance in developing related agencies, not having them simply for the sake of keeping up with the district or national program.

As goes the Sunday school, so goes the church. Sunday schools are known by the churches they build, and churches are known by the Sunday schools they maintain. It is time for us to move forward with a sense of urgency and with a passion for souls in the great work of Christian education.

GIRLS—OPPORTUNITY FOR EVANGELISM

Speaker: **MRS. BILLIE DAVIS**

Moderator: **MRS. GOLDIE ANDERSON**

Panelists: **MRS. T. A. GIANOPULOS, MRS. J. DERALD MUSGROVE, MRS. WILLIAM VENSKE**

Recorder: **MISS CHARLOTTE SCHUMITSCH**

BEFORE WE CAN DISCUSS in any meaningful way the subject of winning girls to Christ, we must consider the general concept of evangelism. It is with an understanding of this concept as a basic premise that all Christian effort must begin. In my opinion there is no technique nor gimmick which can be relied upon to aid in winning girls if we lack an understanding of the ultimate purpose of gospel work.

I. Evangelism as a Guiding Principle of the Church

The why of evangelism goes back to the why of creation. God desired companionship. Nothing in the realm of nature nor of angels met His specifications. I like to think that God not only required companionship, but compatibility, since such is necessary in an intimate, sharing situation. For this reason He created a man and created him *in His own image*—so He and His creature could have something in common.

Such a creature would, of course, have a conscious will, an intellect, and the ability to find satisfaction (emotions). By his very nature man would tend toward the fulfillment of his purpose. He would survive, he would procreate, and he would be able to understand his relationship with God.

The experience in the Garden of Eden was made possible because man was such a creature —a creature with appetites and the ability to

exercise judgment and will. Because man made the wrong choice under pressure from Satan, he fell from grace. After the Fall, man still retained the same appetites and instinct. But since now he was subject to the whims of the devil, his appetites could be perverted.

The Fall did not change God's purpose for man. God wants man to fulfill his true destiny: to exercise his privileges, to be mature and consciously aware of his place in the eternal plan, to be a friend of God. So God gave man the opportunity to choose all over again. He sent His Son, the Lord Jesus Christ, to make a reconciliation between God and man. The death of Jesus on the cross atoned for the original sinful choice and opened the way for man to be what he was originally intended to be—a conscious being intellectually, emotionally, and spiritually compatible with God.

Jesus spent His brief earthly life in demonstrating His work. He had in mind one principal goal—to establish a means by which the results of His life, death, and resurrection might be made known to all the world. Through His example and teaching He made plain the plan of God. At the close of His earthly ministry Christ turned the perpetuation of His work over to the Church.

The purpose of the Church, as we see it, is to keep on doing what Jesus came to earth to do—to reconcile the creature and his Creator so man may share the glories of God's presence for eternity. The Church must make man aware of God's purpose and give him an opportunity to make a decision.

II. Evangelism as a Specific Function of the Church

It might be said that there are two manners in which the idea *evangelism* is conceived. First there is that which might be called "specialized evangelism."

The "revival meeting" is a typical example of this type. It is a specialized effort of the church, limited rather rigidly by time boundaries, during which the aim is immediate overt expressions of conversion. Other examples of specialized evangelism are decision days in the Sunday school; personal witnessing where the aim is immediate response of conversion; certain types of jail, hospital, and street services; distribution of evangelistic literature (that which stresses the one overt confession of faith); and children's revival efforts.

Most Christians recognize another type of evangelism which we shall call "total evangelism." This type aims to create environments and provide stimuli which will guide the individual into fulfillment of his destiny as a child of God. The "total evangelism" concept develops from the fact that the immediate overt expression of a decision and the stimulation by a worker or an instrument such as music or literature, which leads up to an overt expression, are but a small part of the actual evangelistic activity of the church. The urging by a worker is almost incidental to the experience of a convert. It is the moving of the Holy Spirit upon the mind and will of the individual which brings about conversion. Therefore, whether the external push comes from a tract, a sermon, a Sunday school lesson, or admiration for a Christian friend, "evangelism" is accomplished.

Total evangelism may be understood to include four phases.

A. UNDERSTANDING

An individual must know what salvation is and how it may be obtained. He must be able to connect the need he feels within himself (the God-quest) with the message he hears. Therefore, evangelism begins with the teaching which brings about an understanding of God's plan and man's relationship to it. Such teaching may be accomplished quickly if the hearer has had other experiences which have brought him to

"the point of readiness." It is possible that only one tract or one sermon may do it. But experience and logic lead us to believe that such cases are rare. The usual process can be described best by the Bible words: "Precept upon precept; line upon line, line upon line; here a little, and there a little."

B. FEELING

After the mind forms concepts "understands" the nature of God's plan, then the emotions respond. An individual realizes that here is the answer to his doubts, fears, and yearnings. He comprehends a little of the greatness of God's love for him, and the sacrifice of Jesus for his sin. Feelings of contrition, personal responsibility, indebtedness to Christ, and repentance follow.

C. COMMITMENT

Feelings of contrition for sin and gratitude to Christ lead to the act of "accepting Christ as Saviour," or "confession of faith," or "getting saved." Nothing should be done to depreciate the importance of this phase. Nevertheless, a danger is inherent in the emphasis which may be placed upon the actual moments of triumph. For they may be followed by a spiritual letdown. There may be a tendency for the church to feel that the work of evangelism is finished and that all other Christian activity is mundane.

The truth is that commitment to the Lord usually is not complete at the point of overt expression of surrender. It does not end at the altar; it *begins* there. There remains the development of serenity and confidence in Christ. Care of new converts is as much a part of evangelism as getting sinners to the altar.

D. EXPRESSION

After the conversion of an individual, the church has more responsibility than ever. Now a new recruit must be fitted into the program. No born-again one can sit happily by in the church. A part of his salvation is a desire to express his love for God through witness and service. If the desire to serve is repressed, the convert will become restless and feel unworthy.

In order to have a complete program of evangelism the church must: (1) Be diligent in the teaching of the Word and of Christian principles; (2) provide a climate for the development and expression of feelings of contrition, repentance, and love; (3) give opportunities for the overt confession of Christ and the commitment of the entire life and human faculties to Him as Christian maturity is developed; (4) put forth every effort to train and enlist every Christian in a definite program of service, so each conversion begins a new cycle of evangelism.

III. Evangelism a Process of Stimulating the the Internalization of Values

Up to this point we have considered evangelism in general, making no specific reference to the theme of winning young girls to Christ. The reason for this is that I feel there is too much emphasis upon something called "child evangelism" by persons who seem to know little of what the concept of "evangelism" involves. The popular idea of child evangelism which conceives it as a little revival meeting seems out of tune with reality. Child evangelism is nothing more nor less than the principle of providing a program of total evangelism which begins with children and includes elements which meet the needs of various age and sex groups.

What actually happens when a person of any age "accepts Christ" is that he now views as his own certain values which already exist outside himself. This is called in psychology "the internalization of values." Jesus died for all. Still an individual must say for himself, "He died for me." All an evangelist can do is make individuals aware of the fact that salvation is available.

In the example of personal salvation we can see plainly enough that the values must be internalized—the individual must accept for himself, with a conscious knowledge of what he is doing. But in the everyday practice of our church work we tend to forget the principle entirely. We say, "Do this because I say it is right." And much of our "evangelism" among children is based on little more than the smug declaration that "it was good for Paul and Silas, and it's good enough for you."

The point is not that the gospel was *good* for Paul and Silas, but rather that it met certain specific needs of the individuals. To assume that a young girl needs and desires the same sort of satisfactions as does her mother or teacher is a tragic mistake. In fact, to the youth of today anything that satisfied parents and teachers must be dull and square and out of step with the "in" thing.

IV. Understanding the Young Girl in Contemporary Environment.

In order to apply the gospel truth, to make it appear as relevant as it really is to the young girl, and to guide her to accept or internalize Christianity, it is necessary to know what a girl is like, how her concepts develop, and what environmental factors tend to shape her growth.

During the periods of infancy and childhood there are not too many differences in the characteristics of boys and girls which will be significant to us as Christian workers. In other words, most principles of evangelism will apply to both sexes. However, there are a few marked differences of which we should be aware. Following are a few pertinent factors unique to the concept "girl."

A. BIOLOGICAL FACTORS

1. Girls tend to be stronger in infancy than boys.
2. Usually girls grow more rapidly during the early years.
3. Usually girls surpass boys in motor skills which emphasize precision and lag behind boys in skills of speed and strength. (This is at least in part socially determined.)
4. Girls master speech sounds more rapidly than do boys, and they tend to develop larger vocabularies and speak in more complex sentences.
5. Sex emotions begin to appear about the third year.
6. Up to eight years of age, there is little self-consciousness concerning the body or the opposite sex.

B. PSYCHOLOGICAL FACTORS

1. Girls develop emotionally more rapidly than do boys.
2. Girls tend to be more "imaginative" than boys.
3. Girls quickly make ideals of socially attractive people, while boys choose more remote heroes.
4. Girls tend to be interested in school subjects which involve language usage, while boys lean toward mathematics and natural science.
5. Girls evidence interest in grooming and appearance earlier than boys. By the age of ten or eleven tidiness is a fairly high value for girls, but much less so for boys.
6. Most "typically female" personality traits are socially conditioned but are nevertheless important to a study of girlhood because the child naturally tends to develop as expected. She conforms to socially accepted patterns.
7. Girls tend to be religious, to have great interest in the supernatural, to accept the mi-

raculous. They seem to prefer formality in religious activities. They are impressed by stately music, religious pictures, and objects.

C. SOCIAL FACTORS

1. Girls develop qualities of leadership rapidly; by the eighth year they are likely to be "bossy."

2. Girls are more willing to play boy roles and to include boys in their play than are boys to play girl roles or include girls.

3. Girls are generally less likely to start quarrels and to retaliate than are boys; they are more aggressive when playing with boys than with other girls.

4. Girls are generally less interested in competitive activities.

5. Girls start to form gangs later than do boys and usually are involved in smaller gangs; but girl gangs are more exclusive, more secretive, and less likely to include members of different ages or social or ethnic backgrounds. Girls are more cruel to outsiders.

6. Girls tend to have slightly more "social insight" than do boys.

V. The Relationship of the Girl to the Church

A study of girls is more than a matter for a few Sunday school teachers and children's workers; for with the girls, whether we like it or not, rests much of the destiny of the church. By the time girls reach adolescence they already outnumber boys in most churches.

Every effort should be made to provide an environment where a young girl can develop naturally into a mature Christian woman, capable of serving in the church and finding the individual fulfillment she seeks. The church should encourage a girl in her best qualities, such as her proficiency in language, her social insight, her cooperative tendencies, her strength in leadership. It should give positive attention to helping her overcome her worst tendencies: the exclusive or snobbish bent, the bossiness, submissiveness to patterns of unworthy ideals.

The church should provide the girl with an opportunity to train for the work it will one day ask her to do. It should offer satisfying social experiences. It should consider her love for the beautiful and orderly in religious activities and refrain from the notion that children need all noise and motion. But, at the same time, it must be careful that religion is not just a set of rules and ceremonies. The church must give her properly prepared teachers and adequate facilities

for learning. It must see that the truth is related to her needs as an individual, and as a member of a group of contemporary children.

Most important of all, there must be a working principle that the girl has as much to offer the church as the church has to offer the girl. The girl will someday teach its classes, play its music, marry its pastors, mother its children, and carry most of the burden of its social service outreach and its upreach in prayer.

VI. Making Knowledge Effective in Practical Action

At this point we have discussed the concept "evangelism" and the concept "girl." It remains for us to consider briefly how we can bring the two together in practical situations. Of course, the basic principles which we have considered lead automatically to some conclusions.

Probably the most important single factor is the attitude of the worker. If he draws a logical conclusion from the facts we have considered, he will see the girl as a human being passing through a given stage of development. The aim is to cause her to accept the gospel as real and necessary to her, at the moment, according to her present ability to comprehend and respond.

The worker must avoid the attitude that since most young people seem to leave the church when they reach adolescence, the only hope of keeping the girl is to give her strict rules and discipline. Actually many studies show that the more rigid and dogmatic the training in childhood, the more likely the adolescent is to doubt the religious concepts he had formerly accepted in an unquestioning fashion.

The attitude of the worker must be that the child sincerely wants to know and to do what is right. Questions of children through the age of twelve are usually sincere. Girls are more articulate than boys. Do not discourage their questions, for one day a sullen, shut-in teen-age girl may need you, and you will have closed the door to her.

The physical setting has much to do with the impression children form of the church. Probably this is more significant in the case of girls, for they tend to notice an object as a whole unit and be impressed with the total effect, while boys tend to be interested in smaller details. Any room used for teaching should be as attractive and comfortable as possible. Girls like religious pictures, crosses, crowns, communion tables, choir robes, pews, and decorative window treatments. They would rather put their offering into a silver plate than a limp old bag or a crayon box. They like songbooks, even if they can't read, and if possible they should be given an opportunity to handle them.

More important than any other factors are order, good taste, and a feeling of quiet warmth. Music that is soft and sentimental reaches them best. Generally, a serious demeanor on the part of the worker is more effective than a clowning style.

Presentations to young children should consist mainly of Bible stories which involve characters and action; and of simple modern stories which treat situations within the experience of the child.

There should be a minimum of allegory and very little symbolism, until about the tenth year. Girls of ten and eleven are beginning to be interested in mystery and secret societies, so symbols may become exciting to them at this time.

Most girls enjoy knowing about customs and dress of faraway lands. They are not as interested in remote heroes or stories involving sports or war. Girls love to pretend and can be led to see themselves in a story. They like to act out parts, read dialogue, wear costumes, and manipulate materials.

The method of presentation to children, no matter what the subject, should be a teaching method rather than a preaching style. Children's workers will be more successful if they are careful not to baby-talk their audience. Girls need an example of correct, standard speech and a well-modulated voice. Keep elaborate presentations such as magic tricks for special occasions only. Simple visual aids and filmstrips which tell Bible stories are best. When the aim is evangelism, do not let the equipment outshine the message.

As a general rule, the same children should not be coaxed to make public declarations over and over again. Sometimes it is better to have the Christian children go apart first to pray in a separate room. If they are treated in a general decision effort just as are the unconverted children, they may become confused. It is better to lead children to express love for God in conversation and in kind deeds and witnessing to others, than to have them continually making religious motions and noises which may not be properly internalized.

By the time a girl in our modern society is eleven years old, she is already beginning to face some of the problems and exhibit some of the characteristics which we attribute to the teen-age period. It is a great mistake to let this time sneak up and take us by surprise.

Girls grow up more rapidly because of the small and noisy world in which they live. The girl becomes restless and dissatisfied with her homelife. She is lazy and rebellious; and she and her mother, who used to be so close, start to bicker. The mother is hurt and unhappy. The girl feels misunderstood and confused. The only thing that has any real meaning for her may be her friends, her gang, her peer group.

The importance of the peer group subculture has become extremely marked in our society. The church has an opportunity now which it must not overlook. It is organized in the Sunday school and with other groups, such as the Missionettes, along peer group lines. Instead of bewailing the sad state of affairs, now the church can show itself flexible and wise and hospitable. It can help the gangs to form inside it instead of outside. It can make itself relevant to the needs of those it would serve.

The girl who dreams of being a woman, independent and special, is feeling the tug that God put into her nature, the pangs of spiritual hunger, the God-quest. This is the point at which she is most "ready" to receive the gospel and make its values her own. The church will destroy itself if it does not recognize that she represents the *greatest evangelistic opportunity in the world.*

Panel Discussion and Open Forum

The mission of the church is to perpetuate the work of Christ. An excellent way to reach unsaved girls is through summer Bible camps. Parents will often allow their children to attend a church-sponsored camp even though they would not permit them to attend an Assemblies of God church. The preaching and teaching at camp is geared to the age level of the children in attendance.

Girls who see other girls serving the Lord are encouraged to continue their own Christian walk. Counselors have a wonderful opportunity to reach girls who find it difficult or impossible to communicate with their own mothers.

The local church needs to provide opportunities for girls to find the same blessing in worship and at the altar as they find at camp. Often, however, children find no one to pray with them in their home church.

Too often times of extreme emotionalism are followed by spiritual deflation.

There should be a place in every church where

people can find God at any time. If possible, every church should have a counseling service. Every teacher should be a counselor. Workers need to be soul winners. We need trained workers to teach, to counsel, to love, to pray, to be "mothers in Israel." WMC's could be a great help to girls along this line.

It is so easy to neglect our own children while taking care of others. Children are a gift of God and need to be taught to fear God. We sometimes leave it to spiritual environment to win them to the Lord. It is the obligation of mothers to win girls to the Lord. Time should be taken to explain and answer questions. Many mothers do not make time for their own girls.

A traumatic experience does not shape character as much as repetition of an experience. Learning comes from repetition. Classes should be provided for very young children to teach them about salvation, baptism, and communion. Never shut the door on any child's question. Children do what adults expect of them. They should be taught to pray while they are very, very young.

The best avenue to reach outside girls is through our own children. Evangelistic services should be taught to pray while very, very young. to win souls. Children do witness and have faith to pray for needs. It is important that children are not driven away when they are in their "pretending years." Always give them the benefit of the doubt.

HELPING NEW CONVERTS GROW

Speaker: **RALPH HARRIS**
Moderator: **ROBERT EASTLAKE**
Panelists: **JOHN BOSTROM, H. MAURICE CADWALDER JR., PHILIP CROUCH, ARTHUR SHELL JR.**
Recorder: **GLENROY SHEDD**

WHAT WOULD YOU THINK of parents who rejoiced over the birth of a child, then left the baby alone so that soon, without anyone to feed and care for it, it died from neglect? Do you agree this would be a criminal attitude and action? Yet this is the very crime which many churches have been and now are guilty of committing. In fact, our entire Movement has fallen short, for many new converts have been lost to the cause of Christ because we have failed to take care of them properly.

Let us illustrate this way: If we may judge by the sale of our literature, we have about 180,000 teen-agers in our churches. If we were to retain all of them, about every five years we would add nearly half a million people to our membership.

Here is additional proof. Again using the sale of our literature as a guide, we can safely say that we have had about 150,000 juniors in our Assemblies of God Sunday schools each year for the past fifteen years. If we had retained all these juniors (and the goal of every teacher in the Junior Department should be to win every child to Christ before he leaves the department), we would have about one million more members in our churches than we had fifteen years ago.

Let us use another basis of measurement. Sunday school Checkup reports show that over the past few years an average of 85,000 people a year accept Christ as Saviour. In ten years this would amount to 850,000—not far from the one-million mark.

These facts should not only shout loudly in our ears but should grip our hearts. Where are all these people? Where are the hundreds of thousands of people who have knelt at Assemblies of God altars during the past fifty-four years of our existence as a Movement? Many, of course, have passed on to be with the Lord, but it seems conclusive that the capacity of all our churches put together today would not begin to equal the number of those who once found Christ as Saviour and now no longer attend our churches.

What is the reason for the great loss of converts? Is it the fault of the evangelists? Of the pastors? Of the Sunday school teachers? Of the study materials we have used? Perhaps no one could come up with a conclusive answer to these questions. Possibly all or most of these factors are involved. Our chief focus of attention then should be to find a solution to the problem so this terrible attrition does not continue.

May I suggest the following: "The job's only half done when the sinner's been won." It is fine to talk of reaching the lost, but to do an effective work we must also develop, activate, and promote a definite program for retaining new converts.

One of the great experiences of my ministry

103

was participating as a pastor in the Billy Graham Crusade held in Seattle in 1951. It was my privilege as a member of the personal workers committee to help train more than one thousand personal workers; to serve as a counselor to whom personal workers brought new converts after they had dealt with them; and to help assign new converts to cooperating churches for follow-up.

The very effective follow-up program of the Billy Graham Crusades was just beginning under the leadership of Dawson Trotman, who had developed the Navigators Program during World War II. During the six weeks of the campaign a series of early morning meetings was held with pastors and other local church leaders in which Mr. Trotman spelled out for us the principles of convert conservation. At the heart of the program was the Navigator's Bible Memorization Program in which we memorized 108 Scripture verses, arranged in topical form.

It was a thrilling experience for me to follow these principles with converts assigned to our church as a result of the crusade and to see that this system really worked. Based on my own experiences as a pastor, I have developed in recent years some materials designed for the purpose of guiding new Christians into a successful, happy, effective, and mature Christian experience.

First, we must make sure that converts are led into a definite experience of the new birth. *Second*, the convert must be helped over those crucial first few days of his Christian experience. *Third*, he must be guided into patterns of Christian living which will stay with him throughout his Christian life and enable him to become a mature Christian.

I. A Solid Foundation

In many cases it is probably true that we have lost new converts simply because the person's experience was not well grounded. Though he may have been stirred emotionally, he did not surrender his will. He may have gone to an altar because many others were doing so. He may have been influenced merely by a speaker's personality. He may have been touched by some sad story.

No experience will be adequate unless it is based upon the Word of God. Emotions vary, and experiences may differ, but the Word of God is unchangeable. The seeker must possess a complete faith and trust in what the Word of

God says. He must also exercise his human will in the determination to follow Christ.

How are we going to achieve this goal? We must train our personal workers more effectively. We must get them into the Word themselves. We must show them how to use appropriate Scripture passages. We must help them know how to lead a person to a decision; and that decision must be based on the Word of God and must include a definite commitment by the seeker, one which involves the exercise of his will.

II. Those First Crucial Days

The first week is a critical period for a new convert. In fact, the devil often makes a counterattack within twenty-four hours, trying to convince the new convert he has acted foolishly. The new convert needs to be warned against Satan's tactics so he will be prepared for them. There should also be a personal contact with the new convert within twenty-four hours. He will need help.

Now, about that first week. For the benefit of new Christians, a small booklet has been prepared entitled *Now What?* Covering the basic aspects of the Christian life, it takes the questions which normally occur to a new convert and tries to answer them in simple, concise language.

Now What? explains the meaning of the new birth and what it means to be a child of God. It emphasizes the need for development in the Christian life and deals with those elements which will help the new convert grow spiritually. It shows him how to read the Bible with understanding and how to pray effectively. It explains how to overcome temptation and emphasizes the baptism in the Holy Spirit as the normal experience for every Christian. It deals with Christian stewardship and the responsibilities of the Christian life, emphasizing the need for becoming a part of a local church. It deals with principles of conduct and how a Christian can learn the will of God.

One of the important features of *Now What?* is the emphasis on getting into the Word of God. Covering the first week of the new convert's life as a Christian, it takes him through the Gospel of John, three chapters a day. It also gives questions based upon those chapters, thus leading him into a simple method of Bible study. It also provides suggestions on verses to memorize. By the end of that first week, if the new convert has followed the suggestions made in

Now What? he will be well on his way toward a successful, happy Christian life.

III. Patterns of Successful Christian Living

Most of us know what is necessary for enjoying a successful Christian experience. We know a successful Christian is one who has made a special place in his heart for the Word of God. He knows the meaning of the new birth and that he has been made a partaker of the divine nature. He knows he must be a witness and that salvation is only the beginning of the Christian life which has as its final objective maturing into the image of Christ. He knows the baptism in the Holy Spirit is important in this kind of life; he knows he must find and fulfill God's will; and he recognizes that he is a steward of all that God has given him.

Fine! But how do we help the new convert develop into this kind of Christian? It does not just happen; there must be a planned program which will produce this result.

It is highly probable that the first six weeks of a person's Christian experience determine the kind of Christian he will be. Will he be a generous giver to the work of God, or will he think he has done well if he gives God a "tip"? Will he be a regular reader and student of the Word of God, or will he for the most part give little place to the Bible? Will he be a person of prayer? Will he be a regular attendant at the house of God? The answers to these questions will probably be determined in the first few weeks of his experience.

In order to provide a means for training these new converts, another book is in the process of preparation. It bears the title *Spiritual Sponsors* and is designed to help pastors train established Christians so they can in turn help new converts develop in their Christian experience. This material was used in 1967 and 1968 in the AIM (Ambassadors in Mission) program and proved successful. Plans are now underway to include this book, along with *Now What?* and other materials, in a special packet to be used for evangelism by our assemblies.

Here is how the program will work: as a follow-up to *Now What?* a mature Christian should be assigned to each new convert. He will serve as a spiritual buddy to him, especially for the first six weeks of his Christian life. He will provide him not only with spiritual but social fellowship. He will help him become integrated into the life of the assembly. In six visits, each at least one hour long, the spiritual sponsor will deal at length with the matters discussed in *Now What?* Also provided will be cards for memorization as a means to help the new convert get into the Word and help the Word get into him.

If all goes well, by the end of six weeks the new convert will have become a regular part of the church family and be well on the way toward spiritual maturation. Eventually he will also become a spiritual sponsor and a wonderful cycle will continue on and on.

New converts are like babies in the home. We must take care of them and help them get firmly established in the Christian life. If we take good care of them when they are young, they will take care of our church and our Movement when they grow older.

Panel Discussion and Open Forum

General reaction to the presentation indicated a desire for helps in the area of conserving new converts. Most agreed the new convert should be given printed helps immediately and should be visited within twenty-four hours if at all possible. Some felt the pastor should make the first call, and others thought it psychologically advantageous for a lay person to make the visit. It was noted lay persons used in this capacity would have to be specially trained, usually by the pastor, to guide the new convert into the Word of God and not become involved in personal and family problems. Ideally, the pastor should make all the contacts, but it is physically impossible for him to do so and carry on his other responsibilities.

It was generally agreed the greatest help for new converts is getting them into the Word of God. Some ways suggested for instructing in the Word were: using the "Foundations for Faith" course in a special training class; having a new converts Sunday school class using some of the undated manuals; encouraging personal Bible reading using modern translations; conducting Bible studies in the midweek service or some other time in the church program; and instructing the convert on what religious literature and radio and TV broadcasts he should patronize.

Several ways of conserving new converts emerged from the discussion. Though none of these is sufficient in itself, the combined effect of using several should be most helpful: (1) The new convert should receive personal instruction in the Christian walk either from the pastor or a lay person capable of the task. (2) The new convert should be made to understand there is more to being saved than having a good feeling inside. His feelings may be entirely different the following morning but this does not negate his salvation. (3) If possible, place the new convert in a new converts class and follow that up with a Bible doctrine class. (4) Provide the new convert with literature which will help answer the common questions every new convert faces. It may be possible for the pastor to make tape recordings of answers to specific questions and allow the new convert to listen to them, thus conserving the pastor's time but keeping a personal touch in the contact with the new convert. (5) Encourage water baptism as soon as possible and practicable. (6) Enroll the new convert as a church member as soon as possible. (7) Offer help, prayer, support, and encouragement to the new convert. Don't lower standards to accommodate wrong habits but don't immediately condemn the individual because of his habits either.

In every contact and effort put forth for the new convert, love must be shown. A "computerized" follow-up program will leave the new convert cold. He needs to see and feel the love of Christ in the Christians with whom he has joined himself.

It is incumbent upon the pastor to provide the inspiration from the pulpit necessary to a growth atmosphere in his church. This will be a significant encouragement to the new convert. In addition to the encouragement coming from the pulpit, however, there must be a warmth expressed from the pew, making the new convert feel welcome and loved. Helping new converts grow is the responsibility of the total congregation, not just the pastor and a few specially trained lay-persons. The new convert should be accepted into the church circle, guided into spiritual growth, and encouraged to make other converts, thus beginning a new cycle.

LEADING A SOUL TO CHRIST

Speaker: **SAM JORDAN**
Moderator: **HARRY MYERS**
Panelists: **ELLIS DAMIANI, WALTER HANSON, W. J. WIND**
Recorder: **WILDON COLBAUGH**

BEING A SOUL WINNER must be the Christian's goal, and he must be conscious of soul-winning possibilities at all times.

I. Soul Winner's Goal

"For where your treasure is, there will your heart be also" (Luke 12:34). If a Christian's interest lies in soul winning, then he should and will constantly meditate, study, and research the subject—praying and talking to God about it and systematically practicing it.

"Study to show thyself approved unto God, a workman that needeth not to be ashamed, rightly dividing the word of truth" (2 Timothy 2:15). Fulfilling this command has a double effect. First, the soul winner is conscious of and sensitive to the leading of the Holy Spirit when God has a particular harvest for him to reap. Second, God can trust him to accomplish this harvest because the soul winner has availed himself of the necessary knowledge.

The one who wants to win souls must be willing to be persistent in pursuing that ability. The soul winner must determine not to be denied. Without question a person will lead people to Christ if he has this as his purpose and properly studies for it. As the Psalmist put it: "They that sow in tears shall reap in joy. He that goeth forth and weepeth, bearing precious seed, shall doubtless come again with rejoicing, bringing his sheaves with him" (Psalm 126:5, 6).

II. The Holy Spirit

The Holy Spirit is the key to soul winning. The most difficult thing for us to remember is that we can do nothing eternal without the Holy Spirit. It is possible for us to become skilled and accomplish some things here on earth by our own might and power with our training and abilities, or by such leverages as money and prestige, but these things alone will never accomplish eternal matters.

Man can make up his own mind to do certain things. However, one of the laws of God is that man cannot simply decide for himself or make up his own mind to accept Christ as his personal Saviour. Nor can anyone talk a person into a genuine conversion. Without a supernatural drawing of the Spirit of God, he cannot come to Christ. This is emphasized twice in the Book of John: "No man can come to me, except the Father which hath sent me draw him: and I will raise him up at the last day" (John 6:44). "And he said, Therefore said I unto you, that no man can come unto me, except it were given unto him of my Father" (John 6:65).

Man does have an important role to play in leading a soul to Christ, and the soul winner must realize his responsibility in this matter. His job is to tell the prospect about the plan of salvation, and in doing so he becomes a "preacher." "How then shall they call on him in whom they have not believed? and how shall they believe in him of whom they have not heard? and how shall they hear without a preacher? and how shall they preach, except they be sent? as it is written, How beautiful are the feet of them that preach the gospel of peace, and bring glad tidings of good things" (Romans 10:14, 15).

Christians can become discouraged in soul winning if they do not understand this important work of the Spirit. We do not reach everyone we talk to, but we can continue to sow the seed wherever the opportunity arises. If, however, we press for a harvest before the Spirit is ready, the decision will be physical and not eternal. God will not always strive in the same way with each individual. We must seek to lead a soul to Christ when God is dealing with him. We then become partners with the Holy Spirit. He, the leader with all the necessary spiritual power, and we, the physical equipment, work together in this matter of winning souls.

III. Faith

We must be aware of the importance of faith in the process of a soul finding salvation. The law of heaven is faith, and faith seems to begin where the five senses stop.

An individual has only a small amount of faith born to him. It is not enough to accept God as a fact. Therefore, he must come in contact with God's Word in order for his faith to grow to the size of acceptance. "So then faith cometh by hearing, and hearing by the word of God" (Romans 10:17).

It is not possible for the natural man to understand God and His plan of salvation—that man must have faith: "But without faith it is impossible to please him: for he that cometh to God must believe that he is, and that he is a rewarder of them that diligently seek him" (Hebrews 11:6). Salvation must be preceded by faith: "For by grace are ye saved through faith; and that not of yourselves: it is the gift of God" (Ephesians 2:8).

Effective witnessing comes as a result of having genuine faith and a desire to give God the credit for all things. We must learn too to communicate or transfer our faith to others: "That the communication of thy faith may become effectual by the acknowledging of every good thing which is in you in Christ Jesus" (Philemon 6).

Communication of our faith becomes effective when we have made a friend. We do this by being friendly, compassionate, and by giving of ourselves unselfishly. The prospect senses quick-

ly if we have a selfish motive or are insincere. When this is the case, our efforts shall profit us nothing (1 Corinthians 13:1-3). But when the prospect is convinced that our interest is not selfish, he will be willing to engage in conversation.

IV. Conversation Leading to Decision

"Jim, do you ever give much thought to spiritual matters?" (Listen closely to his reply and discuss with him any comments he might make.)

"Where do you think a person goes after he dies?" (After his answer converse with him concerning his answer; but no matter what his answer is, do not criticize him for it. Remember, you are in a conversation.)

You are interested in determining if he knows what a Christian is, and you cannot ask him if he is one, as this would tend to insult him. He lives in a "Christian" nation. He is not a Communist or Buddhist; he is "Christian." You cannot ask him if he is saved because he may not be acquainted with church talk and therefore would not understand your question.

"What would you say a Christian is?" (More than likely, he will give you several things that he thinks a Christian should do.) Immediately agree with him that a Christian does do these things, but tell him you were not asking what a Christian did, but what a Christian is. Most of the time they will say, "I never thought of that. Give me a hint."

1. *Take out your New Testament and turn to Romans 3:23:* "For all have sinned, and come short of the glory of God."

Most people use the stock excuse: "I am as good as so-and-so; and if they make heaven, I will too." Tell the prospect that God is comparing us to His glory, or Jesus, in this verse.

2. *Now turn to Romans 6:23:* "For the wages of sin is death."

Say something like: "Because we are all sinners, we are earning a wage, and that wage is death. Not just physical death, but the wages of sin is spiritual death. Man is born to die two times. The word *death* means 'separation.' The first death comes when the body is separated from the spirit; then there is the second death, when the spirit is separated from God."

3. *Now turn to Romans 5:8:* "But God commendeth his love toward us, in that, while we were yet sinners, Christ died for us."

Tell the prospect: "Most people have a sense of right and wrong; and when they have a wrong habit, they generally want to change that bad habit before they come to church. But Christ died for us while we were in our sins, not after we cleaned them up; so we come to Him just as we are because He loves us so much."

4. *Now turn to John 3:16:* "For God so loved the world, that he gave his only begotten Son, that whosoever believeth in him should not perish, but have everlasting life."

5. *And then turn to Romans 6:23:* "But the gift of God is eternal life through Jesus Christ our Lord."

Here it seems best to communicate by using an object such as a pencil to represent the gift of God. Place the pencil inside the Bible, saying, "The gift is in the person of Jesus Christ and in order to receive the gift of eternal life you must accept Christ—just as you receive this pencil from my hand."

"Now that we know where the gift is (in the person of Christ), where is Christ?"

6. *Now turn to Revelation 3:20:* "Behold, I stand at the door, and knock: if any man hear my voice, and open the door, I will come in to him, and will sup with him, and he with me."

Say: "Now we know the gift is in Christ, and we now know that Christ is standing ready to come into you and to bring the gift and live with you, if you will open the door. How do you do that? By calling His name and asking Him to come in and cleanse your heart and dwell in your life. When you ask Him to come in, a miraculous thing happens."

7. *Turn to John 1:12:* "But as many as received him, to them gave he power to become the sons of God, even to them that believe on his name."

At this point ask Jim to allow you to pray for him. "God, in the name of Jesus bind every spirit that would hinder Jim from calling upon the name of Jesus, and set him free." ("Wherefore I give you to understand, that no man speaking by the Spirit of God calleth Jesus accursed: and that no man can say that Jesus is the Lord, but by the Holy Ghost" [1 Corinthians 12:3].)

Until the Holy Spirit sets him free, a man is bound from calling Jesus the Lord. After we have talked to God and set the soul free, we then stop talking to God. (*But do not say amen.*) Turn your talk then to the individual and ask him to call on Jesus by name and to ask Him to come in.

8. *After this is done, then strengthen his faith by turning to 1 John 1:9:* "If we confess our sins, he is faithful and just to forgive us our sins, and to cleanse us from all unrighteousness."

Ask him, "Do you believe Christ heard you and came in?" If he says, "I hope so," or "I feel better," then you must give him further instruction. Let him read 1 John 1:9 again. Ask him, "Did you confess your sins?" "Yes." "Then you are not sure Christ did His part?" Stay with this until faith grasps the truth that the Word means what it says, that if we do our part, God will do His part. Then his salvation is based on his faith in the Word of God.

Take him to church and spend time with him!

Panel Discussion and Open Forum

Winning souls to Christ was set as a major goal of the apostolic church. "Let all the house of Israel know . . ." (Acts 2:36). To continue winning souls we must keep this objective before us at all times. This is true both of the church and of the individual.

It is evident that less emphasis is given to direct soul winning in our churches today. Many other interests have pushed aside our deep concern for the eternal welfare of the souls of men. The need for new and attractive church buildings, the demand for improved standards of living, the accelerated pace of modern living, and the constant moving from one city to another have all dulled the sense of responsibility for the unsaved. In order for a spiritual awakening to occur today, we must again realize the value God places upon winning a single soul to Christ. When this is again of primary importance to the church, we will have revival.

Question: Where does this concern first begin?

It must start within the heart of the individual worker who must maintain such communion with God that his personal life reflects it. He has a twofold purpose in living such a life. First, to please God; second, to influence the sinner to accept Christ as Saviour. Thus his whole life is affected by his attitude toward God and the unsaved.

Question: What obstacles must be overcome to be effective witnesses for Christ?

Fear is a major hindrance. Satan uses this as one of his chief weapons to silence the Christian worker. What the sinner may think or say about the worker takes on distorted proportions. It seemingly prevents all communication between the Christian worker and the sinner concerning spiritual things. But this does not need to continue to thwart personal witnessing.

The Holy Spirit is important to soul winning for He will fill the life of the worker with confidence—confidence that living for Christ is the best way in the world to live. When the worker realizes that the Holy Spirit prepares the sinner for the harvest, he is less afraid to speak to him about his soul's welfare. As time passes, he will learn to work with the Holy Spirit and can more readily lead sinners to a decision for Christ.

One of the most important ingredients needed in the Christian's life to make him an effective soul winner is love. Love must fill the life of the Christian worker. Christ is love and when He possesses the life completely, love will flow out to the unsaved. Possessing this love is not automatic. It must be sought. Through fasting, prayer, and study of God's Word it will develop in the worker's heart. Wherever he goes there will emanate from him this God-given love, and sinners will be drawn by it, both to the worker and to his Saviour.

Success in witnessing depends largely upon the worker's own attitude toward and dedication to Christ. If he recognizes the necessity to own Him as Lord and Master of his life, then he will be concerned that the unsaved know Christ in this way too. This being true, he will spare no effort to reach the lost.

It was concluded that workers must set a goal in reaching the lost. It is not enough to just wait for witnessing opportunities; we should prepare for them.

MINISTRY OF OUR CHURCH MUSIC

Speaker: **PAUL FERRIN**
Moderator: **PHILIP WANNENMACHER**
Panelists: **MAX ELEIOTT, MRS. NORMAN FIELD, LAWRENCE LARSEN**
Recorder: **MRS. WILLIAM KIRSCHKE**

IN THE HISTORY OF RELIGIONS Christianity is the only one that has developed music as an important part of worship. In most other religions the chant and the dirge are being used. It is certainly true that wherever the name of Christ has been received, He has placed a song in the hearts of the people. Therefore, we can easily see that Christians are the only people who have something real and vital to sing about in a world filled with tensions and fear.

Pentecostal people are a singing people. When the sinner comes in contact with Christ through an experience of salvation and then receives the reality of the fullness of the Spirit through the baptism of the Holy Spirit, music becomes an integral part of his worship, and his very soul cries out in praise to God. This can best be done through music, whether it be in the sanctuary as the congregation lifts up its voices in song, in listening to the soloist or choir, around the altar in a time of prayer, or driving along in the automobile.

When we realize how important music is to worshiping God, then we can see how very necessary it is for singers and musicians to be a channel through which this praise and worship can flow. This will not only give opportunity to the participant himself, but should encourage the entire congregation to enter into a spirit of worship.

Music is a ministry. Long before the minister stands to give his message, the ministry of music has either prepared the hearts for this message or left the service with a cold, unmovable spirit and the pastor will find it difficult to minister.

It is my firm conviction that the spiritual life of a singer or musician should be considered ahead of his musical ability. As a musician, I want to obtain perfection in my musical program as much as anyone; however, I must achieve what musical perfection I can with people who are totally dedicated to God. Often the choir or orchestra member who does not contribute the voice of a Lanza or the tone of a Mendes will enhance the spiritual condition of your musical department by his prayer life and close communion with God. He too must have the opportunity to praise God through the medium of music.

Just as the minister presents the story of Jesus Christ in simplicity and then digs into the Word of God to present deep spiritual truths, so the musical program of a church must include all types of music. The simplest of gospel songs along with the sacred classic anthem will give a well-rounded message to the congregation. The anthem should never be used to educate people. It has its place in worship because of the deep message it has to share. Usually the anthem is based on Scripture set to music. Nothing is more thrilling to the choir member than to sing scriptural text. On the other hand, the simple gospel melody must not be neglected because it can easily touch the heart of the listener.

To develop a successful musical ministry it

will be necessary to use a great amount of planning and rehearsing. However, the director must never become so involved in this planning and rehearsing that the Holy Spirit is neglected. In addition to your already prayed-over and planned program, God may direct the pastor or minister of music in a last-minute change needed for that certain service. Often this last-minute change will be the musical message which God uses to bring His blessing to the people.

An effective church musical program should include a variety of musical groups, both vocal and instrumental. While the church choir is the backbone of the musical program, the following musical groups may be used—depending upon the size of your local church: the sanctuary or church choir; youth or teen choir; junior, primary, and cherub choirs; ladies ensemble (about nine or twelve voices); male chorus (any amount); small mixed ensemble (about fifteen or twenty voices for specialized work); male and mixed quartets; male, ladies and mixed trios; soloists in all voicings.

The use of instruments will not only give additional variety in the church musical ministry, but will often involve young people and older ones alike who would not have an interest in the vocal groups. Perhaps you cannot start with a complete orchestra or band, but the various instruments can be used to form duets, trios, quartets, and small ensembles. As the interest grows from seeing and hearing the smaller groups, eventually a church band or orchestra will come into existence. The various instrumental combinations can also serve as accompaniment to the vocal groups.

Throughout the year there are many opportunities for special musical presentations. Today there are a wide variety of Christmas and Easter cantatas. These cantatas will enable you to use the entire vocal and instrumental groups in your church. Around Thanksgiving a musical harvest festival is appropriate.

Music should play an important part during the missionary emphasis of your church. There are missionary cantatas as well as beautiful gospel songs and hymns with a missionary theme.

The use of patriotic music can be an effective part of the services around Memorial Day or the Fourth of July.

In considering the ministry of music in the church, we must include more than the special music. The atmosphere of worship should begin with the first note of the prelude. If there is no Sunday school class in your sanctuary, the organist or pianist should begin playing as soon as the people begin entering the sanctuary. If there is a class, however, the musician should begin the prelude as soon as the class has dismissed in prayer. A processional for the choir should lead into the opening call to worship by the choir as soon as they are standing in their place.

The song service should bring the people to a spirit of worship, preparing their hearts for the prayer-time.

Two musical presentations are usually satisfactory for the morning worship service. The choir and a quartet or solo will give the balance needed for this service.

There are various "closing" songs that can be used. I feel this part of the service should be very flexible. The service will sometimes end with a general altar call or it may have a final benediction. If a choral benediction is desired, this must be used only when the service is dismissed altogether. If the service ends with a general altar call, something more suitable should be used.

Pentecostal churches have always been known for their Sunday night evangelistic services. Countless people have made a decision to accept Christ through the ministry of music, before the message was ever brought.

A brilliant, lively, and happy gospel song or chorus is the ideal beginning to this evangelistic service. This will help to bring the entire congregation into a receptive frame of mind. This is an excellent place to use a combination of instruments and choir.

A good, lively song service should follow. Again, may I urge you to use very familiar gospel songs and insert new songs or choruses that have been previously rehearsed with the choir and instruments. This is the service where a wide variety of musical numbers should be used. I believe a musical "package" is very suitable for the Sunday evening service.

It is often very effective to use the choir for the invitation, singing appropriate numbers. Using the choir on the invitation is a lever for the director whose choir members feel they should be allowed to sit in the audience after the musical part of the service is over. I feel the choir is needed not only to sing during the invitation but to back the pastor with prayer.

The midweek prayer service is sometimes forgotten when it comes to special music. Its needs are different from all other music. Usually a solo, duet, or trio would be suitable. The number should be of a devotional nature and in keeping with the service.

Other than the pastoral staff, the musicians in the church are perhaps the most known and recognized members of the church. Therefore, their spiritual lives and Christian conduct are of utmost importance. A well-behaved, smiling choir will let visitors know that your church has people that are happy, vibrant Christians who want to do their very best for the Lord.

The anointing of the Holy Spirit is the key to a successful ministry of music. We can have the finest talent in the city and rehearse the music until we know it by memory; but if the Holy Spirit does not take control, all of the efforts are in vain, and hearts and lives will go away untouched and unmoved. If, however, the choir and musicians are channels for the free flowing of the Holy Spirit, the musical department of the church truly becomes a ministry in music.

Panel Discussion and Open Forum

Few theologians have ever valued music more than did Martin Luther. In a preface to a songbook published in 1538 he wrote: "Experience testifies that, after the Word of God, only music deserves to be praised as the mistress and the governess of the emotions of the human heart, by which emotions human beings are ruled and often torn asunder by their masters. A greater praise of music than this we cannot imagine.... It is out of consideration for this power of music that the fathers and the prophets willed, and not in vain, that nothing be more closely bound up with the Word of God than music."

In the words of Ulrich Zwingli, the great Swiss scholar and reformer, "No teaching, no injunctions, sink so deeply into the heart of man as does music."

The pastor and minister of music must be agreed in concept of evangelism. They must decide on definite objectives for the music ministry of the church.

Question: Where are we going in presenting our choir music, special numbers, programs, etc?

There is a danger of too much *performance* and not enough *ministry.* Beware of the audience becoming spectators. Everyone must participate in worship.

Question: What can be done about the lack of respect during the prelude, offertory, etc?

Any order of service becomes ineffective if it becomes a *form.* Instruction is needed emphasizing the *ministry of music* in every part of the service. Ushers should be instructed to refrain from seating people during a special musical number.

The altar song or song of invitation is usually better if sung by the choir or soloist in order to not detract the attention of the congregation by looking for a song in the hymnal.

Question: What general guidelines for music are suggested?

Adapt the music to the character of the church and the locale. There should be a variety of sacred music presented in the church services in order to minister to everyone in the congregation.

Question: Should musicians be paid?

Remuneration for music ministry should be determined by the situation of the person involved, whether full-time in music ministry or making a contribution for the joy of service. Appreciation should be expressed by the pastor to those who participate in music ministries.

THE MIRACULOUS IN EVANGELISM

Speaker: **WARD WILLIAMS**

Moderator: **J. PHILIP HOGAN**

Panelists: **MELVIN HODGES, ANDREW TEUBER**
DERRELD WARTENBEE

Recorder: **ROBERT CUNNINGHAM**

TODAY QUESTIONS ABOUT MIRACLES are raised everywhere. Believing that miracles are for today and that God answers the fervent prayers of righteous men, we will consider five questions on what the Bible approves and disapproves concerning miracles; we will then conclude by presenting the four miracles essential to our personal salvation.

I. What Is the Pentecostal Message?

There is only one gospel—the one proclaimed by Paul in 1 Corinthians 15: (1) Christ died for our sins; (2) Christ was buried; (3) Christ rose again and was seen by many witnesses. This is the message of every evangelical church and it is our Pentecostal message—there is no other!

What is the difference, then, between Pentecostal churches and others? This is explained by Acts 1:8: "Ye shall receive power, after that the Holy Ghost is come upon you, and ye shall be witnesses unto me." The Pentecostal message is *Jesus, preached in the power of the Spirit.* There are Biblical teachings concerning miracles, healings, sanctification, the Second Coming, and other truths, but the gospel is that *Christ died for our sins* and was raised again for our justification.

The purpose of miracles is not to glorify man nor to call attention to any person. We read Christ's statement that "when he, the Spirit of truth, is come . . . he shall not speak of himself . . . he shall glorify me" (John 16:13, 14). When we

are led by the Spirit, it is Jesus who is glorified—not man. Lest someone should say, "But we have a new revelation, and God is doing a new thing today," we would call attention to Galatians 1:8 where Paul declares, "Though we, or an angel from heaven, preach any other gospel unto you than that which we have preached, . . . let him be accursed."

II. Is the Ability to Work Miracles the Test of a Scriptural Ministry?

In 1 Corinthians 12:29 Paul asks, "Are all workers of miracles?" and plainly expects a negative answer. In Galatians 5:19-26 the works of the flesh are contrasted with the fruit of the Spirit. Here the marks of spirituality are not stated in terms of ability to work miracles, but in quality of character, attitudes, and traits of personality.

The attitude of Paul toward the operation of the spiritual gifts apart from a correct attitude of heart is given in 1 Corinthians 13 where he states that though we speak with other tongues, or prophesy or understand or have such faith that we could move mountains, yet have not love, then we are nothing. So the test of a scriptural ministry must be found basically in the fruit of the Spirit.

III. What Is the Relationship Between Believers and "Signs"?

From Mark 16:17, 20, we learn that signs shall follow them that believe. As the early Christians

114

went everywhere preaching the Word, the Lord confirmed the Word with signs following.

The reverse order is condemned by Jesus as recorded in four places in the Gospels: Matthew 12:39; 16:4; Mark 8:12; and Luke 11:29. Jesus told the people not to look for signs. He declared that an evil and adulterous generation seeks after a sign. We are not to follow after those who make signs the major feature of their ministry—to do so is to make ourselves a part of an evil and adulterous generation. The warning is given in Mark 13:22, 23: "False Christs and false prophets shall rise, and shall show signs and wonders, to seduce, if . . . possible, even the elect. But take ye heed: behold, I have foretold you all things." *A truly Pentecostal person has signs following him, but is not himself a follower of signs.*

IV. In Regard to Miracles, What Do We Oppose?

A. WE OPPOSE THE VIEW THAT WE SHALL EVANGELIZE THE WORLD THROUGH MIRACLES

"If they hear not Moses and the prophets, neither will they be persuaded, though one rose from the dead" (Luke 16:31). People who are not open to the Word of God will not be open to the evidence of miracles. In Ephesians 6:17 we learn that the sword of the Spirit is the Word of God. 1 Thessalonians 2:13 speaks of "the word of God, which effectually worketh also in you that believe." We expect to bring salvation to as many as will believe by the proclamation of the Word of God in the power of the Spirit.

B. WE OPPOSE THE VIEW THAT THE GIFTS OF GOD ARE ONLY FOR A FEW CHOSEN MEN.

The purpose, operation, and control of spiritual gifts is given most clearly and fully in 1 Corinthians 12, 13, and 14. In 12:7 we learn that the manifestation of the Spirit is given to *every man* "to profit." In 12:11, after the various gifts have been listed, we learn that "all these worketh that one and the selfsame Spirit, dividing to every man severally as he will." The gifts of God are for every child of God through faith in our Lord Jesus Christ.

C. WE ARE OPPOSED TO SUPERSTITION.

For generations one large branch of the professing Christian church has claimed to have weeping statues, bleeding pictures, and visions of the Virgin Mary.

D. WE ARE OPPOSED TO DECEPTION.

On Mount Carmel when the fire came in answer to Elijah's believing prayer, it was obviously of God! But there are those who, instead of using water as Elijah did, would pour on gasoline. In such cases we are never quite sure whether God or human psychology is responsible for the resulting fire.

E. WE ARE OPPOSED TO THE COMMERCIALIZING OF THE GOSPEL OR OF THE GIFTS OF THE SPIRIT.

The Protestant Reformation began when Martin Luther protested against the sale of spiritual benefits in the form of indulgences. As Protestants we still oppose the distribution of blessings, the guaranteeing of financial prosperity or any benefits from God in consideration for money paid into the hands of any so-called representative of Christ.

When Simon the sorcerer would have given money in exchange for the power to bestow the Holy Spirit, Peter refused him with the words in Acts 8:20: "Thy money perish with thee, because thou hast thought that the gift of God may be purchased with money. . . . Thy heart is not right in the sight of God."

V. In Teachings About Miracles, What Do We Approve?

A. AS BIBLE BELIEVERS WE TAKE OUR STAND WITH THE GREAT PROTESTANT DOCTRINE OF THE PRIESTHOOD OF ALL BELIEVERS.

In 1 Peter 2:5 believers are called "an holy priesthood," and in verse 9 "a royal priesthood." We would, therefore, reject the view that any group of men has more direct access to God than any true believer.

B. WE BELIEVE THE GIFTS OF THE SPIRIT ARE FOR ALL BELIEVERS, TAKING OUR STAND ON 1 CORINTHIANS 12:7, 11.

C. WE BELIEVE THAT ALL SPIRITUAL TRUTH NECESSARY FOR SALVATION, EDIFICATION, AND ETHICAL GUIDANCE IS CONTAINED IN THE OLD AND NEW TESTAMENTS.

While we believe that neglected and ignored truths can be recovered—as was true at the time of the Protestant Reformation and again at the beginning of the modern Pentecostal movement, we believe that in regard to any new thing which is not clearly stated in the Scriptures: "What is new is not true."

D. WE BELIEVE THAT EVERYTHING GOD HAS FOR HIS PEOPLE IS FOR THE ORDINARY CHRISTIAN WHO WILL READ, BELIEVE, AND CARRY INTO PRACTICE THE BIBLE IN ALL HUMILITY, SINCERITY, AND GODLINESS.

God does heal, and miracles are for today! We can have them in our own lives and in our own local Assemblies when we walk the Bible way and pay the price that God requires.

Miracles today arrest the attention of men and point them to the reality of the invisible God. We thank God for the truth of divine healing. We must never cease to preach it, believe it, and give it the emphasis it should have in a New Testament church.

But we must realize that healings only minister to the temporal, bodily needs of the believers. For the long reaches of eternity, four miracles are important above all others: the Incarnation; the resurrection of Jesus Christ; our new birth; and our future, personal resurrection. These are the miracles which must receive the major emphasis in a true-to-the-Bible Pentecostal ministry.

Panel Discussion and Open Forum

Question: Are people saved through miracles or through the preaching of the Word?

In response to this question, the speaker told of a marvelous healing he witnessed at an Indiana camp meeting in 1966; a girl's ankle actually grew two and one half inches in about forty-five seconds; and yet the audience, he said, was not greatly moved. If there is unbelief in people's hearts, miracles will not necessarily convince them.

Romans 10:17 was cited: "Faith cometh by hearing, and hearing by the Word of God."

It was also pointed out that many scriptures illustrate the fact that miracles often produce faith.

One panelist said miracles have stirred the people of Latin America and caused them to come to hear the Word. He said it is important, however, that the evangelist exalt Christ and lead the people to put their faith in the Scriptures. Some advertising stresses the miracles more than the Miracle Worker; it draws more attention to the evangelist than to the Lord. Miracles are not given for novelty; neither are they given just to produce large crowds. The goal is to get people saved and established as active members of a functioning church. He told of various fields where many thousands have been saved and multitudes of churches started as a direct result of meetings in which God performed miracles.

Another panelist said there are three major reasons why God sends miracles: (1) To demonstrate the Lord's compassion for sick and suffering humanity; (2) to bring glory to God, not to man; (3) to publicize the power of the Lord.

He cited many scriptures to underscore these points.

Question: What should be our relationship to independent evangelists who reportedly have a very effective ministry with miracles of healing in their meetings?

The criteria by which the Assemblies of God approves various types of ministries was cited. This requires a proper accounting of funds; their books should be open for inspection. Some of these evangelists would not need to be independent if they would submit to the criteria.

A panel member quoted Revelation 2:2: "Thou hast tried them which say they are apostles, and are not, and hast found them liars." He said true apostles are willing to be tried by the church. "If sign workers were willing to be subject to their brethren and to let the church judge them, they could be conserved and helped and their ministry would be very fruitful."

The speaker said more people are being healed in local churches from week to week than are being healed in the big meetings. He quoted one of the best-known of the so-called "healing evangelists" as saying that about ten percent of the people he prays for get healed.

A panelist read what James wrote about calling the elders to pray for the sick. In the days of Paul, he said, the people could not travel long distances to attend the apostles' meetings, so they called the local elders, whose praying brought tremendous miracles. These elders were not especially gifted men but they could pray the prayer of faith.

It was pointed out that healings are not the only kind of miracles. There are mighty miracles of conversion and miraculous answers to prayer in evangelism. If God gives a special message that just meets the need of a particular listener at a particular time, that also is miraculous. All the gifts of the Spirit are miraculous and should operate in evangelism.

Question: What should be the frequency of messages in tongues in our services?

Paul's admonition to the Corinthians was cited: there should not be more than three messages in tongues in a public service, and not this many unless they are interpreted. The speaker compared it to eating pie. Each piece of pie is good, but after you eat one or two pieces, any more would fail to serve a good purpose. So each message in tongues is good, but after there have been two or three, any more would not be profitable.

Question: "Do we see as many miracles of healing today as in former days?"

Various pastors told of miracles they have seen in their churches, including marvelous healings that have occurred recently.

But someone said there ought to be more healings, and all the panel members agreed. When asked why there are not more healings, several mentioned the sovereignty of God. One pastor told how miracles of healing occur when he prays for the sick, and yet his own daughter remains afflicted. Another said God healed him of one disease but did not heal him of another.

A missionary told of mission fields where great revivals were seen at one time, but when evangelists would return to the same place for a second meeting, they would fail to see another great move. Evidently God moves in certain situations at certain times for His own good purposes. His sovereignty must be recognized. Since it is difficult to have a second great revival in the same place, it is very important that the fruit of a great revival be preserved through proper teaching, follow-up, and the planting of churches.

A panel member emphasized it is not enough merely to believe in the miraculous. "We have to be gripped by it, and pray, and break through in active faith, and claim God's promises. We have to see our place in God; we have to rise and expect God to move; we need to fast and pray; we must wait on God to see His power manifested in the working of miracles. There is too much negativism among us. Jesus cannot do many mighty works in some places because of our unbelief; but where there is active faith and expectancy, we find the power of the Lord is present to heal."

Another minister declared we need to dig out some wells that were dug by our forefathers; we need to make the valley full of ditches if we expect an outpouring. We need to fall on our knees and seek God for another great revival of miraculous nature and of miraculous proportions.

The general feeling, to which all the speakers agreed, was that there ought to be more miracles in our evangelism activities. One pastor said, "I pray this Council on Evangelism will help us to reevaluate our position and send us back to our Assemblies determined to seek God until the signs follow. God help us to fast and pray and seek the Lord until we see a restoration of the miraculous as in the early days."

OPENING NEW CHURCHES

Speaker: **EARL BLYTHE**
Moderator: **JAMES KING**
Panelists: **EVERETT COOLEY, JAMES MAYO SR., ROBERT SCHMIDGALL**
Recorder: **RUTH LYON**

WHY ARE WE SO CONCERNED with opening new churches? A simple answer is, "Everyone has a right to hear the saving gospel of Jesus Christ at least once."

If men are lost and I know how they can be found, how great is *my obligation*? If men are in darkness and I have the light, how serious is *my responsibility*? And if men are dying of spiritual hunger and I have the "bread of life," how can I excuse *my failure* to feed them?

Someone wrote: "We need one hundred thousand new churches in the next twenty years." He further said, "Every Protestant church in America should build one new church in the next five years." As members of the Assemblies of God, we should do our part.

Why are we so concerned with opening new Assemblies of God churches? Someone answers, "I could find an easing of conscience ... if through the ethnic religions souls were being saved, but this is not the case. In Hinduism millions are told there are three hundred million gods. In the Communist world millions are told there is no God. Millions more believe Allah is God and Muhammad is his prophet. Romanism points still more to the queen of heaven. The cults, sects, and philosophies only add to all this confusion."

Without doubt we are facing an unprecedented dilemma. If present trends continue, the world population will double by the year 2000. By 2050, should Jesus tarry, it will have quadrupled. About 150 babies are born every minute. Of these, 103 are in Asia, Africa, and Latin America.

The churches, all of them together, are not keeping pace with this phenomenal growth. By the year 2000 the church will account for less than 25 percent of the world's population. What then? If we just carry on at our present rate of involvement in prayer, money, and soulwinning, the entire Christian enterprise will be reduced by 50 percent within a few years.

I. The Mission—Missions

We are concerned about opening new Assemblies of God churches because missions is the very center of New Testament Christianity. God's mission was missions; Christ's mission was missions; the mission of the New Testament Church was missions; and the mission of the twentieth century church must be missions!

A. THE TRINITY

1. *God the Father* sent His Son to a lost world because He loved (John 3:16).
2. *God the Son* came, lived, died, was buried, and arose from the dead.
3. *God the Holy Spirit.* "When he is come he will reprove [convince, convict] the world of sin, and of righteousness, and of judgment" (John 16:8). This is missions!

B. The Apostles

In Matthew 10 Christ sent the twelve apostles on a preaching mission to the lost house of Israel. They were empowered to heal the sick, cleanse the lepers, raise the dead, and cast out devils. They were instructed, "Provide neither gold, nor silver, nor brass in your purses. . . ." That sounds like home missions in the twentieth century!

C. The Disciples

In Luke 10 Jesus appointed other seventy also and sent them two and two before His face into every city and place where He Himself would come.

D. The First Church in Jerusalem

The first church was empowered with the Holy Spirit enabling them to witness "both in Jerusalem, and in all Judea, and in Samaria, and unto the uttermost part of the earth."

Following their personal Pentecost, they witnessed and continued steadfastly in the apostles' doctrine and fellowship . . . and . . . from house to house, did eat their meat with gladness and singleness of heart, praising God, and having favor with all people. And the Lord added to the church daily such as should be saved" (Acts 2:42, 46, 47).

The first church was to begin its witnessing and soul winning in Jerusalem—*at home*. This was, and is, home missions! It took this church some seven years to accomplish its task. At the end of this period, it was said of them, "Ye have filled Jerusalem with your doctrine." There were literally thousands of believers in Jerusalem at the close of this seven-year period.

II. How the Church Grew

The first twelve chapters of Acts show the church at Jerusalem in transition. It is the pattern of growth and progress. Christianity literally swept from the capital of the Jewish world to the capital of the Gentile world.

The church in Jerusalem had become established; it had become strong spiritually, numerically, and financially. They had the necessary strength and finance to branch out into Judea and Samaria. Thus they obeyed the second part of Acts 1:8. Some ten years later all Judea and Samaria had heard the saving gospel of Jesus Christ.

During those years of home missions endeavor, the church had been growing spiritually, numerically, and financially. They were then ready to undertake the task of fulfilling the last part of Acts 1:8. They began to branch out in every direction with the gospel of Christ. Some sixteen years later "the uttermost parts" had been reached! *Think of it*—one generation evangelizing the then-populated world.

I do not believe we can overemphasize the importance of a strong local assembly, section, and district. In fact, we must be strong spiritually, numerically, and financially if we are to reach the uttermost part of our sin-sick world. If we are to accomplish our God-given task in this generation, we must renew our consecration and dedication and double our efforts.

After the outpouring of the Holy Spirit on the Day of Pentecost, the followers of Christ presented the claims of the gospel with new zest and power. It is evident that neither they nor their message was accepted in the synagogue. They were criticized, threatened, arrested, jailed, beaten, and some were killed. They were excommunicated from synagogue membership and were not welcomed to the services. We read in Acts 4 that the disciples went to their own company, made their report, and lifted up their voices to God.

In Acts 12 Peter was released from prison by angels and went to the house of Mary where many were gathered together praying.

In Romans 16:5 Paul said "Likewise greet *the church that is in their house.*" And in 1 Corinthians 16:19 Paul said, "The churches of Asia salute you. Aquila and Priscilla salute you much in the Lord, *with the church that is in their house.*"

Thus, we note that churches opened in homes —the home of Mary, the home of Aquila and Priscilla, etc. The church in Philippi had its beginning down by the riverside. Simon Peter opened a church in Gentile territory—the house of Cornelius.

This gospel was preached at crossroads, in homes, on the streets, in jails, under the stars, in cities, and in islands of the seas. The first church was truly a missionary church—branching out in every direction and establishing churches whenever and wherever possible.

III. Opening New Churches—How Important?

Gayle F. Lewis, former assistant general superintendent and executive director of Home Missions, said, "We are fast coming to the realization that strengthening the home stakes is not just an incidental matter, but one of vital importance.

119

The future usefulness of our Movement actually depends on it."

Former General Superintendent Ralph M. Riggs described home missionary workers as "the fingers of our Movement reaching out into new areas to enable our church to move forward in its great program of going to all the world—community by community, town by town, city by city. Each step is taken by some person obedient to the Great Commission. The pioneer pastor is the heart of our Movement for he carries feelings of love for the lost, love for the Master, and faith in God, which are characteristic of our great church. He is giving tangible expression to all those God-given feelings which lie inherent in every member of the Assemblies of God."

What kind of person does it take to open new churches? A spiritual pioneer has been described as follows:

He is a man whose calling is not human, but divine.

His conquest is not by the might of men but by the power of God.

He is more concerned with the will of God than with the will of man.

He is ready to serve rather than to be served.

He is more interested in souls than in salary.

He must share what he has received, rather than receive what he can persuade others to share.

He depends more on prayer than on popularity.

He has a passion rather than a profession.

He is a man of the Word more than of human works.

He is all that he is because he is a man of God.

Christians must be willing to do more than just *read* about inner-city problems, juvenile delinquency, the ravages of the ghetto, and moral decay. They must go where these people are and see it, smell it, bear it, feel it. We cannot relate to man's basic need of God unless we can speak to him in the context of his life.

How important is it to open new churches? It was important enough for the compassionate Saviour to declare: "Go out into the highways and hedges, and compel them to come in."

If the church today is to fulfill the Great Commission and reach the unreached of this generation, it must determine a plan of action and develop a program that will enable us to get on with this God-given task. The plan that will work in my district might not work in your district, but there is a workable plan and program for each district in our Fellowship. It is our responsibility to find and develop that plan and program.

Panel Discussion and Open Forum

One panelist stated we can never lose by investing in new churches. He cited an example of a seven-year-old church in his district which last year was able to pledge $10,000 to foreign missions. He said the investment in the church did not equal that amount.

Another panelist remarked he would not minimize the necessity for a strong home base, but many pastors are trying to get a strong church first—and they never get there. Every church should be reaching out. A family never gets smaller by having children. He said his church never lost by reaching out and starting new churches, but continued to gain. They started three churches in one year and 17 churches during 23 years.

It was the consensus that churches should not wait until they have everything. We need to get souls in mind instead of just churches. Of course, people have to have a place to go to church when they get saved. New churches can begin in open-air meetings, vacant church buildings, halls, vacant store buildings (with some renovation), etc.

Question: At what point should a smaller congregation think of reaching out into a neighboring community or suburb?

Be guided by God's will. Vision, conviction and faith are important.

It was the consensus that Assemblies of God pastors of established churches need faith to *branch out.* The need is not among the people, but rather among the leadership. Some denominations buy more property at the time they establish a pioneer church. Then when the time is ripe, they build a good church on the property. All agreed we need to reevaluate our church extension program. Of course, we need to be strong financially, but we also need to be strong spiritually.

Question: Who is supposed to open the churches?

Some say, "Let the district do it." But it is the ministry of the church to open new churches.

Question: How are we, as a Movement, going to start churches *en masse?*

If the district sponsors a work, seldom can it sponsor more than one a year. One answer would be to inspire our ministers to get a vision for the salvation of lost souls. They must see opportunities for reaching people they can't get in their churches.

Keep a group of enthusiastic young people involved and happy by starting a new mission. A deacon of one church became the pastor of the second church they started in a section others had considered unreachable. In nine weeks' time the mother church had bought a lot, built a tabernacle, and had 182 in the Sunday school.

A panelist cited the Brazil revival where the Assemblies of God has 1,500,000 church members; this was accomplished largely through the mother church method.

Question: How do we start when we have caught the vision?

Discuss your vision and plans with sectional ministers. This strengthens the work. Then get the entire district behind the project.

Question: What if you have already gone that far? Do you make a survey? Do you get nearby churches to assist the pastor in distributing gospel literature?

A branch Sunday school is an excellent way to begin a new work. Take a census or go from door to door; have a VBS. Use a team of college students and conduct services each night.

The speaker said we cannot overemphasize the importance of the church, section, and district in the church extension program. Districts need a financial program to be able to give assistance to pioneer churches. We need to think in terms of salary, property, and erection of a building.

A panelist mentioned that it is important at the beginning of a new work to give the pastor support. He said we need to hit harder in more populated areas. His district concentrated on one at a time and started three new churches. They guaranteed $100 per week plus housing and utilities. They would underwrite what the church could not handle. They asked several of their established churches to contribute. With support from the beginning, each new church has grown rapidly. These churches are soon self-supporting.

If pastors and churches will cooperate and participate in the home missions program and take their young people to home missions rallies, young people will get the vision.

Question: What about a provision for evangelism in the pioneer church?

In Michigan the district appropriates a certain amount for evangelism. For instance, four evangelists went to four different churches, ministering two weeks in each place. An amount of $3,200 was designated for this ministry.

It was agreed that pastors too should be challenged for home missions work—to make themselves available to God. Many become settled in established churches and lose the pioneering vision. If a church can establish another church that has an effective ministry, it will have multiplied its ministry many times.

The focus of attention kept coming back to the importance of vision on the part of the pastor, the congregation, the section and the district, with total commitment and involvement. The preparation of the home missions worker begins in the local church and must not be overlooked. Also, responsibility falls upon our colleges to include practical home missions courses in their curriculum.

OUR MISSION TO YOUTH

Speaker: **ROBERT PAGETT**
Moderator: **DERALD MUSGROVE**
Panelists: **RON BURGESS, K. K. JOHN, WAYNE KRAISS**
Recorder: **VERNE MacKINNEY**

IT SEEMS AS IF DANIEL 12:4 is being fulfilled before our very eyes: "Many shall run to and fro, and knowledge shall be increased."

The number of college students has arisen at a phenomenal rate, from 200,000 in 1900 to four million in 1963. There are more than six million students in universities today, and authorities project up to 10 million students by 1970. In 1900 one in 25 high school graduates sought a college degree; today nearly one-third do. Collegians are not only increasing numerically, but they are making their number felt.

There is a transition in collegiate thinking. As little as two years ago, collegians were philosophizing that "life is too short for the heroic or the unusual . . . the course of least resistance in life's curriculum is the most popular."

Just a year ago one analyst diagnosed the collegian as one "whose only ambition is to fit squarely and comfortably in place in this world when he finishes college." But with a general rise of dissatisfaction among today's collegians, this is no longer true. Some of the problems expressed as recently as two years ago are still with the college-age person. But that is where the similarity stops, for there is today a dramatic and phenomenal move among collegians to right what they feel is wrong.

Today, the advocates of student power want just that power. "Student power" says Edward Schwartz, 24, president of the National Student Association and a moderate, "means not simply the ability to influence decisions, but the ability to make decisions."

Students' number one dissatisfaction is the "system" or the "establishment," and they rise up against it. There is a phenomenal rise of dissatisfaction among students around the world. Not only do they protest at Berkeley and Columbia and more than 100 universities in America, but in countries such as West Germany, Italy, France, Great Britain, Spain, Czechoslovakia, and Poland. These students are overwhelmed by the sheer size and impersonality of the university and, for that matter, the world outside the campus. Everything seems to come in mega-packages, mega-versities, megalopolises, megatons—and most chilling of all, megadeaths.

We have created the first generation of young people who have been taught to do nothing but buy and consume. As in the scriptural account of a longing father and his prodigal son, we find the situation the same; only we have provided a better pigpen for the prodigal.

There is the feeling of *emptiness*. It is a cry for something beyond. Man was made to know God, so he can have everything, yet feel empty.

There is the feeling of *loneliness*. They can be in the crowd, yet for a fleeting moment they sense a tremendous feeling of loneliness. *Look* magazine states that more than 1,000 students committed suicide last year. Part of the why is

122

that tremendous sense of loneliness in the life of every person who has neglected that dimension of his life that needs God.

There is the feeling of *guilt*. A Harvard psychologist claims that a feeling of guilt is one of the underlying problems of people today.

There is the *fear of death*. No one young or old escapes this fear, and without resurrection life there is nothing to look forward to but eternal death.

To those committed Christians close to the college scene, these developments hint at an atmosphere for a spiritual revival not seen since the great revivals of the late eighteenth and early nineteenth centuries at Yale, Harvard, and Princeton Universities. The fears and anxieties of students and their statements, actions, and reactions of the last few months indicate a whitened field, ready for harvesting.

America's leaders of tomorrow and the many thousands of foreign students, who almost without exception are the cream of the crop of their homeland, are the greatest potential for positive spiritual force in the world today.

The first key to evangelism on the college campus depends on the person—the committed person, committed to the Lordship of Christ.

I feel there are a number of imperatives that must be resident in the life of a person before he can be effective on campus. He must: (1) realize the Christian purpose in life (Mark 16:15-18; Matthew 28:19, 20); (2) understand the Spirit-filled life (Romans 8); (3) speak the Word with boldness (Acts 4:31-33); (4) realize authority given by Christ (John 1:12; 15:7); (5) "become image bearers, not image builders" (John 12:32), which means presenting the Christ image and not the self-image.

The popular opinion that you have to be a hippie to reach a hippie is false. We are to live holy lives without spot or wrinkle. A holiness of life has a tremendous impact. Living it is the greatest force for evangelism on the college scene today.

The second key to evangelizing the college scene is an authoritative proclamation of the gospel. For everyone wanting to reach an intellectual society, I am certain that 1 Corinthians 1:17-31 holds principles that will disarm and direct this group to God. The message has its own built-in power. "Faith cometh by hearing, and hearing by the word of God" (Romans 10:17).

The third key for reaching the campus crowd is the personal witness. This can be utilized through group involvement. I am talking about the organized group with the purpose of evangelizing. This gives the timid or weak Christian the confidence inherent in numbers.

If a group program is utilized, it does not need to copy directly one which has worked in some other location. The most effective program will always be the one which comes about by prayer and by the inspiration of the Holy Spirit. At all times the aim of the person involved should be to present Christ to another person regardless of the method employed to gain the initial contact.

Such things as coffee houses, singing groups, literature-saturation campaigns, door-to-door contact, dinners, socials, Chi Alpha, koinonia groups, will be useful to reach the campus crowd if the above imperatives are understood.

The church has a heavy responsibility in training and developing persons qualified to witness to college and career young people.

Chaplains have noticed the Biblical illiteracy of Assemblies of God servicemen. Far too many of our young people have a first- or second-grade knowledge of Biblical principles that they carry with them to the secular college campus.

The following are some suggestions I would like to give as to how we can alleviate the problem:

1. *We need to develop a graduated Bible doctrine course* from the earliest age on up for the purpose of establishing a person in his faith, preparing him to reach a world in need of Christ.

2. *We need to develop a Biblical training course commensurate with the secular training received from grades 1-12.* Some of our Bible college courses such as Biblical Introduction, the Pentateuch, the Minor Prophets, the Major Prophets, the Gospels, the Epistles, Systematic Theology, Personal Evangelism could be introduced at different levels of our training and not just presented at Bible college. For if the statistics I have are correct, four out of five of our Assemblies of God young people never enter the doors of our Bible colleges.

I don't believe it should stop with high school. College-oriented Bible study courses for those attending secular colleges should be developed and taught by qualified teachers. This program could be developed and promoted through Chi Alpha.

We need to develop a program that will mature our young people in the physical, social, mental, and spiritual dimensions of their lives.

The balanced life of a Christian, with every

compartment saturated by the Holy Spirit, will go a long way in the development of lives fit and prepared to evangelize the college and career and foreign students of today.

It seems that many of our young people have never learned to live the Christian life in the world. They live with complexes and "hang ups," and lists of dos and don'ts, instead of living lives of moderation, guided by the Biblical principles.

Remember, it's not just the program that will reach a generation, but more important, it is the lives of persons controlled by and living under the direction and guidance of the Holy Spirit.

Panel Discussion and Open Forum

It is imperative that we reach today's college students. In the years to come they will be making the big decisions both in business and in politics; they will be the people with the money because of the increased earning power of college graduates; and they will be acceptable in foreign countries when missionaries will no longer be welcome.

One Assembly used the following approach to reach the foreign students enrolled at the university. From the college records they secured the names, addresses, and nationality of all foreign students. The church purchased bilingual Bibles from the American Bible Society. The CA's then visited each student and gave him a copy of the Scriptures.

It was pointed out that fifty percent of the Communists in foreign countries became Communists in American colleges and universities. It was also stated that one foreign student in our colleges reached with the gospel was as valuable as a missionary we would send to that country.

Local pastors were encouraged to welcome college students and use them in the church where possible.

Where the pastor was not a college man himself, he was counseled to keep to the Word and be an expert therein, rather than to try to downgrade the teachings in subjects with which he was not acquainted. He was cautioned to be honest with the students and have Biblical answers for the stands he takes on various aspects of holiness. He should be strong on doctrine.

Pastors were encouraged to get to know the college students as individuals and try to overlook the outward expressions of clothing and hair that signify rebellion. The kids are looking for truth and will accept it when logically and honestly presented by a concerned pastor.

Poor relations between the local church and the college students have lost an estimated twenty percent of our college age people, and another thirty percent marry out of the church. It is important from this point of view to keep our young people in touch with each other through the local church and such college organizations as Chi Alpha.

Chi Alpha, the college scene CA group, was pointed out as an ideal arm for reaching the non-Assemblies of God collegian, both domestic and foreign, as well as making a rallying point for our own young people on the secular campus.

It was suggested that the larger colleges and universities should have full-time pastors assigned to them, as they constitute a very vital home missions field. It was pointed out that such pastors should have college background themselves and seminary training, if possible.

It was felt that the Assemblies of God college student is the best means we have of reaching the other college students. In this connection, it was pointed out that many Pentecostal students are very poorly equipped doctrinally to cope with the college scene. They know all the Bible stories but can't seem to relate them to doctrinal principles. There was a call for more doctrinal teaching at all levels.

The matter of suitable leadership for the Chi Alpha group was mentioned and also the possibility of having student centers on secular campuses for Assemblies of God students. It was stressed that Chi Alpha leadership should be high caliber, spiritually strong, and without reproach.

OUR WORLDWIDE RESPONSIBILITY

Speaker: **RICHARD DORTCH**

Moderator: **WESLEY HURST JR.**

Panelists: **THOMAS CUNNINGHAM, GEORGE W. FLATTERY, CHARLES GREENAWAY**

Recorder: **MRS. ANGELINE TUCKER**

MISSIONS IS WORTHY OF MEN and means equal to the task of preaching the gospel "to every creature"! The men who called for the first General Council of the Assemblies of God believed this strongly. The great priority of that first meeting was our worldwide responsibility. The quality of early missionary personnel clearly indicates the importance they placed upon world missions. At the first General Council fifteen foreign missionaries were listed. In four years the missionary family had grown to seventy-three. There could be no doubt that much attention was focused on our worldwide responsibility.

I. The Origin of Our Responsibility

When a study is made of Assemblies of God missions, one sees the forces available to the church of God. It clearly discloses the processes and the elements of power bringing the work of missions to pass. The dynamics in the Pentecostal church are in Assemblies of God missions.

A. DIVINE RESPONSIBILITY

"And they were all filled with the Holy Ghost" (Acts 2:4). This is where missions begins! "But ye shall receive power, after that the Holy Ghost is come upon you: and ye shall be witnesses unto me both in Jerusalem, and in all Judea, and in Samaria, and unto the uttermost part of the earth" (Acts 1:8). The Holy Spirit must assume leadership at every level of missionary enterprise. Just as the Holy Spirit was the determining factor in Early Church missions, our church today needs the dynamics of the Holy Spirit in proportion to our mechanics. The tendency is to reorganize the structure.

The Pentecostal missionary program should be simple in organization and ample in power! Fulfilling our worldwide responsibility will not be in the strength of our machinery, but in the power of God. The winning of the lost to Christ is a superhuman task. But God's power is available to us! A recognition of this fact is fundamental to success in any missionary program today.

B. HUMAN RESPONSIBILITY

It has always pleased God to use men as conductors of His power. God used Peter to proclaim the gospel, and three thousand were saved. Stephen gave his testimony with such power that young Rabbi Saul's conscience was goaded. Through Paul, God spoke to the Gentile world and changed it for all time. The faithful ministry of the modern missionary continues to reveal that the Holy Spirit uses human instrumentality, awakening the world and moving the hearts of men toward God.

C. MATERIAL RESPONSIBILITY

"And all that believed were together, and had all things common; and sold their possessions

125

and goods, and parted them to all men, as every man had need" (Acts 2:44, 45). In the early days of the Church there was a definite financial policy; nothing was left to haphazard methods. When the Christians scattered and the rapid spread of Christianity came, the doctrine of stewardship began.

Money is an agent of great power in the world. The church in the modern era has advanced wonderfully in its thoughts concerning money and its uses. With a gospel adequate to regenerate the world, we are often impotent to answer the call of the nations—largely through lack of funds. The love of money and its misuse are today, as always, a paralysis upon the spiritual power of the church. When we deal more fairly with God in money matters, we can renew our Pentecostal experience and carry out our worldwide responsibility.

II. The Object of Our Responsibility

"When I consider thy heavens, the work of thy fingers, the moon and the stars, which thou hast ordained; what is man, that thou art mindful of him?" (Psalm 8:3, 4). Man is at the center of all things. Small though he is, he is God's prime consideration in worldwide responsibility. It is man for whom God gave Jesus to be a ransom. Jesus came "to seek and to save that which was lost"! Man not only needs to be saved, but he is worth saving, and that is the object of our responsibility—that is the goal of missions!

A. THE GOOD NEWS OF SALVATION

This is where our responsibility begins—to tell the "good news." "For God so loved the world, that he gave his only begotten Son, that whosoever believeth in him should not perish, but have everlasting life. For God sent not his Son into the world to condemn the world; but that the world through him might be saved" (John 3:16, 17). This is the "good news" of the gospel for man, all of man—body, mind, and soul. It is for all men, the high and the low, the rich and the poor, the learned and the unlearned. Our responsibility is to bring men to new lives of righteousness—from sin, selfishness, and self-indulgence. This is the good news of salvation—for the individual and for the nations.

B. THE GOOD NEWS OF MAKING GOD REAL

There must be a better life, and we must all bring this life to others. We intensively realize God's redemptive purpose in Christ when we accept Christ as our personal Saviour. Entering into this experience, we have a normal impulse to tell others about the Saviour we have found. We should naturally want to be a "sent one"— a missionary to our neighbors as well as to those afar off who have never heard of Jesus. This experience is so vital that a sense of obligation should be the program of our lives. Our churches must never consider missions extraneous to the Christian life or something tacked onto the church program. Each church and member must see missions as a passion burning in the heart of God, and this fire must flow from the Eternal to every Christian heart.

III. Our Outreach

What shall our method of response be to our worldwide responsibility? H. Leo Eddleman says that "to promote the conversion of unbelievers or of adherents of a non-Christian faith is either the sheerest presumption or the holiest of all endeavors."

"And Jesus came and spake unto them, saying, All power is given unto me in heaven and in earth. Go ye therefore, and teach all nations, baptizing them in the name of the Father, and of the Son, and of the Holy Ghost: teaching them to observe all things whatsoever I have commanded you: and, lo, I am with you alway, even unto the end of the world" (Matthew 28: 18-20).

We must have "all power," go to "all nations," be "all things," and know that "all presence" is with us.

A. POWER

"All power is given unto me in heaven and in earth." We must believe that God has given us a living, vital role to play in worldwide responsibility! The Assemblies of God is a movement of power—Holy Spirit power! The Lord's concern for missions is so profound that He pledged the resources of the universe to its support.

The program of the local church can be greatly enhanced when it gives proper attention and place to missions. This is a program of power. It is on the basis of power that missions operates in foreign lands and at home, and this authority is justifiable. The first missionaries and their successors needed the encouragement and assurance that God Himself was a God of missions who would uphold and support them in their labors. This is true of the local congregation that believes and practices the program of missions.

126

B. Program

"Go . . . make disciples . . . baptizing . . . teaching." Here are four phases of complete missionary activity. Only one comes in the imperative mood, that is, a direct command: "Make disciples." The going, the baptizing, and the teaching are accessories to the primary function, which is to induce men to become disciples of Jesus and His way of life.

Missions is a program for the local congregation. Any church that is not helping make Christ known through missions around the world is not heeding the last express command of its Lord. The blessing in training workers right at home, in seeing them prepare themselves further in college, and to ultimately see them working on some field is one of the great strengthening forces of a local congregation. Many churches here at home have their missionary program as the central part of their entire outreach. These are churches that are alive, vital, forever reaching out, and they attract young and old alike because of the challenge of the task.

C. Presence

"Lo, I am with you alway, even unto the end of the world." This is Christ's promise to those who carry out His Great Commission. Christ has commanded us to go, but missions is so urgent to our Saviour that He marches with us in this great battle for souls. A going church is a growing church, and a growing church will have missions as its solid foundation. Our worldwide responsibility can only be met through local congregations who commit themselves to depend upon Christ's presence to anoint them to carry out the task that the Master has committed to them.

Panel Discussion and Open Forum

Missions actually began when "they were *all* filled with the Holy Ghost." When Christ gave the Great Commission, He did not demand that which is impossible. But the Great Commission does imply that every Christian should be a "sent-one."

Question: How does the Holy Spirit guide us?

The Holy Spirit speaks in various ways to the individual Christian, but He also speaks through "the brethren" or committees.

Some felt that a need in itself is a *call*. If this were so and carried out on a mathematical basis, most missionaries today would be working in India where there are over half a billion people in desperate need—numerically more overwhelming than the need in Africa.

Someone else felt that the combination of a need with the health, proper education, and ability of a particular person to meet that need could constitute a call. One missionary, because of training received while a cadet at West Point, had been able to save the lives of thousands during the Boxer Rebellion in China.

Others felt that to effectively minister in a given area one must feel a definite *call*.

A panelist commented, "I don't care what you have in methods and means, including excellent building facilities and ample finances, unless the pioneer or mission church be born first in the heart of the pioneer pastor or missionary, it will be a still-born church. Unless God plants the work of missions in the heart of our youth, missions will never work."

To do justice to our worldwide responsibility we must be in tune with God and be *where* He wants us *when* He wants us. God sees the need. As we answer His call, He will make available His resources. "Pray ye therefore the Lord of the harvest. . ." (Matthew 9:38). If we see a need and begin to pray ourselves, others will join in prayer, and God's power will be released.

Question: How can a missionary best get the message of missions across to people so they will be moved to help meet the need?

It was felt that the secret lies in being able to communicate with the pastor prior to the missionary service, sharing the need and burden with him. The pastor is the key to the personnel and financial resources of the church. If he senses the burden and has a vision of our worldwide responsibility, he will share it with the church.

One panelist commented that: the Lord pledged *all* the resources of His kingdom to back missions. Yet the greatest obstacle to the advance of our missions program is selfishness among Christians.

Many feel that we in the Assemblies of God have given all we can to missions, that we have reached the saturation point. But in 1967 there were eleven hundred Assemblies of God churches which did not give a missionary offering. There were hundreds more who sent less than $100 during the year. Twenty-five percent of our churches contributed only 1.4 percent of the total giving. So we have not reached the saturation point in missions giving.

Two-thirds of the world has yet to learn of Christ. This is God's work, and He will supply.

127

Each church and each pastor must ask, "Are we concerned with building *a* kingdom or are we truly building *the* Kingdom?" The plush curtains of our own churches are in many ways more of an obstacle to the advancement of the Kingdom than are the Iron and Bamboo Curtains of other lands.

Another commented that any man who contributes in any way to missions is a part of God's worldwide program. We must realize too that raising money for missions, when used correctly, is a spiritual ministry.

Missions demands a certain element of sacrifice. One panelist reported: "Early this summer Ovid Dillingham, missionary to South India, said, 'I would give anything to see a church in Bangalore.' Only a short time later his youngest daughter Susan was killed in an air crash in Calcutta. She was preceding her parents in order to enter school at the beginning of the term. A memorial fund in Susan's honor will be used to build a church in Bangalore."

The work of missions is twofold. We must first evangelize, and then we must make disciples.

A missionary-evangelist mentioned that he has been around the world five times conducting evangelistic campaigns. Thousands have been saved. But converts cannot live on evangelism alone. They must be taken care of and taught.

We must depend on the Bible schools to train men who can make disciples out of the converts.

Question: What is "making a disciple"?

A field secretary replied: "Each pastor forms a class for teaching new converts the simple doctrines of the Bible. Each person is then given a place where he can witness and work. Other new groups are then formed."

A panelist added: "I've just returned from a trip to the mission field where I visited all kinds of churches from large evangelistic centers in big cities to small brush arbors on the backside of the mountain. What impressed me most was the starry-eyed enthusiasm of many young pastors. The missionary had multiplied himself many times by training and sending out nationals who were first converted and then made disciples. They were reaching multiplied hundreds—evangelizing and then disciplizing."

The greatest power in coping with the population explosion is to plant a strong autonomous church in each land. There is still a place for mass evangelistic efforts by missionary-evangelists appointed for that special task, for national evangelists whom we hope the Lord will raise up, and for overseas evangelists in specific locations. But to fulfill adequately our worldwide responsibility we must train the workers who will in turn evangelize and disciplize their own people. In this way the remaining two-thirds of the world can be reached.

OUTREACH THROUGH TV AND RADIO

Speaker: **RAYMOND SCHOCH**
Moderator: **ROY WEAD**
Panelists: **EDWARD BERKEY, CORBETT CRACE, THEODORE VIBBERT**
Recorder: **LELAND SHULTZ**

IT DOESN'T TAKE ANY MORE EFFORT to speak to two hundred than it does to two million. It depends on your connection, your relationship to that two million.

For a long time we have thought we have delivered our souls by going into a town and starting a church and reaching a few hundred for God, while forgetting that the rest of the town is just as important to God as the two or three hundred we touch.

We find that Coca Cola, for example, doesn't open a small auditorium and start out to train a half a dozen people that Coca Cola is the best thing on earth. Immediately they weigh one thing—how they can touch the most in the town at one time.

My church ministry reaches out every day of the week to millions of people through radio. We now have three broadcasting stations and are building a fourth. The fourth is a color television station that will influence ten million people.

Let me share with you a section of Scripture I think speaks of television. "How beautiful *upon the mountains* are the feet of him that bringeth good tidings" (Isaiah 52:7). Television transmission antennas have to have the highest peaks. The next verse says, "Thy watchman shall lift up the voice; with the voice together shall they sing: for they shall see eye to eye, when the Lord shall bring again Zion." This is the day when the Lord is bringing again Zion. Through the mountains they shall see eye to eye. That is television!

What is the greatest compelling force in the world today? Television! People are buying things they don't want to buy; they are being sold on things they don't want to be sold on. The whole power of the nation today is regulated by what we are impressed with by television. This is the great compelling force.

I believe Moses was the greatest man who ever lived, next to Jesus. But everything that Moses had been trained for and geared for and what he had planned for, he never attained because he did one thing wrong. What was it? *He wouldn't change his method.* They needed water —the same old problem. But when Moses came to the rock the second time, he hit it instead of speaking to it; and God said, "For that, Moses, you're not going in."

The Assemblies of God is the greatest Pentecostal organization in the world. Do you know how many missionaries we sent last year? Less than 100 new missionaries. If we had sent 10,000 missionaries last year, we wouldn't have even begun to scratch the surface of the need. The population explosion alone demanded 10,000 more missionaries. Other Pentecostal churches didn't even make missionary replacements last year.

God is going to have His will done in spite of

men or devils. Well then, we had better get our ear to the wind and find out what God is doing. God knows that in this hour radio and television are the way to reach the masses for the glory of the Lord.

My engineers have developed all kinds of things for the glory of God. They are now working on an ear-plug radio just the size of the little plug that you have on the transistor radios. It has a photo cell on the outside—a photo battery you turn to the light. You can raise or lower the volume only by turning your ear away from the light. We can buy them from Hong Kong for twenty-five cents each. We can pretune them to a gospel station, and from sheer novelty people will listen to the gospel of the Lord Jesus Christ by the millions.

My friend, invading a town and having several hundred in your church does not relieve you of the responsibility for the rest of that town. Not when Coca Cola doesn't rent a building that seats 500 for the purpose of selling its product. And you have the greatest product of all. Some day the merchandisers of Coca Cola are going to stand before the judgment bar of God and condemn you because you didn't utilize the communication tools for "selling" the gospel to the people of your community.

You will never have a problem of the Holy Ghost moving upon your church if you are doing the will of God. It's not all-night prayer meetings —although it may take an all-night prayer meeting to get you there. It's not even more evangelism. No. It is sensing that what you are doing is in the absolute center of the will of God.

If you will find the means of God's choosing for reaching the lost, you can't keep the money out of it. You can't keep the glory off of it. You can't keep the power off of it. Your efforts will just flow with a dynamic of God when you get into the center of the purpose of God.

I dare you, I challenge you, I put the responsibility on you. God will hold you responsible if you are ministering to dozens when with the same amount of energy you could minister to millions.

Panel Discussion and Open Forum

Question: How can a local church secure a place on television?

1. Sell yourself to the station management to secure time.

2. Watch for new stations opening in the area and approach them ahead of time to buy time.

3. Be sure that you approach them with the highest possible quality program of broad enough scope to be of listener interest.

Question: What is the best time for a television or radio program?

The time must be determined by the type of community you live in, the listening audience of the station and its habits.

We need to advertise the fact that we are on the air and to spend time and money helping to build an audience. This will not only give the program a greater listening audience, but also puts the program in a better light with the station, as they are always concerned about audience response and audience building.

Question: How do radio and television compare today?

According to the largest surveying company in the nation, TV is no longer the major mass media of the world. Radio is now number one in mass communication and still offers a great challenge to those who want to disseminate the gospel.

Radio holds a large intrigue to people outside of our nation, as most of them listen to radio constantly. When it comes to preaching the gospel with the objective of securing a decision, radio has some advantages over TV, since with the radio speaker the listener becomes concerned with, "What is he saying to me?" On television the viewer is asking, "What does he look like?" "How is he dressed?" "What kind of production are we seeing?"

Question: Will we be having a telecast originate out of our General Council headquarters?

The group recommended that the General Council give serious consideration to producing a national telecast.

PARTICIPATING IN COMMUNITY ACTIVITIES

Speaker: **HASKELL ROGERS**

Moderator: **ROBERT GRABER**

Panelists: **HOWARD CUMMINGS, CHARLES R. HEMBREE, H. PAUL HOLDRIDGE**

Recorder: **DAVID LEWIS**

COMMUNITY ACTIVITIES CAN BE A prime area of evangelism for the alert and progressive church which evaluates, selects, and participates in wholesome civic affairs.

We know it is the will of God to evangelize the world. Just as certain is the assertion of the Scriptures that the Church is God's chosen instrument to effect this evangelization.

I. The Field

Jesus said, "The field is the world" (Matthew 13:38). This field is growing. The world population explosion is reaching proportions that are hard to imagine. As the world population expands, the challenge of evangelism increases.

A. IT MUST BE ENTERED

It would be ridiculous to assume that a reaper could stand at the edge of the harvest field and expect the stalks of ripened wheat to assemble themselves into sheaves and move out to the reaper. So it is the height of folly to assume that the Church can fulfill its ministry of world evangelism by building a fine and efficient organization with elaborate educational and social facilities and by displaying human ability and talent. God has a plan of world evangelism in His Word, and this plan has never failed to accomplish His purpose. His plan calls for a *moving out* into the harvest fields.

B. VISION IS NECESSARY

But laborers must have vision before they will go. "Where there is no vision, the people perish" (Proverbs 29:18). An essential prerequisite of evangelism is a valid vision of the lost, needy, distressed, and confused world. It was said of Jesus, "But when he saw the multitudes, he was moved with compassion . . ." (Matthew 9:36).

II. The Agency

In His prayer Jesus referred to the fact that the Church was "in the world" even though they were not "of the world" (John 17:11, 16).

The Church is the agency for worldwide evangelism. A Christianity that does not begin with the individual is not true Christianity, but a religion that ends with the individual is certainly not Christianity. Any analysis of evangelism reveals that it requires a dissemination of the message of redemption among men, and the Church is God's instrument for that purpose.

A. INDIVIDUAL INVOLVEMENT

How well is the Church fulfilling its ministry in the world? Remember the field is not the Church, but the world.

The evangelistic church will address itself to the world through a dedicated laity. To go into *all* the world, witness must be given in the office, in the stores, in the shops, on the farms, and in the filling stations. Our light must shine in the political realm, in the service club, in the school, in welfare assistance, in the PTA in social betterment efforts, and wherever the Christian works and serves. This witness will have to be given by the individual Christian.

B. Time to Awake

We must awake to the fact that we have been depending on the organization-filled First Assembly of God of Anywhere, U.S.A., and its scheduled evangelism program to effect evangelism, rather than depending on the individual believers. In the Early Church "they that were scattered abroad went everywhere preaching the word" (Acts 8:4).

III. The Channels

To consider opportunities for evangelism through participation in community activities we must narrow our attention to channels by which we can disseminate the gospel locally.

A. A Work to Do

The Church has been entrusted with the Great Commission. Jesus said to the nucleus of the New Testament Church after His resurrection: "Ye shall be witnesses unto me both in Jerusalem, and in all Judea, and in Samaria, and unto the uttermost part of the earth" (Acts 1:8). It is the consensus of most Christians that to accomplish our mission we must begin at home, in Jerusalem.

How can this be accomplished? Would participation in various community activities be helpful? What are the opportunities for evangelism through these channels? What are the dangers?

There is no question about the emphasis on community affairs in the Bible. The Old Testament has much to say about special events and activities, many of which were of a religious nature and yet were conducted as community affairs.

Any community activity that brings people together affords an opportunity to spread the witness either directly or indirectly. One case in the ministry of Jesus was the marriage feast at Cana (John 2:1-10).

This is not to imply that participating in a community activity will afford an opportunity to proclaim the gospel. But many activities give opportunity to establish communication with people, some of whom might be influenced to hear the message within the church later. But

participation in such activities will not result in people "flocking to your church."

B. Be Contemporary

If the Church is to be a saving agency in any generation, it must be concerned about the problems of that generation. We must see that there is no incompatability between the Church as a fervent evangelistic organization and the Church expressing itself by a diversity of ministry through regenerated members in all available channels presented in community service. Paul said, "... that I might by all means save some" (1 Corinthians 9:22).

C. The Church in Dialogue

The Church has to be in contact with the unbelieving world to understand it. It is only as the Church listens to the world's reaction that it can really apply the gospel to life.

1. *Citizenship.* One observer states, "Politics and government always stand in need of more Christian voices. Merely to criticize and never participate in political planning will hinder rather than help the Christian cause. ..."

2. *Welfare.* Such ministry affords wonderful opportunities for witness. At most, this participation would be a fringe involvement since most of this is sponsored by state or federal governments, even though in the past this was completely handled by the church.

3. *PTA.* The church through its pastor and dedicated laymen may witness effectually through participation in such community work as the PTA. This also affords opportunity to witness vocally on many occasions.

4. *Ministerial Associations.* Usually this relationship offers many opportunities to witness through preaching and other kinds of community action sponsored by the associations. Many times these have resulted in further opportunities to witness to individuals and lead them to a personal experience of salvation.

5. *Fairs.* County and state fairs afford a wonderful chance to install booths to display and distribute literature. We belong in places of community activity like this. Jesus continually walked the paths of men and "came to where they were" (Luke 7:36; 10:33; 19:5).

6. *Parades.* We have used floats to convey the gospel and on some occasions presented gospel singing and messages.

7. *Social betterment.* Service clubs and social betterment projects offer opportunity for evangelical witness for Christ. The better things of

our civilization are the result of the ministry of the Church. Wherever it has carried the gospel, the Church has brought civilization with its hospitals, homes for the orphans and the aged, help for the poor, clothing for the naked, freedom, and liberty. All these results of the gospel are also channels for further gospel witness.

D. BECOME INVOLVED

The Church is weak, fearful, powerless, and anemic because it will not accept the challenge of an encounter with the world. Jesus said regarding His Church, "I have sent them into the world" (John 17:18). We certainly will not have this encounter with the unbeliever inside the four walls of the church building if we are unwilling to move out there where they are.

E. SOME PRECAUTIONS

A balance must be kept between the religious and secular, between the spiritual and material. Evangelism should not be equated with welfare activity, social action, political and legislative effort for building a better world through abolishing poverty and crime. These are good, but they are not the primary work of evangelism. The main objective in participating in community activity should always be to witness for Jesus Christ.

Every true Christian has such concern for the mental, physical, and spiritual welfare of people that it is an easy matter for him to be swept out into the midstream of a good cause which might become merely a substitute for real evangelism. At this point a Christian could become overinvolved in political issues, social betterment projects, service clubs, and welfare activities. These may all be good, but they are not to have first place in the work of the Church.

There are dangers! We should watch the matter of involvement at the risk of compromise. Many times the testimony of both the individual and the church is strengthened when they say no to an invitation to participate. We must guard against being caught in the current as was Lot whose testimony became a joke to those in Sodom.

The alert church will be wise in evaluating these opportunities and involving itself only in those which are wholesome and vital and in which the message of God through His Son may be manifest by this participation.

Panel Discussion and Open Forum

Since we now live in an era when it is increasingly difficult to get lost men inside our churches, our primary concern must be to take the gospel to them. Pentecostal people should be encouraged to become active in political realms. Some may be able to run for offices.

Many great men of the Bible were involved in political and governmental activities, such as Daniel and his three companions in Babylon.

It was noted that the churches that have stayed out of politics have been most successful in evangelization. Yet we need individual Christians from our churches who will penetrate every level of our society. Let the church be the church and the pulpit be used not for politics but for the declaration of the gospel. The church can encourage her sons to become involved in the world of politics, not just for involvement's sake, but as a means of exposing men to a personal witness. Many Christian statesmen of our day have successfully done this.

A pastor from Alabama stated, "I feel that the greatest indictment against the church of the Lord Jesus in our century is our stand (or lack of one) on racial problems. We must search our hearts to see if we have any type of racial misunderstanding in attitude or in action."

There is little to be gained by joining the pickets: in fact, a stand must be taken against lawlessness. But this does not answer the real problem: What are we going to do to evangelize 28,000,000 American Negroes? We are beginning to make certain advances. Most of our churches need to be made aware of what is being done and what can be done. We need some solid Biblical teaching on the subject of prejudice. We must cease viewing men as black or white and see them as individuals with souls that need God.

Question: How can a church move out to reach men at all levels of society?

In many cases the bridge must be through one or two key individuals, either the pastor or a layman who is capable of overcoming such barriers. Fear often holds us back from witnessing to those we feel may be our intellectual or social superiors. The truth is that all men have a "God-shaped vacuum" in their souls that only God can fill. The hunger of man is one. No one, poor or rich, should be neglected in the ministration of our witness.

There are times when involvement with a ministerial association may be a means of reaching men with the Pentecostal witness. However, the

Assemblies of God does not have affiliation with the National Council of Churches and takes a stand against the organized ecumenical movement. Affiliation with some church groups would damage the pastor's influence in the community.

But affiliation with acceptable associations will give the minister openings to speak in schools and on radio and in other community religious services. Each case must be evaluated individually.

THE PASTOR—LEADER IN EVANGELISM

Speaker: **V. ERNEST SHORES**
Moderator: **R. D. E. SMITH**
Panelists: **CHARLES CRABTREE, EMMITT FOSTER, ROY HARTHERN**
Recorder: **JACK RISNER**

WITH MANY, it is the common concept that a pastor is to minister to the spiritual needs of his people. He is to teach them, comfort and encourage, hold them together, and help them in the many problems that life presents. However, the Scripture has made it plain that the ministry of a pastor is more than this. He is to take the lead in evangelism and he is to encourage—even urge—his people to get the good news of salvation out to all men.

Before the pastor can accomplish this, he must have a vision for evangelism. "Where there is no vision, the people perish" (Proverbs 29:18) has a twofold application. Unless the Christian has a vision, those who are lost will never hear the message that Jesus saves—and they will certainly perish. But this passage also means that unless the church of Jesus Christ has a vision for lost souls, she also shall perish. The fountain of her spiritual life shall dry up and no longer produce, and she shall die. Most assuredly then, the pastor who is the leader of the church must have this vision for evangelism.

A pastor must also have a burden for evangelism. Though a vision and a burden are closely related, there is a difference between the two. A vision could be defined as seeing the need, and a burden as having a deep spiritual concern for the need. This deep spiritual concern is a necessity and is born of hours spent in the presence of God, until God Himself gives the burden that is needed. Only then can a pastor go out and really accomplish the work that must be done.

A vision and a burden are prime requisites before the pastor can lead in evangelism. There are many avenues by which he may accomplish this work: He can begin teaching special groups and presenting the great need, the methods of meeting the need, and the responsibility of the church. Thus the pastor is able to convey to his people necessary knowledge and help them with the tools they can use to implement this work.

But such endeavors alone leave a great gap, for the majority of people will never attend a class. The pastor must also, through his pulpit ministry, cause the people to be conscious of the vision and the burden he feels. There must be preaching from the pulpit emphasizing the need for all people to share the gospel of Jesus Christ with the unsaved. If only the few who are inspired and trained in special classes are challenged with the need, the work will only be half done. The entire church must be challenged.

The pastor must lead his people into the field, setting before them the pattern of personal witnessing. By sharing with his people his experiences and his rejoicing over the soul that has been saved, he will thus encourage them to become involved in this great ministry.

Jesus said, "Pray ye therefore the Lord of the harvest, that he will send forth laborers into his harvest" (Matthew 9:38). How can we as pastors

135

pray for the Lord to send forth laborers into the harvest until we have first made the full consecration of our time and service?

We must base our vision upon Christ's claim on the souls of men. It was to save lost mankind that He came into the world; no other reason, no other purpose. His life and His ministry, His suffering, His death and resurrection, and His ascension back to the Father were all done that men might be saved. He ever lives to make intercession for men, that they may be forgiven their sins and be made children of God, making it possible to spend eternity with the Father.

Men sell their souls for the pleasures of the world, for position, for wealth, for many things; but Christ has first claim. Beginning with the pastor, the Christians have the responsibility under God of presenting that claim and of urging that it be fulfilled.

For too long we have talked a "good game" but we have failed in the real test, the test of producing for Christ. As pastors, we have had many classes, instructed many people, and have endeavored to challenge many lives. Countless numbers now have the knowledge of the message of salvation, a vision of the needs of lost men, an understanding of the method of presentation, and tools with which to work. Some have absorbed the truth of these over and over again, and now action is demanded!

We do much talking about soul winning, even do much to prepare ourselves to reach souls, but seldom use the tools we have at hand. Very few ever go where the sinners are. Very few ever reach out to the lost to win them for Christ.

The pastor must set the example before his people. He can promote mass evangelism by encouraging evangelistic efforts in the church and arranging for them. We can no longer allow the enemy of the souls of men to keep us from renewed efforts to reach men for Christ because of past failures, lack of success, or excessive costs. There is no cost too great to win men for Christ. We must renew our evangelistic efforts in special revival meetings, in street corner preaching, wherever we have opportunity of reaching the masses for Christ. This was the pattern of the Early Church. This has been the pattern of evangelistic movements from then until now, and again you and I must assume this responsibility.

Furthermore, the pastor must practice evangelism in the regular meetings of the church. How often we have been aware of the fact there were more unsaved people in our Sunday morning service than on Sunday night or any week-night of a revival effort. Why not preach an evangelistic sermon at least occasionally on Sunday morning, giving an altar call, and believing God to reach these hearts and bring them to Himself?

The pastor can also lead in evangelism by organizing special efforts in reaching out for souls. There are those who with a little encouragement would join a team and go with someone more experienced and a little stronger in the faith to invite people to church. Then when the door is opened, these willing workers will witness to the unsaved about the Lord Jesus Christ.

There is one last emphasis. Follow-up is essential. We may do all that we can think of doing, and our efforts may be crowned with success. We may see souls find Christ. What then? Will we leave these souls to fend for themselves?

Our work is not finished with the initial witnessing, even if it is crowned with a soul accepting Christ as Saviour. We need to stay in contact with that individual and tie him to the church, where he will hear and learn the Word of God, that he may grow in grace and in the knowledge of the Lord and Saviour, Jesus Christ.

Panel Discussion and Open Forum

In Ephesians 4:11, 12, Paul gave a mandate to the pastors to train or teach the saints so that the church might grow. The pulpit ministry alone is not enough; there must be an outreach through the people.

One panelist reported that he preached nine months on evangelism and instituted door-to-door witnessing. As a result thirty-two were saved in two weeks' time. A "buddy system" was instituted to follow up each new person or family saved. Someone in the church of similar interests, culture, or background was asked to take a new convert as a "buddy" and to invite him once a month to have dinner with him and to meet with him periodically.

The pastor is the key individual in training others for personal witnessing and in the evangelistic campaigns of the church. If the pastor does not show his support of the evangelist and his messages and in prayer around the altar, then the evangelistic meetings cannot succeed.

If the pastor uses a Sunday morning evangelistic message, it would be good to announce it ahead of time and urge the people to bring unsaved friends.

Question: What do you do with a convert

who does not easily fit into the culture or class of people in your church?

Some of us think only of the initial decision, but what about the development of Christian character and life? There must be a realization that a man's eternal reward is determined by his life here. A real burden (love) knows no color, or race.

Question: Are we being over-programmed to the loss of real evangelism?

Not if we turn every organizational effort into a soul-winning effort. Then it is not a burden but a tool.

Question: How can the pastor lead in real evangelism efforts when there are so many other things to do?

Our basic call is to the ministry, not to business. It is possible to become involved in so many other activities that the real reason for our ministry is lost. We may even become so busy with our board meetings and committee meetings that we lose sight of the fact that Christ sent us to feed the sheep and to lead them in bringing forth more souls.

Question: How do we get evangelists into home mission works?

If even a small home missions work would budget for a year toward an evangelistic meeting, it would be able to set aside the needed finances for the evangelist. Also, there are many evangelists who are ready to give a portion of each year to ministry in home mission works.

Question: What is the basis for a burden?

Prayer! If a pastor is willing to set aside time and really seek God, a burden will come. He may then desire to set aside a special time for the people to join him in prayer. He may be the only one present at these prayer meetings at first; but if he insists on this time with God, God will surely send others to join him and will also send the answer to his prayers.

We must be careful that we do not institutionalize soul winning and relegate it to only those who have had certain soul-winning courses. Every person who has been born again should be encouraged to be a witness and a soul winner.

We are too inclined today to use only those who have years of experience as Christians. We must learn again that the newly converted person many times has fresh energy and new anointing and needs to be guided by the pastor or another leader in the church. These new converts may be able to accomplish much more than some of the old-timers in the church who have lost their vision and burden.

We are losing too many of our new converts by not following up. There should be a planned program using material such as the booklet, *Now What?*

Every area and organization within the church should be organized to be active in soul winning, with the pastor setting the pace and leading the way.

THE PASTOR'S PULPIT EVANGELISM

Speaker: **KENNETH SCHMIDT**
Moderator: **BERT WEBB**
Panelists: **JAMES HENNESY, JAMES KOFAHL, THOMAS PAINO JR.**
Recorder: **DAVID KNIGHT**

WE HAVE BEEN BORN into the greatest age of communication the world has ever known. With communication bringing so much scientific progress before our eyes, sometimes the simpler and commonplace things of life appear unessential. When this happens, we end up with "scientific giants and moral pigmies!" We may call this the "age of the blundering of the brilliant."

Too many have looked at evangelistic preaching as commonplace, as almost menial and practically unessential. But the Word of God says: "For whosoever shall call upon the name of the Lord shall be saved. How then shall they call on him in whom they have not believed? and how shall they believe in him of whom they have not heard? *and how shall they hear without a preacher?*" (Romans 10:13, 14).

Preaching is communication of truth through personality! Preaching is anointed evangelism in the pulpit; it is the gospel with maximum power. So we may face our theme with the realization that the Word of God teaches us *"it pleased God by the foolishness of preaching to save them that believe"* (1 Corinthians 1:21). When we speak of the pastor's pulpit evangelism, we are talking about a communication that pleases God and that we cannot do without! And the religious denominations that have quieted and overlooked evangelism in the pulpit have lost their effectiveness for the gospel.

Webster's Dictionary gives the definition of the word *evangelism* as "a preaching of, or zealous effort to spread, the gospel, as in revival meetings"!

Let us never minimize the accomplishments of the evangelistic pulpit, for God has used anointed men in times of great moral darkness and national frustration to bring revivals. In the Old Testament, men like Asa, Samuel, Jehoash, Hezekiah, Josiah, Elijah, Elisha, Jonah, Haggai, Zechariah, Ezra, and others are examples.

Look at Peter's evangelistic sermon on the Day of Pentecost. It was instrumental in that great revival in Jerusalem. Or look at the great revival when Philip went down to the city of Samaria, *and "preached Christ unto them."*

Unlimited results are obtained when our pulpits radiate evangelism.

History tells us that the Italian revival under Francis of Assisi, who had a simple evangelistic message, was of great proportions. Thomas of Celano states, "His words were like fire, piercing the heart!" This is an evangelistic pulpit which is a persuasive, passionate approach and appeal.

Another Italian example of evangelistic pulpit preaching is Savonarola, who from the pulpit of St. Mark in Florence shook the people till the crowds were so great he had to move into the large cathedral. He preached day after day to throngs. History reports, "Tears gushed from their eyes; they beat their breasts...they cried unto God."

Time hinders us from talking about such anointed men whose pulpits were aflame with the fire of evangelistic messages. Men such as Wycliffe in England, Huss in Bohemia, Martin Luther in Germany.

Then there was John Calvin of France, Wesley and Whitefield of England, Griffeth Jones and Daniel Rowlands of Wales.

When Whitefield heard Rowlands preach, he said, "The power of God...under the ministry of Mr. Rowlands was enough to make a person's heart burn within him. At seven of the morning have I seen perhaps 10,000 from different parts, in the midst of a sermon, crying and ready to leap for joy."

Look at history and realize that the pastor's pulpit evangelism has played a tremendous part in even bringing the gospel down to us who live today. Think of the pulpits of Spurgeon, Finney, Banks, Moody, and Talmadge.

Christ's life on earth is an example of an evangelistic pulpit from beginning to end. His disciples could not comprehend His motivation and passion for the lost. He told such stories as the lost coin, lost sheep, the prodigal son.

Christ refused to involve His pulpit in the irrelevant and unimportant! They constantly sought to sidetrack Him, but He cried, "I must work the works of him that sent me, while it is day: the night cometh, when no man can work. As long as I am in the world, I am the light of the world" (John 9:4, 5). Jesus refused to be derailed from His main purpose on earth, which was "to seek and to save that which was lost"!

Our pulpits are filled today with everything but evangelism. We have so many sidelines that we find today's pulpits "majoring in minors," and the unsaved go through the church like water flows over a dam! We do not obtain, nor are we in many cases able to retain, because of the loss of the evangelistic flame in the pulpit.

It is a trick of Satan to get us so wrapped up in sermonizing on the nonessentials and to get us so involved in the organizational structure and problems of our society that we become heavy on diagnosis and weak on prescription. Our pulpits become a "drag of negativism instead of a push of positivism"!

It is easy to slip into becoming "church introverts," with our messages only geared with modern problems and trends, instead of having an evangelistic impact on our church and community!

For Christian people to see and feel an altar call is effective in developing a compassion for the lost. An altar call is not just conducive to sinners and backsliders to step out for Christ; it also opens a channel for the Holy Spirit to work with the saints, developing a compassion for the lost and reiterating to them that the church is a "lifeboat" on a rescue mission, and not just a "pleasure boat" on a cruise.

Panel Discussion and Open Forum

Of all the needs of the church today with respect to our mission of ministering to the world, without a doubt one of the greatest is that of evangelistic pulpits. Though the term does suggest the art of preaching evangelistic sermons, there is definitely much more involved. For to have an effective evangelistic pulpit not only should the sermon be evangelistic, but everything in the service should point toward the saving of the lost.

Every preacher should recognize first of all that he has been sent, commissioned by the Lord Jesus Christ. Second, he should understand the purpose of his being sent: to preach the gospel. He is not sent to sermonize or philosophize, but to preach the gospel in simplicity.

The wise pastor will make the Sunday night service truly evangelistic by preaching evangelistic messages. He should not be deterred in this purpose because of an absence of unsaved in the service. Rather he should be encouraged by the thought that when the constituency of the church knows there is going to be an evangelistic message preached, they will then bring the unsaved. But they must have this assurance!

Just as a fish is not caught until he is in the net, so the unsaved has not been reached until he is praying to God for forgiveness. This points up to us the necessity of an efficient, Spirit-anointed altar call. The preacher must follow through with his altar call if his message is to be truly evangelistic. This is not the proper time for a new face or voice in the pulpit. The rapport between speaker and audience must not be disrupted.

An openness to the leading of the Holy Spirit cannot be overemphasized. He knows the needs and the needy. And He has the key which will unlock the heart. The preacher who desires souls for God will not be hasty in concluding his altar call, for he knows that the Holy Spirit is dealing with lives, and decisions of an eternal nature are being affected.

The pastor, recognizing the teamwork characteristic of the evangelistic pulpit, will build toward and upon this factor. He will engender a spirit of harmony among those participating in the service by meeting with them periodically to inform them of the importance of their position, to make requests or suggestions which he feels will be beneficial to the services, and to pray with them.

PENTECOST IN OTHER CHURCHES

Speaker: **JOSEPH FLOWER**
Moderator: **HERMAN ROHDE**
Panelists: **FULTON BUNTAIN, CHARLES W. H. SCOTT, JOHN WILKERSON**
Recorder: **MALCOLM CAMPBELL**

I. Survey

A. BACKGROUND

1. *The Pentecostal phenomenon.* The Book of Acts records an outpouring of the Holy Spirit on the Day of Pentecost and on subsequent occasions when speaking with tongues and other manifestations of the Spirit occurred.

Similar outpourings have occurred during times of spiritual renewal, in the Early Church, and throughout church history among isolated groups, as for example, among the Montanists, Albigensians, Cevennes, Waldensians, and Irvingites.

2. *The judgment of Christendom,* for the most part, has been that the speaking with tongues and other supernatural manifestations of the Spirit served the purpose of *temporary signs,* witnessing to the induction of *specific* groups of believers into Christ's body, the Church, and attesting to the authority of the twelve apostles. Generally it is considered that speaking with tongues ceased with the passing of the apostles and has no distinctive relationship to the experience of the Spirit's infilling. Subsequent reports of speaking with tongues are looked upon as spurious, psychologically induced gibberish, or possibly demon-inspired. Those throughout this Church Age who would admit the possibility of genuine speaking with tongues inspired by the Spirit would consider it a fringe phenomenon as a sign, bestowed sovereignly by God, and in no way essentially related to the Spirit's infilling.

3. *The early twentieth-century Pentecostal outpouring.* With the turn of the century and outpourings of the Spirit throughout the world, attended by speaking with tongues and other miraculous gifts, a definitive theology has evolved linking speaking with tongues distinctively to the experience of the Spirit's infilling as the initial, physical evidence. This has become a major point of doctrine and practice in a number of denominations and churches that have sprung up worldwide. Its numerical strength has been assessed at approximately ten million. In many countries it is the predominant evangelical force.

B. THE NEO-PENTECOSTAL MOVEMENT

1. *Beginnings.* Since the middle of the twentieth century, observable for at least the last decade, the Pentecostal phenomenon has been occurring among individuals and groups affiliated with most of the old-line denominations. These people give little indication of separating from their churches. Most, though not all, accept the Pentecostal position on the experience of the Spirit's infilling that speaking with tongues is an integral component of that experience.

2. *Names.* Some have not hesitated to attach the name "Pentecostal" or "Neo-Pentecostal" to

this, but to many, such names as the "Charismatic Renewal" or "The New Penetration" are more acceptable. Many who are critical toward it would dub it "The Tongues Movement," as they have the older Pentecostals.

3. *Leaders*. As in the outpouring of the Holy Spirit in Pentecostal fashion during the first half of this century, this penetration of old-line denominations does not have any single leader.

4. *Extent*. It is practically impossible to know how many are directly affected, but its impact is certainly considerable. In many localities prayer groups have been formed. Robert Walker, editor of *Christian Life* magazine, has stated that hardly a major city in the United States is without such a group.

It has also been reported that 75 prayer groups with Spirit-filled members are meeting weekly in the San Fernando Valley of Southern California. These groups meet for discussion, spiritual fellowship, and the operation of the gifts of the Spirit. They are usually apart from the regular activities of established churches; but where local leadership is favorable, the Pentecostal manifestations have come out into public view.

5. *The depth of penetration among the denominations is considerable.*

a. *Among Episcopalians*. The Rev. Dennis Bennett, former rector of a large Episcopal church in Van Nuys, California, now pastors in Seattle, Washington, where Pentecostal phenomena regularly occur. He has also had an extensive influence on the movement throughout the United States.

Other prominent Episcopalians who have lent support to the movement include: The Right Rev. Chandler Sterling, bishop of Montana; the Rev. Morton T. Kelsey of Monrovia, California, who although he has not himself spoken with tongues, has written a sympathetic book entitled, *Tongue Speaking;* John L. Sherrill, senior editor of *Guideposts* magazine, who has written a book entitled, *They Speak With Other Tongues,* which recounts his personal search and experience; Dr. William Standish Reed, a surgeon who regularly contributes a column to *Christian Life* magazine and who has actively promoted the movement; Dean Weaver of St. Paul's Cathedral in Detroit, who promotes speaking with tongues in the church services there; the Rev. Michael Harper of the Church of England, who is editor of the *Pentecostal Renewal* magazine and author of a book, *As at the Beginning*.

A joint statement was issued by representatives of the Assemblies of God and the Protestant Episcopal Church after a second meeting together, acknowledging the work of the Spirit in each group. The text of this statement was released in the January 20, 1963, issue of *The Pentecostal Evangel*.

Dr. Donald Coggan, Archbishop of York stated in a sermon in St. Paul's Cathedral in London on October 24, 1964, that the Pentecostal movement is one of the most extraordinary features of religious life in the twentieth century. He further stated that "its roots are in the New Testament, even if some of its fruits are, to our thinking, not always in strict accord with New Testament teaching."

I personally attended a Full Gospel Breakfast in Poughkeepsie, New York, on Saturday, April 20, 1968, which was largely attended by Episcopalians. Many of them gave evidence in their testimonies of a tremendous spiritual experience which changed their lives.

b. *Among Presbyterians*. We can only briefly refer to a number of Presbyterians who speak with tongues: the Rev. James Brown of Upper Octorara Presbyterian Church in Pennsylvania; Catherine Marshall Le Sourd, authoress and widow of the famous chaplain of the U.S. Senate; McCandlish Phillips, New York *Times* reporter; Colleen Townsend Evans, former Hollywood starlet and wife of the pastor of the Bel Air Presbyterian Church; Dr. McCord of Princeton.

It is reported that 600 of the membership of the huge Hollywood Presbyterian Church speak with tongues. Dr. John A. MacKay, retired president of Princeton Theological Seminary, has stated, "If it's a choice between the uncouth life of the Pentecostals and the esthetic death of the older churches, I for one choose the uncouth life."

c. *Among Lutherans*. The Bethany Fellowship of Minneapolis is an offshoot of the Lutherans; and the gifts of the Spirit, including speaking with tongues, are manifest among them.

It has been estimated that 250 of the 5,000 American Lutheran churches have groups that speak in tongues. The Rev. Larry Christensen is a prominent Lutheran leader in the "charismatic renewal."

An Assemblies of God church on Long Island has had regular meetings each week for many months ministering to denominational people, many of whom have been filled with the Spirit and spoken with tongues. I personally ministered at one of these when a local Lutheran minister's wife received.

The Pentecostal Evangel of February 6, 1966, quoting *Pentecost* magazine, stated, "Over 100 university students, young pastors, and workers in the Finnish Lutheran Church have been baptized in the Holy Spirit. This movement which has begun in the State Church emphasizes evangelism and strongly opposes worldliness and modernism."

d. *Among Baptists.* Baptists who have participated in the movement include the Rev. John Osteen of Texas; the Rev. Howard Ervin, formerly pastor at Atlantic Highlands, New Jersey, and now dean at Oral Roberts University; Thomas Hunter of Temple Baptist Church, Albany, New York.

The Pentecostal Evangel of April 2, 1967, quoting from *Christianity Today,* reports that "Dr. Francis E. Whiting, director of the Department of Evangelism and Spiritual Life of the Michigan Baptist Convention (American Baptist Convention) speaks in support of present charismatic works of the Spirit, declaring the choice is Pentecost or holocaust."

e. *Among Mennonites.* The Rev. Gerald Derstine led a remarkable revival in Minnesota in the mid-1950's during which the Holy Spirit was poured out, resulting in many speaking with tongues. "Concern," a pamphlet published by Mennonites, is sympathetic toward a true, scriptural Pentecostal experience.

f. *Among Methodists.* The Rev. Jolly Harper, Methodist district superintendent in Shreveport, Louisiana, with 50 ministers under his supervision tells of "a great gladness in my heart" when he first spoke in tongues.

The Pentecostal Evangel of June 2, 1968, reports that in a revival with Evangelist Paul Olson in Monrovia, Liberia, Dr. J. Bolton Williams, pastor of the Mt. Scott Methodist Church of Cape Palmas, Liberia, (the church President William V. S. Tubman attends) told the audience: "There was a day when I used to make jokes about these tongues-speaking people, but now I am one of them. I am not ashamed to stand with you Pentecostal people tonight. I assure you that the Holy Spirit has revolutionized my life and ministry."

g. *Among Roman Catholics.* A considerable number of Roman Catholics have experienced the Pentecostal infilling and speaking with tongues, particularly among university students and professors. Favorable articles have appeared in many Catholic publications.

Many Catholic groups have invited Pentecostals to speak to them on the subject of the Holy Spirit. Dave Wilkerson has spoken to a group of seminarians. In May 1968, a seminar was held in a school for nuns, and also in a school for priests, with about 150 persons present. Of these, 30 received the infilling and spoke with tongues.

h. *Among others.* There are reports of Pentecostal manifestations among Congregationalists, Reformed, Evangelical, Churches of Christ, Christian Advent, Christian and Missionary Alliance, and in fact nearly every denomination. There has never been a time when other church groups have been so open to listen to what Pentecostals have to say. I have personally participated in a number of sessions of dialogue. As someone has said, "Pentecost is not a denomination; it is an experience."

6. *Student groups.* Speaking with tongues is reported to have "erupted" in student fellowship groups on many campuses—Yale, Princeton, UCLA, Stanford, Massachusetts Institute of Technology, Notre Dame, University of Michigan, Duquesne, Fuller Seminary, Wheaton College, Westmont College, and other campuses.

7. *The secular press.* Most newspapers have carried articles on tongues or the charismatic renewal by such writers as Louis Cassels, religion editor for United Press International. The New York *Times* and *The National Observer* (October 26, 1964) devoted considerable space to the matter. Many national magazines, such as *Time, Newsweek, Coronet, Life,* and *The Saturday Evening Post,* have carried articles on the subject.

8. *The religious press.* Of course, Pentecostal publications have widely publicized what is taking place. Of the non-Pentecostal magazines, *Christian Life* has given much favorable and objective coverage, reporting outpourings of the Spirit in many old-line denominational churches. About four years ago, articles on speaking with tongues began appearing in many religious periodicals, including *Presbyterian Life, Bibliotheca Sacra, Moody Monthly, Christian Herald, Christianity Today, Eternity, The Alliance Witness,* and *The Sword of the Lord.*

A few books approving the neo-Pentecostal movement have recently been published, among these being: *Tongue Speaking,* by Morton T. Kelsey; *They Shall Speak With Tongues* by John Sherrill; *Studies in Ecstasy,* by Bernard L. Bresson; and *Pentecostalism,* by John T. Nichol. On the other hand, several books have recently been published in opposition, some of the most significant being: *The Modern Tongues Movement*, by Robert G. Gromacki; *What About Tongue Speaking?* by Anthony A. Hoekema; *Glossolalia*, by Frank Stagg, E. Glenn Hinson, and Wayne E. Oates; *Speaking in Tongues and Divine Healing*, by Robert P. Lightner.

II. Appraisal

A. Strengths

1. *It reaches people that old-line Pentecostals could probably never reach with a life-giving truth and experience.* The earlier Pentecostal movement has been outside the mainstream of the established denominations. This neo-Pentecostal movement is within the established denominations. While not generally warmly received by the leaders, it is in many instances tolerated. Some are forced to this by its world impact and are manifesting greater tolerance than those of the previous generation. Some sincerely consider it has a spiritual contribution to make to those churches.

In most instances it does not affect the public worship services of the churches, but this is not universally so. Individuals often meet together somewhat clandestinely in small prayer groups. Some churches have extra services for a Pentecostal type of worship, but regular services remain traditional.

Could this be the beginning of a greater outpouring of the Spirit previous to Christ's return such as Dr. Charles S. Price foresaw? We can only stand back in awe at the sovereign ways of God, which are "past finding out."

2. *It has been characterized by an openness and simplicity of faith.* Some degreed persons have become disenchanted with the inability of their educations to give them satisfaction in Christian experience and effectiveness in Christian service. Now through the Pentecostal experience they have found Christ has become a reality and relevant to everyday living.

3. *This neo-Pentecostal movement has displayed a return to a basic spiritual hunger for the Word* and a thirst for the living water of the Spirit.

4. *In many instances there has been an unmistakable quickening of the Spirit of God,* both individually and corporately.

5. *Many lives have been changed for the better,* with the giving up of sinful and destructive habits.

6. *The movement has been characterized by* a zeal that is almost apostolic, and reminiscent of the degree of zeal that Assemblies of God believers demonstrated a generation ago.

7. *The educational background* of many in the neo-Pentecostal movement, along with their new spiritual understanding, qualifies them to represent and project Pentecostal theology.

8. *From their vantage point they are in a position to promote* the Pentecostal experience among denominational people.

9. *Most of the neo-Pentecostals are not given to some of the emotional excesses* and fanatical practices that have at times been associated with the Pentecostal movement, which have been a stumbling block to many.

B. Weaknesses

1. *There seems to be a tendency toward gullibility among some*—accepting everything that appears to be supernatural as from God.

2. *In a few cases there have been emotional excesses*, but these have been rare. The strictly disciplined intellectualism of most of the leadership has limited these excesses.

3. *Some have gone astray by seeking personal guidance through prophecy* or tongues and interpretation.

4. *Some have fallen prey to "spiritual pride"* or pride because of presumed spiritual superiority. Some have also been inclined to look down on the older Pentecostals as socially and intellectually inferior.

5. *In some instances speaking with tongues has not been accompanied by a marked change in moral standards.* Things we generally consider wrong and sinful, such as drinking, smoking, theater-going, card playing, dancing, immodest conformity to worldly standards in dress and outward adornment, have been tolerated and condoned by some who have claimed a Pentecostal experience.

In making this criticism we should also confess our own shortcomings. There has been an unmistakable lowering of our own standards; and if we are to continue to have God's blessing upon us, we must shore up the defenses.

6. *Some have given a misplaced emphasis, or an overemphasis, to speaking with tongues.* Such have been more occupied with the gift than the Giver.

7. *Others have not given tongues the distinctive relationship to the Spirit's infilling* that we believe is given by the Scriptures. Some look upon it as merely one evidence of the Spirit's infilling, among others.

8. *There has been some misapprehension of the nature of the gift of tongues.* It has been looked upon by some as more mechanical than supernatural, and there has been some tendency to reduce it to a rationale and explain it psychologically.

9. *Many have been influenced in interpreting Pentecostal phenomena and passages in the Scriptures by traditional and secular concepts.* One example is an expressed Roman Catholic interpretation that speaking with tongues on the Day of Pentecost was a miracle of hearing rather than a miracle of speech. Another example is the view that speaking with tongues in the Book of Acts was in foreign languages, but the phenomenon at Corinth was something different, some kind of ecstatic speech.

10. *There is a tendency to hold onto the traditions, forms, liturgy, and sacraments of the institutional church* and make the Pentecostal experience an added dimension thereto. Most see no inconsistency in such problems as the theological conflict between the Pentecostal infilling and the sacrament of confirmation. Some church leaders delight in the fact that those involved in the charismatic renewal become more devoted to the institutional church.

11. *There is a possibility that through absorption of the neo-Pentecostal movement by the denominations it will become smothered and lost.* In a few instances, especially where the leadership is involved, whole churches have been affected for the good; but in most cases it is an empty hope that the churches can be changed.

It was probably the salvation of the Pentecostal testimony that the denominations rejected it in the first half of this century. The fact the Pentecostal movement is now firmly established with a distinct identity will probably be of assistance in keeping the Pentecostal experience alive among those who are maintaining their church connections.

12. *There is frequently an identification of the neo-Pentecostal movement with liberal theology and ecumenism.* It is true the liberals are often more open and receptive to the Pentecostal message than many fundamentalists and evangelicals.

Many do not interpret what is taking place as a compromise with the modern ecumenical movement which is endeavoring to bring about a structural unity, but rather they see it as an indication of a spiritual hunger among many caught up in the ecumenical movement and a desire of many of these for a true unity of the Spirit.

III. Relationship

We ask ourselves the question: Is there any basis for dialogue or fellowship between the older and the newer Pentecostals? By the very nature of Christ's body there is a basic unity and fellowship that is implied. Unfortunately, there are issues that keep members of His body apart. Where there is a common faith and experience, there should be a drawing together. But it must be recognized that there are still doctrinal and practical distinctions, in addition to denominational barriers that stand between to separate us. Everyone who is truly led of the Spirit should seek to circumvent these distinctions, without compromising to do so.

A. CAN WE CONTRIBUTE ANYTHING TO THE NEO-PENTECOSTALS?

We do have something from past experience to offer. They have a right to expect to see the fruits of Pentecost in us, and only as they see these can we contribute much to them.

B. CAN WE LEARN ANYTHING FROM THEM?

We can learn that an experience need not be highly emotional to be genuine and that emotionalism in itself is not necessarily spirituality. We can also learn that it is not intellectualism or education that is the enemy of spirituality, but pride of intellect.

There are some traditional concepts that we hold that might stand a little closer scrutiny from the perspective of the neo-Pentecostals and also that of the non-Pentecostals. To do so could enable us to purify our own doctrinal position and enable us to be more effective in dialogue with others. This is not to imply, however, that our basic Pentecostal position is in error.

C. WHAT SHOULD BE OUR ATTITUDE?

We should not be defensive or apologetic. If it should appear that many of them are not seeking our fellowship, perhaps we are somewhat to blame in that we have shunned contact with them. There is nothing like contact to dissolve imaginary barriers to fellowship. If they do not measure up to our standards, let us not assume an air of superiority, but by our own godly influence and genuine Christian love help them to see what God expects of His Spirit-filled saints.

Panel Discussion and Open Forum

Question: What should be our attitude toward those of other denominations who are interested in the ministry of the Holy Spirit?

We should be available to talk with these friends from the Scriptures and pray with them. Any leadership role should be a humble one. We should welcome them heartily but not pressure them to change affiliation. An additional service during the week primarily for sharing with them is advisable. Exemplary lives, natural operation of the Spirit in our meetings, and good literature draw them and help them. It is important to emphasize the inner moving of the Spirit and yieldedness to God rather than techniques of receiving the baptism of the Spirit.

Question: How can Assemblies of God people develop an attitude of welcome to these inquirers?

The pastor has responsibility for his congregation in this area and should cultivate a magnanimous feeling among his people. It will also help if Assemblies of God people become more effective, zealous, fruitful, and spiritually active. Then they would not be as sensitive about being excelled. Also Assemblies of God believers should become more able to explain their position scripturally.

Question: Should we encourage Spirit-filled denominational people to stay within their churches?

Sometimes there are values in staying with the old-line church as an influence. Some Spirit-filled persons attend their old church on Sunday morning and an Assemblies church on Sunday evening. Special mid-week services for them are helpful.

There is a danger that their spiritual development will be stunted in the home church. The biggest conflict comes with Roman Catholics because of the institutional authority, liturgy, sacraments, etc. However, many Roman Catholics feel their main loyalty is to Christ, their allegiance to the church being in letter only, since they disagree with it. It is felt that if we are alive spiritually and have an appealing invitation, Spirit-filled people will join us.

Question: Do these denominational people receive the baptism of the Holy Spirit in a manner different from us?

Circumstances have varied and are often different from what we are accustomed to. Often there is no high emotional pitch. Some new Pentecostals have prayed with the laying on of hands, some seated quietly, and many exhibit a new on-going moving of the Holy Spirit in their daily experiences.

Question: Many members of other denominations who claim the infilling of the Holy Spirit do not follow the code of conduct that we do. Three basic questions are involved. Does this cast doubt on the validity of their experience? What can we expect to develop in those individuals? What should be our attitude toward them?

Regarding the question of the validity of the infilling in view of worldly behavior, one panelist pointed out that the original outpouring of this century came to holiness people, but because they were hungry, not because they were holiness-oriented.

The opinion was expressed that the experiences usually are genuine, but that teaching is desirable. From the floor also came the comment that outward standards can be deceptive relative to inner purity, and that Assemblies of God people often have something to be desired in conduct. Another view is that lack of teaching is responsible for divergence when the Holy Spirit comes, and that the elements of worldliness will drop off, since worldliness is incompatible with the moving of the Spirit. Another reaction expressed that the Holy Spirit will deal with people individually about these matters.

Question: What effect does this outpouring of the Holy Spirit have on our general approach and goals?

It is imperative for us to keep our own experience alive. We must be worthy of leadership. We must cultivate a rich operation of the Spirit in our midst. We must consider the picture we are presenting to the Christian world. We must follow proper priorities. We must be yielded to God to answer the questions our culture is asking in the way He would have us answer.

Question: What about interaction with those Spirit-filled persons of other denominations?

Some of the most fruitful experiences of sharing the ministry of the Holy Spirit have come from association with other ministers. In some areas there are restrictions on the sharing of pulpits which inhibit this activity.

REACHING AND RETAINING TEENS

Speaker: **WILLIAM THORNTON JR.**

Moderator: **MARVIN GORMAN**

Panelists: **BOBBY BROCK, RICHARD COOK, SAM PETERSON**

Recorder: **MRS. ROY TREGENZA**

JESUS SAID THERE WOULD BE a future generation with certain characteristics to indicate that the end is near. In other words, there is an 'X Generation' at some point in history where all the signs will converge."—Billy Graham, in *World Aflame*.

As we think of the topic before us, we are immediately conscious that in all probability we are talking about reaching and retaining this prophesied "X Generation," the generation that "shall not pass, till all these things be fulfilled" (Matthew 24:34).

I. The "X Generation"

1. *First, we are amazed, overwhelmed, at its size.* The youth problem is larger today by the sheer weight of numbers. Advertisers, politicians, entertainers, writers, anyone who reaches for the American public cannot ignore its young people. To refuse to "think young" would bring economic disaster to industrial America, leave the houses of entertainment empty, and cause history's greatest stockpile of consumer goods.

2. *This "X Generation" is informed, in touch, and mobile.* Modern communication and transportation have made this possible. Young people have never lived in so small a world. Tokyo is closer to them than the county seat was to their grandfathers. Students at Berkeley have a genuine empathy with the students of Paris. They are communicating. And they are traveling.

3. *This "X Generation" lives in the city.* Megalopolis is on the drawing board. The individual is feeling stifled by the press of the mass. The groan and cry for individuality and freedom seems to be the death rattle of an old way of life. The closer we get to it, the more Huxley's *Brave New World* appears to be a nightmare—a mass, ordered, sterile, amoral, "perfect" society; a brainless, heartless, programmed Utopia. Mr. Teen is resisting it. Sometimes he hates it. Sometimes he loves it. Sometimes he fears it. He is its child. The teen we are speaking of reaching and retaining is in the city—and the city's name is Sodom.

4. *The "X Generation" is integrated.* It is more than racial integration. This society is moving with rapid pace toward total integration—socially, economically, and culturally. Your teen mingles. He speaks a different language, at least the words have different meanings. Unless we hear what this generation is saying, we will not be able to speak to its real need.

5. *This "X Generation" is wise.* Sophistication is a badge the teen wears. He is digging, asking, searching, weighing. "Because I said so" is no longer a satisfying answer. Today's youth want to know reasons, and they must receive logical ones. They are questioning moral codes, laws, standards, philosophies, and behavioral patterns that have existed in society without question for generations. Some of history's greatest changes in the realm of sexual mores, religious philoso-

phies, and political concepts are taking place in the world of youth. The teen has been taught to think. And he is fighting for the right to express his thoughts, surprising and sacrilegious as they may seem to a passing generation.

II. Guidelines for Reaching and Retaining Teens

1. *We must try to understand.* Understanding itself is the first requisite. We will need to know as much as possible about today's youth to reach and retain them. For example, we will need to know the facts about marijuana and the other drugs so readily available. We need to know what Mr. Teen is thinking, what he is reading, what movies he is seeing (the review section in most Sunday papers will give you this), what his teachers are telling him—in short, what he is absorbing and what is absorbing him.

Understanding is not the whole answer to the communication gap between generations. But it is the first step. It establishes dialogue. There is some degree of intelligence in exchange of ideas instead of blind stabs at each other. Someone said, "We shout at each other across the seas of misunderstanding." Certainly this is happening in our homes, and too often in the context of church life.

2. *We are responsible to provide today's youth with an authority structure.* One of the great human paradoxes is that while man strives, sometimes violently, against it, he needs authority. He survives only within such a structure and responds best to a figure of authority.

Authority structures, recognized in the past, are being undermined today. The state is being resisted as a figure of authority. The home, perhaps the main authority structure in any sound society, is losing its prestige. The world's last hope is the Church. We must not fail. This is the nature of religion—it has the last word. A church without authority is a farce. And unless this authority is expressed by firm positions on current trends, issues, concepts, and behavioral fads, the church is an enigma. A church on fire with authority is the only saving agency the world has ever known.

The Church derives its authority from the Word of God. A mysterious, divine, community conviction brought into existence the Book we call the Bible. The church spoke, and the Scriptures were canonized. The church in each generation is responsible to "recanonize" this Holy Book. Unless today's church does—unless the Bible becomes God's Word to us now and here,

a living and redemptive force in every Christian's life—the Bible is but a dead book.

3. *We must be convinced that today's youth need spiritual experiences.* Codes of Christian ethics, psychology, and mental gymnastics will not suffice. Only the impress of the divine Spirit is life-transforming and redemptive. This emphasis on spiritual experiences is our Pentecostal distinctive. It must be insisted upon, preached about, "programmed in." Our youth must be led to the altar, to the prayer room, and taught to linger "until."

4. *We must have faith and patience.* Parents, educators, as well as the church in many instances, are running scared. Ineffective, failing, perplexed—today's adult world finds itself with gigantic problems and very few solutions.

The Bible has the answer. That answer is the spiritual renewal of the individual. Educators and legislators have proved that you cannot impose the Christian ethic on an unregenerate society. Now the church is trying to change society with an outsized emphasis on social action.

The church, then, has become a part of the problem and cannot be a part of the solution. Rollo May asks the question in *Psychology and the Human Dilemma*, "Is not one of the central problems of modern Western man that he experiences himself as without significance as an individual?" When the church loses this sense of the significance of the individual and begins to concentrate on Christianizing the mass, all is lost. The clear emphasis of the Great Commission is that we preach to reach, and we teach to retain.

There ought to be provisions in the youth program for social interaction, recreation, and activity—lots of it. But we already have learned that these things alone will not reach nor retain in the saving sense of which we speak. Only gospel preaching and Christian teaching will do that with lasting results.

III. "How To" Methods and Programs

We are all aware that in youth work you never arrive. Youth programs are fluid, unpredictable, fluctuating. *Change* is the watchword. A general outline of our church's ministry to its youth is as follows:

1. *Sunday school is for teaching, pure and simple.* This is a no-nonsense hour devoted to God's Word. We endeavor to constantly emphasize this to our staff.

2. *The CA service is for training.* Participa-

tion is stressed. I have yet to find anything superior to our own *CA Guide*.

3. *For five years we have operated with varying degrees of success what is called a Youth Center.* This is for recreation and evangelism. The schedule has been shifted from time to time, but the general idea is that teens arrive after school and begin participating in sponsored recreation. A meal is served at 5:45. At 6:30 a short, simple youthspiration service is held. The dress is informal. The approach is casual. A film, a speaker, a musical group is usually the order of the service. There is little singing. It is not a worship service. An appeal is made for decisions as often as the Holy Spirit directs. Recreation, fellowship, and personal counseling are continued until 9 p.m.

There are many innovations to programming for a youth department. Finding a program that fits your current situation is of prime importance.

Panel Discussion and Open Forum

One pastor compressed his youth-approach into four essentials: availability, communication, motivation, and involvement. He stressed the point that motive is more important than method when seeking to reach teens. We must seek to harness youthful boldness. Give them a goal, then let them get there with their own ideas.

In every part of our society youth are asking for a greater voice. To earn this right to speak, involvement in the youth program is a prerequisite. One national youth organization has observed that for everyone involved in the youth program, you may expect ten in the audience.

The youth leader needs to get out of the sanctuary with his teens. He must seek to discover their thought patterns and motivations. Teens want to be involved in the actual program planning.

There seems to be a growing lack of leadership or sponsorship from adults. Pastors are not sufficiently involved in the CA program. They treat it as a satellite and commit it to a changing group of young people not yet mature or to a novice youth pastor. There never comes a time when a pastor can turn an entire youth program to an assistant. He is the key. Involvement with guidance is important.

More than one-third of the "retaining" methods suggested by the audience were related to music. Suggestions ranged from organizing a teen chorale to providing band instruments and free music lessons.

Teen understanding and rapport comes with sharing experiences with them. One pastor said that in order to attract "pagan" teens in the inner-city neighborhood they developed the youth center approach offering sports, group activities, and an evening meal. They reach about sixty teens in the summer and 150 during the winter. It is important to keep a spiritually strong nucleus of Christian teens in this kind of a program. Outsiders can overwhelm them.

Most agreed that in communicating with teens, adults should speak their language but not use their words. Teens like adults to understand their vocabulary, but they resent it when adults use their words. When adults try to adopt a vocabulary not natural to them, they appear phony.

Tell the teen-agers what *you* think about questions that confront them when they come for guidance. They may not agree, but they want it straight.

A personal survey of 13 churches with somewhat ineffectual youth programs revealed the following: In eleven churches there was no budget set up for the youth program and activities; in one church there was no pastor participation; in the thirteenth church there was no CA interest.

One person suggested that to program our CA service into a spot in the fragmented midweek service has proved to be a mistake. Another stated that our youth meetings can be more like clubs than evangelistic arms of the church. We must face it. This is a generation that will turn down our packaged programs unless they prove to be relevant.

Age-grouping and obtaining materials for younger CA's appeared to be a major problem in churches of all sizes. Several suggestions were made by the seminar participants.

One said his church divides the total group into teens, college and career, and married couples. They separate for training in the Sunday school hours but come together for worship in the CA service and in planned recreation.

Another reported that instead of dividing their young people they keep them together, offering a program to meet all ages. The youth leadership, with the pastor's sanction, sets aside some of their regular service hours to go out into the community in witnessing activities.

Still another suggested that by keeping all the youth together, regardless of age, the younger CA's will be encouraged by the older

CA's in such things as public speaking, testifying, etc.

Question: Should Assemblies of God teens be sent to witness to hippie and drug addict groups?

The speaker responded: "No. Some of our Assemblies of God teens are too naive. They require special training to witness to these groups. As a pastor I do not send my CA's out alone to any questionable areas. I go with them."

The problem of retaining the teens we are keeping by these various "holding actions" is of supreme importance. Many programs that are used to attract them only show them Jesus Christ in a one-dimensional lordship. They must see Him in three dimensions: in the Church, in the Word, and in a personal relationship to themselves. More than a textual study of the Word for use in Bible quizzing is necessary. Teens must be introduced to a daily devotional confrontation with Christ through His Word.

TODAY'S EVANGELIST

Speaker: **DONALD M. COX**
Moderator: **ROBERT C. JONES**
Panelists: **E. M. CLARK, LEROY SANDERS SR., C. M. WARD**
Recorder: **MARION RAVAN**

THE BIBLE DOES NOT DEFINE an evangelist. However, from the three references where the word *evangelist* is used, we can arrive at a Bible-based definition.

1. Acts 21:8: "And the next day we that were of Paul's company departed, and came unto Caesarea; and we entered into the house of Philip the evangelist, which was one of the seven; and abode with him." This word properly means "one who announces good news." In the New Testament it is applied to a preacher of the gospel or one who declares the glad tidings of salvation.

2. Ephesians 4:11: "And he gave some, apostles; and some, prophets; and some, evangelists; and some, pastors and teachers." In this verse, we discover that the evangelist is given to the Church as a gift from the ascended Christ. So high and sacred is this office that it is mentioned alongside that of apostle, prophet, pastor, and teacher. Evangelists, however, are classed with apostles and prophets as itinerant workers, in contrast to pastors and teachers who are attached to local assemblies. Eusebius, the earliest Church historian, specifically says that those occupying the first steps in succession from the apostles "set out on journeys from home and performed the work of evangelists and preached to such as had not yet heard the word of faith."

The office of the evangelist must be kept in proper proportion and balance. There is a tendency in some quarters to hold this sacred office in contempt. Others magnify the office out of all proper proportion to the other gifts of the victorious Christ.

On the other hand, we must never minimize the work of the pastor and exalt that of the evangelist. Many consider the evangelist a "glamour gift" to the body of Christ and his ministry to be the greatest of all. Sometimes an evangelist will receive more publicity in a two- or three-week meeting than a pastor does in one year. If it were not for the faithful pastors, however, the evangelist would be unable to carry on his evangelistic work. Ephesians 4:11 teaches that all these gifts come from the same Lord for the mutual blessing of the whole church of God.

3. 2 Timothy 4:5: "But watch thou in all things, endure afflictions, do the work of an evangelist, make full proof of thy ministry." The phrase here means "to do the work of preaching the gospel, or the work of one appointed to proclaim the glad tidings of salvation." The words, "make full proof of thy ministry," have both a nautical and commercial meaning.

Paul was saying, "Spread out all your sails. The ship can use all the canvas she can bear. Let the winds fill them all and let the ship go careening along. Fully discharge your ministry as an evangelist to the utmost of your ability. Make full proof of your ministry by doing everything possible with all your might to win souls for Christ."

The commercial meaning of this phrase is

"give good measure." Make the vessel hold a little more. Fill up to the brim your ministry. Fully discharge all the obligations of your office. I believe the work of an evangelist is physically and spiritually the hardest job on earth.

I. Today's Evangelist Meets the Changing Challenges

Essentially an evangelist needs the same equipment, emphasis, and message as those used throughout history. There are incidental changes in methods from day-to-day, but the message is the same—a Bible message of sin, judgment, the need to be born again, God's love and Christ's atoning death, salvation by faith, and the fullness of the Holy Spirit.

Let us briefly consider change in three areas: (1) the intellectual climate, (2) the Electronic Revolution, and (3) the soil.

It is no secret that our congregations are now more intellectually oriented than they were a few years ago. Apparently this trend will continue. Therefore, to meet the changing challenge of the intellectual climate, our message must have *both* emotional appeal *and* intellectual content.

Sometime ago our world experienced what historians called the Industrial Revolution. The Church met this challenge without changing its message, only its methods. We are now experiencing what some call the Electronic Revolution. Our message must be anchored to the Book, but our methods must keep pace with the times if we are to meet the needs of this generation.

Matthew 13 and Mark 4 record the Parable of the Soils. Only God makes the soil; we cannot change it. Some soil is wayside soil, and Satan takes away the Word as soon as it is sown. Some soil is stony ground that has no depth; and although it receives the Word gladly, it cannot produce anything lasting. Some soil is infested with thorns—the cares of the world, the deceitfulness of riches, and the lust of other things—and these choke the Word. But there is some good ground that produces thirty, sixty, and a hundredfold. Check the soil in which you are sowing.

Paul's methods are recorded in Acts 17:2, 3: "And Paul, as his manner was, went in unto them, and three sabbath days reasoned with them out of the Scriptures, opening and alleging, that Christ must needs have suffered, and risen again from the dead; and that this Jesus, whom I preach unto you, is Christ." The word *opening* means "to open thoroughly, or to open up." The word *alleging* means "to set thoroughly by placing one passage alongside another, by the power of the Spirit." By this manner Paul set forth and quoted passages to prove that Jesus was the Christ, the Anointed of God.

Do not be afraid to preach the Word. There must be substance to your message. An effort is being made by some to discredit the value of preaching in soul winning and revival. Great emphasis is put on personal evangelism. I believe with all my heart in the necessity of man-to-man personal witnessing. But I also know that God has ordained that men shall be saved through the preaching of the gospel.

To meet the challenges of this day we must be careful to preach the gospel in the everyday language of the people. It was said of our Lord that *"the common people heard him gladly"* (Mark 12:37).

II. The Relationship of Today's Evangelist to the Local Church

To fulfill his responsibility to the church, the *first* aim of the evangelist is the salvation of souls. The *second* responsibility of the evangelist is the reproduction of the life of Christ in every convert. The *third* responsibility of the evangelist to the church is to produce witnessing converts.

Pentecost may die out unless we maintain this gospel succession. It is the will of God that through our preaching our own private ministry should be reproduced again and again in the lives of those we win for Christ. Luke puts it this way: "The word of God grew and multiplied" (Acts 12:24).

We will deal with the responsibility of the church to today's evangelist in five separate areas.

A. THE INVITATION

An invitation should be extended for one reason and one reason only. Invite the evangelist because he is the best man you can find to do the job you need done at the time.

B. ACCOMMODATIONS

In order to have an evangelist at his best, he should be given a private room in a reputable hotel or motel. Avoid asking him to stay in a home. The evangelist needs privacy so he can pray and study and rest.

C. COOPERATION

The evangelist is not in competition with the pastor; he is there to help the pastor. Sometimes churches and pastors take the attitude, "Well, you are here. Now let's see what you can do." Cooperation is the first step to revival.

D. CONSIDERATION

The evangelist should be allowed to eat his meals when and where he chooses. Many of the men of God carry such heavy burdens and have been in the work so long that they cannot eat many of the things they are expected to eat.

E. REMUNERATION

The Bible says, "The laborer is worthy of his hire" (Luke 10:7); and, "Thou shalt not muzzle the ox that treadeth out the corn" (1 Timothy 5:18). The evangelist depends upon the churches he serves. His traveling needs, his hotel expense, and his food should be paid for by the church over and above the love offering. Today's evangelist has many needs and expenses that the average Christian has never thought of, and the church should do everything within its power to give a generous offering to the evangelist.

Some pastors feel envious of an evangelist for securing a love offering which may amount to more than the pastor's weekly salary. Sometimes pastors, by their stingy attitude toward the evangelist, teach their people to be the same. Remember, Jesus said it is more blessed to give than to receive. He also said, "Give, and it shall be given unto you; good measure, pressed down, and shaken together, and running over, shall men give into your bosom. For with the same measure that ye mete withal it shall be measured to you again" (Luke 6:38).

Some things to remember in the matter of remunerating the evangelist are:

1. His travel expense in coming to you should be cared for by the church.

2. Any time the evangelist takes off during the year to be with his family, such as at Christmas, he will be without income.

3. Any cancellations of meetings during the year leave him without a schedule. If the church has to cancel after confirming a date, the church should pay the evangelist normal salary.

4. His operating expenses are usually greater than those of the pastor because of the nature of his ministry.

5. God's people usually want to give to an evangelist, and they respect their pastor for honoring the needs of God-called evangelists.

6. Remember, dear fellow-pastors, jealousy on our parts of the income or popularity of an evangelist is usually detected by the people.

7. Prayerfully put yourself in his shoes and ask yourself, "How would I like to be treated if I were an evangelist?"

Panel Discussion and Open Forum

Panelist's Question: Isn't it time the Assemblies of God considered setting a minimum salary for evangelists with fringe benefits?

Suggested guidelines from the General Superintendent's office or the Spiritual Life—Evangelism Commission might include expenses that would be similar to the pastor's remuneration for (1) salary, (2) insurance, (3) retirement, (4) travel and entertainment.

The speaker doubted that the answer is a guaranteed salary. A minimum might become a maximum. Perhaps the pastor could see that a visiting evangelist gets 25 percent more than the pastor's own salary. Thus the small church would not be embarrassed while the larger churches could help pick up the load.

A panelist noted that an evangelist must get twice as much as the pastor to exist on the field. The evangelist usually has an eleven-week vacancy in his schedule.

Another panelist declared that he had no faith in a professional evangelist. The evangelist cannot be manufactured. We cannot have the Bible pattern if we continue to regulate and try to make evangelists professional salesmen. The Pentecostal evangelist must have freedom. If everything is regulated—underwritten—you lose freedom. He suggested that evangelists have faith for finances just as they have faith to heal people.

Question: What can be done to finance a revival in a smaller church?

The smaller church can build an evangelistic fund in advance. A percentage of the budget of the larger churches could go into an evangelistic fund for smaller churches.

Question: What is the responsibility of the evangelist?

Encourage, first of all, a sincere involvement of the church people in the evangelistic meetings. It would be worthwhile to bring the evangelist in a week early and pay him a salary to organize, inspire, and involve all areas of the church—choir, teens, workers, etc.

Stop emptying the platform! Keep everyone

on that platform to back up the evangelist. This includes the choir.

The evangelist's responsibility does not end with preaching the message. He must stay in the altar until the last man and woman have touched God. Altar workers can help in this vital personal work at the altar. Battles are fought and won at the altar.

Prepare for evangelistic campaigns in advance. Plan, advertise, involve, build up the evangelist as God's man. Go calling. Build expectancy that God is going to do something in the lives of everyone.

Precrusade planning might involve the following:

1. Encourage the church to undergird the meeting by prayer. Build a prayer band. Come to pray fifteen minutes before every service.

2. Enlist the church to assist the evangelist during the services. Have cards listing responsibilities.

3. Organize a telephone brigade to share the blessing of God with the community.

4. Capitalize on the little people—*children* are the key to attendance interest. Mothers and fathers go out with their children.

Question: What is the ideal relationship between an evangelist and the pastor?

We must recognize that the pastor and all the people should do the work of an evangelist. You can't win a sinner by worship. The gospel is the power of God. Pastor, study the doctrine of salvation and preach salvation. Preach the gospel, give an altar call, and stop the entertainment.

1. The pastor can ask for a testimony and then say, "How many are saved? Lift your hand." Look around and see how many are unsaved.

2. People in the pew can invite those near them to go to the altar.

There should be an understanding between the pastor and the evangelist on what the priorities are. The pastor and evangelist are workers together. They should plan every phase of the meeting—altar workers, choir, Sunday school workers, musicians, ushers—that the outsiders might realize the church means business.

Today there seems to be a conflict between the evangelist and the theologian. This should not be so. The evangelist should study theology.

He should also seek for answers to present-day morality problems. There are many troubled consciences in audiences! Young people are asking, "If Dad was wrong about some things (customs), can't he be wrong about others?"

Question: Why is it so hard for an evangelist to get meetings?

The first three years on the field are an investment. The pastors must get to know an evangelist and his ministry. The beginning evangelist must start somewhere. A new man can share his ministry with the smaller church. God can do big things in little places.

If the pastor and board have a burden for a nearby small church, they could stretch their own church budget and send an evangelist to help the small church.

The evangelist could take the offering during the week for the church budget. He is the man with a burden for the meetings. The pastor can then take up the evangelist's offering on Sunday morning. As the shepherd, he loves the people and is concerned for the church. The people will respond to him.

Conclusion: The pastor, church, and evangelist should share liberally and believe God to meet all their needs.

WHAT MAKES A CHURCH GROW?

Speaker: **MURRAY McLEES**
Moderator: **HUGH ROSENBERG**
Panelists: **THOMAS MING JR., NELSON SACHS, JAMES SWANSON**
Recorder: **PAUL FENTON**

I MIGHT INTRODUCE this subject by simply saying that on Easter past we had an aggregate attendance of 4,500 in four services at First Assembly of God in Eugene, Oregon, with seventy decisions for Christ.

I. What Is Church Growth?

In my opinion church growth is that life-producing principle which God has placed in His church. This life-producing principle must be nourished by good stewardship.

Good stewardship involves several things; among them spiritual thrust and promotional push.

A. SPIRITUAL THRUST

Our spiritual thrust comes from the great statements of the Word. For instance, "I know whom I have believed, and am persuaded that he is able to keep that which I have committed unto him against that day" (2 Timothy 1:12). There are three things involved in this statement —Christian knowledge, Christian persuasion, and Christian commitment.

1. *Christian knowledge.* I know from having been born again, from being filled with the Spirit, from being used in the gifts of the Spirit, from being called of God to preach the Word, from being healed, from personal experiences that Jesus Christ lives and is the resurrected Head of the Church.

2. *Christian persuasion.* Because we have Christian knowledge, we are persuaded. We have come to know Him. His declaration is that He is the way, the truth, and the life. And because we are persuaded, we become persuasive.

3. *Christian commitment.* Since I know whom I have believed, and I am persuaded that He is able to keep that which I have committed unto Him against that day, Christian commitment becomes my position. Many things interest me. One thing *concerns* me, and that is *"that day."* How will I stand? How will those with whom I have to do stand? Because I know and because I am persuaded, I am committed to reaching for Jesus those that come within my particular field of service.

The Book of Acts may be outlined by its record of growth. "Praising God, and having favor with all the people. And the Lord added to the church daily such as should be saved" (Acts 2: 47). "And believers were the more added to the Lord, multitudes both of men and women" (Acts 5:14). "And the word of God increased; and the number of the disciples multiplied in Jerusalem greatly; and a great company of the priests were obedient to the faith" (Acts 6:7). "Then had the churches rest throughout all Judea and Galilee and Samaria, and were edified; and walking in the fear of the Lord, and in the comfort of the Holy Ghost, were multiplied" (Acts 9:31). "But the word of God grew and multiplied" (Acts 12:

24). "And so were the churches established in the faith, and increased in number daily" (Acts 16:5). "So mightily grew the word of God and prevailed" (Acts 19:20).

These Scripture references are notations of increase of numbers or in quality of spiritual life. Some people say they do not concern themselves with numbers. Let me simply say that behind every number is a face, and behind every face is a soul for whom Jesus died. The Lord was concerned about numbers. He permitted one of the books of the Bible to be named Numbers. Thousands are recorded in the Book of Acts finding Jesus as their personal Saviour. To me this is the platform for the *spiritual thrust*.

B. PROMOTIONAL PUSH

The Bible says that David served his generation, and I think we could imply from this that we must serve ours. We are living in a changing world. The methods and techniques which reach one part of the world do not work in another. The message and the dedication may be the same, but the methods do differ. And since we are Americans living in American culture, we must take into consideration that the American culture is the most rapidly changing in the world.

Since 1900 there have been tremendous changes in transportation, communication, and industrialization. As a result of these rapid changes, families have become smaller, juvenile delinquency has increased, and crime has increased. So now we have a new set of problems. But in 1900 God had the answer—as He has always had the answer. At the turn of the century the Pentecostal power fell, and the Great Commission was again emphasized, "Go ye into all the world, and preach the gospel to every creature."

Since we are living in the American culture, what is the best way to preach the gospel to every creature? Well, what have the American people accepted as their values? *Life* magazine carried an article which pointed out that the top 100 men making major decisions for the United States are all businessmen. In other words, we have accepted the American businessman's set of values. These values are free enterprise, hard work, punctuality, neatness, loyalty, individualism, and practical realism.

If these are the values, then we must, wherever possible, flow with them to reach lost souls. A restaurant may have the very best food, but unless people know of it, that restaurant won't move much of its product. Therefore, the restaurant must promote through hard work, punctuality, neatness, loyalty, individualism, practical realism, free enterprise. The same is true with the church. In the American culture we must recognize cultural trends and take advantage of promotion as does the business world. We must become "promoters with God."

II. Why Should a Church Grow?

Church growth is to fulfill the Great Commission. Matthew 28:19, 20 says, "Go ye therefore, and teach all nations, baptizing them in the name of the Father, and of the Son, and of the Holy Ghost: teaching them to observe all things whatsoever I have commanded you: and, lo, I am with you alway, even unto the end of the world." You see, everyone must be reached and taught.

I have always believed that we are not only to be soul winners but we are to be soul developers. It is not an either-or proposition, but it is both-and. We are to reach and teach.

III. What of Church Growth?

Church growth employs the talents of everyone. In the Parable of Talents it is remarkable that the man who had one talent should hide it. There are usually many more one-talented people; and if we can get that one man with that one talent to work, we get about ninety-five percent of the church involved. Wherever there is church growth, there is involvement. Church growth compounds the energy and vision of everyone.

IV. How to Achieve Church Growth

First of all, we establish our purposes, and in establishing our purposes we must be able to justify our program.

As stewards—and a steward is a man over another's household—we are told: "Let a man so account of us, as of the ministers of Christ, and stewards of the mysteries of God" (1 Corinthians 4:1). A steward was one who had charge of his master's affairs—and could use them to his own advantage if he chose. Yet Luke 12:42 reminded him that there comes an hour when he will give an account of his stewardship. In the light of this we must set our objectives.

When you set your objectives in any program for church growth, they must first of all be spiritual objectives. As long as men and women are being saved and your church is on the move, you don't have any great problems—at least problems that cannot easily be solved. Goals such as people receiving the Baptism, individual classes being grounded in the Word of God, training programs for leaders—all of these are part of your objectives and these must be spiritual.

You must also have objectives so far as service is concerned. What do you plan to do for missions? What is happening in your tithing program?

We moved from thirty percent of our congregation as practicing tithers to eighty percent tithers this year, and our giving has gained thousands of dollars every month.

We should have goals for witnessing. I am now attempting to train about fifty couples to be personal soul winners. Our motto is, "Stop trying to win everyone, and win *someone.*"

These are objectives which fulfill our purpose, and our purpose is to serve as stewards over His household.

Once we have established purposes and set objectives, we prepare a program of implementation. This program of implementation involves spiritual exercise. For instance, participation in the stewardship program alone has revolutionized our church.

When you start promoting, you will have opposition. It doesn't make any difference what kind of promotional work you do, there will be people who say, "We haven't got the money"—in other words, the economical resister. There will be people who say, "We can't see the need"—the ignorant people. There are always those who say, "We have done it this way and don't want to change"—that group bogged down in social inertia and who fear the new promotional ideas, especially if they think the new impinges on the mores and customs of bygone days. There are those who reverence the past. They have always had little classes, and they want to continue with them. Then there is the vested interested group—the individual who has held a certain job for a long time.

Remember that the new sounds cold. You will have forces that oppose change; therefore, you have to keep warm, emotional-sounding symbols for the job assignments. When you have to make a change, you must brag nine-tenths of the time on the old ways and one-tenth on the new idea.

One year we decided to take our Sunday school staff, add music, and present the Easter story in drama. We knew that there would be those that would oppose this, so we looked for a scriptural statement that would strengthen and support what we felt to be necessary to reach our generation—a changing culture.

We selected a pageant. It was edited and rewritten by my assistant pastor and Mrs. McLees, and it has been changed over the nine years we have been producing it, but the same essential story is there. This pageant involves the entire Sunday school staff as far as is practical.

We start rehearsals seven weeks in advance. This employs all the talents and abilities of the various people through its production. We advertise on TV, newspaper, lawn signs, bumper stickers, and so forth.

When the crowds come, we use hand counters and tickets, so that we had 4,500 signed tickets telling us whether the person attended church or not. At the conclusion of each one of these productions I preach for fifteen minutes and give an altar call. The results: seventy decisions for Christ were made this year on Easter.

We followed up these contacts with visitation. The visitation, of course, is routine and weekly.

Let me add this. To reach the culture and generation we are in, we are now using a church data processing system which employs the computer. We have complete records on about 1,100 people, and through the computer can look them all over in about a half hour each Wednesday. Assignments are given out to those who do the visitation. The computer tells us two weeks in advance what child is having a birthday and a whole host of other information.

Again let me state, "Church growth does not lend itself to an 'either-or' philosophy, but fits rather the proposition, 'both-and.'" Through this philosophy First Assembly in Eugene has tripled in ten years.

Panel Discussion and Open Forum

This part of the seminar consisted largely of questions to the speaker and panelists.

Question: How do you get an average-size (150) church moving?

Consider what you have (evaluation); find your potential; establish leadership; get everyone working (personal witness); set goals; communicate from the pulpit to the individual; utilize promotion opportunities; let nothing deter; find God's purpose, His will, and His way; change from a come-church to a go-church by winning people on the streets or wherever they are and bringing them into the church.

Question: What about the use of contests?

They are all right if they accomplish the purpose. However, their use should be limited.

Question: Is too much effort being expended in perpetuating the institution? How about making homes more a center of witness?

One opinion was that this should be done. Another pastor reported that they have the Sunday evening service at 6 p.m. Afterward the people who have brought friends with them to the service take them out for refreshments and discuss the service and spiritual matters.

Question: Some people drive past several Assemblies of God churches to get to another Assemblies of God church. Should we encourage people to work in an assembly in the area where they live?

Churches have personalities. People will go where they want to go. Ministers must talk freely when members go from one church to another. Thus they need to have a clear understanding, develop a good working relationship, and maintain friendship.

Question: Does the pastor have to be a different person today?

He must be a strong overseer-leader, out front in ideas and planning.

Question: What about growth in a small church; how is it achieved?

A pastor said that to break the status quo he began to pray. Then he went door-to-door downtown and got acquainted with the businessmen.

Another pastor said he visited the home of each new baby, each newcomer, and all newlyweds.

Question: How do church buildings relate to growth?

The building is a tool which can help growth. The building should lend itself to the dignity of worship. We should build with soul saving in mind. Use of subdued colors contributes to correct attitude and ease of discipline. The building should complement the area where it is located.

Question: How do you get on TV?

The speaker noted that they couldn't buy time, so they made it a matter of prayer. The Lord helped them win the owner of a station to Christ. Then he invited them to have a telecast on his station.

WITNESSING IN PRINT

Speaker: **NORMAN CORRELL**
Moderator: **LOREN TRIPLETT**
Panelists: **B. HAROLD CONANT, FRED LESSTEN, DAVID WOMACK**
Recorder: **MRS. HARRY BROTZMAN**

IN SOLEMN TRUTH I TELL YOU, anyone believing in Me shall do the same miracles I have done, and even greater" (John 14:12, *Living Gospels*).

Is there a man alive who would claim to have reproduced—much less improved upon—the miraculous works accomplished by Jesus Christ while on earth? Yet Jesus Christ said with emphasis that future men would do "the same" works and "even greater ones."

I believe Jesus had in mind quantity of works rather than quality. Perhaps even as He spoke He was looking omnisciently to our own age with its phenomenal technological advances in the processes and methods of communication. If He was, His penetrating glance could not miss the tremendous potential of propagating His message by the printed page.

We have at our disposal today one of the most effective means of spreading the gospel that the world has ever known. The printed page goes where the living voice cannot go. The printed page is often more permanent in its influence than the living voice.

Martin Luther used the printing press to make the Reformation permanent. No wonder the monks said, "If we do not put down the printing press, it will put us down." We fervently hope that this statement epitomizes Satan's sentiments today as he sees the message of Jesus Christ, in printed form, scattered throughout the world.

I. On the Foreign Field

Opportunities to witness in print have never been greater than they are today. The winds of change are sweeping our world. We are fast approaching the end of the colonial era. There are at least thirty new nations with more than 750 million people living in them. Most of these, plus countless millions from older, yet underdeveloped nations, are now beginning to emerge from the long, dark night of illiteracy. Frank C. Laubach, in his book *Literacy as Evangelism*, states that 150 million people have learned to read in the last thirty years and that ten million more are joining these ranks every year.

Missionaries from all over the world tell of the overwhelming demand for literature. There is a reason for this. People have hungry hearts and minds. And this includes the majority who have yet to break the literacy barrier. The danger is that they are indiscriminate in what they read. They eagerly read the literature the Communists give them.

Someone has estimated that the Communists have spent $3.4 billion for literature—enough for four pieces for every person in the world. Seventy percent of all the literature in India comes from Communist presses. The grandson of the late Mahatma Ghandi said, "The Christian missionaries taught us how to read, but the

159

Communists gave us the books." False cults are also busily engaged in literature distribution.

But we are not idle! The Assemblies of God has nineteen major printing complexes placed in strategic locations throughout the world. We are printing literature in more than one hundred languages. The Christ's Ambassadors, through their Speed-the-Light program, have invested funds totaling $477,286.96 to provide these foreign printing plants with the finest equipment available.

Assemblies of God men have played an important role by providing funds for evangelism literature, through Light-for-the-Lost. Since this program began in 1959, a total of over $200,000 has been given. This has been used in its entirety for literature.

The Boys and Girls Missionary Crusade (BGMC) has also made a vital contribution in providing over two million dollars since its inception in 1949 for Sunday school and Bible school training materials.

A wide variety of conventional methods are very effective on most mission fields today. By all means they should be continued and even accelerated. These include mass literature distribution in rural and city markets, in hospitals, in prisons, in public gatherings such as political or sporting events, and distribution of Bibles and literature by colporteurs.

1. *Witnessing with printed Scriptures.* In 1804 when the Bible Societies movement began, the Scriptures existed in only seventy-two languages of the world. And then in one century, more than four hundred tribes of people received some part of the Scriptures. In the first half of this century, five hundred more languages were added until now the Scriptures exist, at least in part, in 1,326 languages throughout the world. The task is not complete, but it is encouraging to know that the Scriptures already are available for well over 95 percent of the earth's peoples.

2. *House-to-house witness and literature distribution.* Such an effort, well-organized and strategically planned, conducted by trained nationals, and with a systematic follow-up plan will reap a great harvest. In one area in Nigeria such an endeavor, combined with an evangelistic campaign, reaped 12,000 decisions. An additional 4,000 decisions were made in follow-up canvassing.

3. *Newsstands and bookstores.* Dr. Clyde Taylor said, "In every mission field of the earth, you will find not only American pornog-

raphy, but national pornography. Let's get gospel literature in newsstands and bookstores sufficiently attractive to compete with the devil's corruption."

4. *Witnessing in print on campuses.* While we are saying that something should be done to prepare and sow the world's campuses with literature, the Communists are doing it.

5. *Bible correspondence courses.* Here is one of the greatest potentials. A North African mission in Tunisia reported forty converts in fourteen years. In desperation they switched to Bible correspondence courses. In twenty-one months they mailed out 17,784 courses, had 1,027 completed courses, and recorded 675 decisions for Christ.

The International Correspondence Institute (ICI) is currently being developed under the auspices of our Foreign Missions Department. This school will doubtless revolutionize this area of opportunity for the Assemblies of God.

6. *Witnessing by newspaper.* In some countries, like Greece, where there is a lack of freedom to propagate the gospel in public, gospel messages may be published in the newspapers and magazines as paid advertisements. This has, according to report, proved very effective. It has been estimated that in some cases one dollar's worth of advertising reaches up to fifty thousand people.

7. *Ambassadors in Mission (AIM).* Each summer teams of carefully selected and oriented youth from the U.S. spend a month overseas teamed with national CA's in a witness and literature distribution endeavor. In 1967, 1,610 decisions in five countries were recorded. The literature centers in salvation, an extensive follow-up system for converts, and a home study course consisting of six lessons. "Spiritual sponsors" from the national church are recruited and trained to continue the follow-up contacts after the AIM teams depart. One of the main objectives is to inspire and set a pattern for the national church to follow on a year-round basis.

II. In the United States

It is incredible that there is such a great demand for reading material in a country that has had so much literature for so long. It seems that affluent Americans have an insatiable appetite for something *more* to read. Obviously a tremendous spiritual vacuum exists in the minds and hearts of people in our own land. Americans may not be as receptive as those in other lands, but the need and opportunity is everywhere about us. Before dealing with specific opportunities there are two factors that we should consider.

First, there is a spirit of involvement that is beginning to grip many of our Assemblies of God people as well as other evangelicals. People who really love the Lord want to be specifically involved in the mainstream of Christian service these days. This is the same spirit that made the Early Church such a fruitful success.

Second, when we talk about witnessing in print, we should remember that giving literature is no substitute for the person-to-person transmission of the gospel. It is an "arrow in the quiver," so to speak. Witnessing and literature go hand in hand whenever possible.

A few choice places and opportunities for literature distribution are professional offices, bus stations, air terminals, halloween trick-or-treat bags, and "tip" tracts for restaurants. Now let us take a closer look at other opportunities.

1. *Witnessing by mail.* One has only to read the daily newspaper to realize the many opportunities of witness. Appropriate literature plus a personal note to someone injured in an accident, someone in bereavement, someone in trouble with the law might be just the right message at the right time. How about sending a congratulatory or commendatory note together with a carefully selected tract or Scripture portion to someone in your community who has excelled or achieved high honors? Why not send the servicemen listed in the paper a New Testament and a copy of *Reveille?*

2. *House-to-house witnessing.* This broad opportunity falls into three categories: (a) literature saturation, (b) religious census, and (c) team witness. I would like to elaborate on the last, for it represents one of the greatest of all methods and without a doubt is the most scriptural.

Acts 5:42, speaking of witnessing by the Early Church says, "And daily in the temple, *and in every house,* they ceased not to teach and preach Jesus Christ." In Acts 20:20, Paul reminded the Ephesians that he had taught them publicly "and from house to house." If you want results, do not wait for people to come to you—*go to the people!*

It is most encouraging and exciting to hear reports from increasing numbers of churches, districts, and even regions that have converged on a specific area, city, reservation, or other "target" for a concerted house-to-house quest

for souls. Youth and adults in evangelism, this is the answer!

3. *Person-to-person witnessing.* Others are using literature to witness. Are you?

Because of the great evangelistic potential of the printed page, the Assemblies of God has launched an Evangelism Literature for America (ELA) program. Briefly stated, its goals are: (a) to develop and provide suitable literature for evangelism, (b) to promote evangelism literature distribution energetically throughout the Assemblies of God, and (c) to make evangelism literature available as reasonably as possible. During ELA's first year (1967), a total of $6,230.60 was received from interested churches and individuals. These contributions made it possible to distribute 214,675 pieces of evangelism literature in various parts of the United States.

An urgent need faces ELA now. The requests for assistance have far outdistanced the limited resources. Let us demonstrate our interest in providing evangelism literature for America. It is suggested that our churches write ELA into their budgets. This, plus contributions from interested friends, will meet a great need.

It would be well to consider briefly some other factors in literature evangelism. First, we must realize that literature is a highly competitive field. Modern techniques have made it so. Therefore, our literature must be of the highest quality in both paper and format.

Second, we must carefully consider content. Fortunately, we have the opportunity to translate the gospel into contemporary language. Unfortunately, too often we use a kind of evangelical dialect that is meaningless to most unconverted people. As one outstanding evangelical put it, "So far as most people are concerned, most of our terminology is just Protestant Latin." We need to rediscover the meaning of the Word in today's world by communicating the gospel in language people clearly understand.

Finally, with all the planning, organizing, training of workers, and with the finest literature —what is all this without the Holy Spirit's power and anointing? It is only by His enduement that God can use our efforts to reach a lost world. The involved Christian must possess, by virtue of Christ's indwelling presence, the power not only to live triumphantly, but also to witness effectively. God is ready to fulfill His promise of power, victory, and triumph. He offers His resources to those dedicated to the task of witnessing.

Panel Discussion and Open Forum

The discussion revealed the following needs:

1. A literature piece applicable to the young couple—especially the housewife.

2. A simple home Bible study course. Make known the one available from AIM—the "Living Word Home Bible Course."

3. Literature pieces that can be identified with the local situation, such as photos of historical landmarks, prominent buildings, etc.

Buzz sessions produced the following:

1. Suggestions for developing a plan of action for the local church to take full advantage of literature evangelism:

a. There seems to be a lack of knowledge concerning what literature is available. More publicity is needed on various soul-winning plans.

b. Use "Living Word Home Bible Course" as a free offer over the radio. Use phone solicitation to give home Bible study course.

c. Set up a booth at fair and other public places for literature distribution.

d. Tract gadget ideas: (1) Kleenex pack with gospel insert to give to hospital patients;
(2) breast-pocket handkerchiefs for men with tract or card with church announcements attached.

2. Because home Bible study or correspondence courses have effectively helped thousands in foreign countries, it was felt that these can also be used effectively in the U.S.

3. Ideas to produce and encourage Christian writers:

a. Conduct essay contests with prizes.

b. Have classes on Christian writing in youth camps and CA's.

c. Include books about writing in the church library.

d. Feature biographies and articles about writers—how they started writing, etc.

e. Conduct writers conferences at General Council and/or regional seminars.

f. Encourage ministers to write down their ideas—many of them don't put them on paper and they throw away their sermon notes.

g. Local church bulletins and church newspapers should encourage people to write testimonies and other articles and then print them.

h. Ministers seminars should have sessions on writing.

THE WORTH OF A BOY

Speaker: **EUGENE MEADOR**
Moderator: **LEON MILES**
Panelists: **JOHN ELLER, HERBERT ELLINGWOOD, JACK KUYKENDAL**
Recorder: **JOHNNIE BARNES**

Tomorrow's world will soon be in the hands of the boys of today. No longer can we assume that it will be a Christian world because other forces are striving to win our boys.

For years the church has been prone to neglect its boys. We need to be aroused to action by Christ's words, "Even so it is not the will of your Father which is in heaven, that one of these little ones should perish" (Matthew 18:14).

Not perish! These words are a ringing challenge to a world where life is cheap and where children are perishing, both physically and spiritually.

Winning boys to Christ is not incidental in the program of the church; it should be the church's greatest imperative. Instead of leaving it to the few who have a natural knack for dealing with boys, we should train many more workers who can, and will, devote their time to winning boys for Christ. When a boy is saved, not only the soul is committed to God but a life for service as well. All that we hold dear in our Pentecostal ranks will be conserved or endangered according to the kind of men the boys of today become.

A beautiful picture of the value that Moses placed upon the "little ones" of Israel is found in Exodus 10: "So Moses and Aaron were brought again to Pharaoh; and he said to them, Go, serve the Lord your God; but just who are to go? And Moses said, We will go with our young and our old, with our sons and our daughters, with our flocks and our herds (all of us and all we have); for we must hold a feast to the Lord. Pharaoh said to them, Let the Lord be with you, if I ever let you go with your little ones! See, you have some evil purpose in mind. Not so! You that are men (without your families) go and serve the Lord, for that is what you want. And Moses and Aaron were driven from Pharaoh's presence" (Exodus 10:8-11, Amplified).

Pharaoh's demand that Israel leave their "little ones" behind in Egypt while the men held a feast unto the Lord is similar to the cunning devices of the devil in our generation. The devil causes worldly men to say, "Why should we trouble children with religion? They are too young yet. They cannot understand; they can take no pleasure in it. At their age it becomes them to play. Let them enjoy their diversions."

Thus the prince of this world, the great Pharaoh of the darkness of this world, would wish to keep our children as hostages. If your house were on fire, what would you think of a person who should say to your father, "Go out as quickly as you can, but leave your children in bed"?

The Assemblies of God needs its sons if it is to keep alive the flame of Pentecostal fire and preserve our heritage.

The life of one boy dedicated to God is of unlimited value to the kingdom of God.

Juvenile delinquency sets an all-time high every year. Satan is bidding an enormous price for the lives of boys. There is a teeming mass of boys around the world who desperately need Jesus Christ.

Without pleading or coaxing, our children come to our altars. A child's heart is so tender, his faith so spontaneous. If we get our children saved, later on we will not be wringing our hands because we have no Christian young people.

Let no mistake be made. The child must be won to Christ or the child will be lost. We have a great responsibility before God in bringing up our children in the nurture and admonition of the Lord.

Moses said to Israel, "Thou shalt love the Lord thy God with all thine heart, and with all thy soul, and with all thy might. And these words, which I command thee this day, shall be in thine heart: and thou shalt teach them diligently unto thy children, and shall talk of them when thou sittest in thine house, and when thou walkest by the way" (Deuteronomy 6:5-7).

Those boys in our churches are perishable. We dare not switch them off the track by carelessness or dullness or severity.

All children grow; but the child whose church guides his development mentally, physically, morally, and spiritually will have a richer life than the one whose training is neglected.

The most fertile and productive field of evangelism open to the twentieth century church is the field of winning boys to Christ. With eighty-five percent of all male conversions recorded before boys reach their fifteenth birthday, it is imperative that every church be made aware of the needs of boys and that each church cultivate a sincere desire to capture boys for the Saviour.

The boy comes without knowledge of God. He must be taught by the church. We must continue to provide for his training and spiritual welfare through every avenue open to us. The Sunday school, VBS, Royal Rangers, boys and girls camps, children's church, and children's revivals are just a few of the ways by which our boys will increase in favor with God and man.

The boy comes without commitments. He must be loved.

Those who would win boys to Christ must first of all love them and evoke their response of love. It is not enough to be concerned for boys who are near and dear to us. The true lover of boys will want for every child what he desires for his own children. Even though the children

of the church are all safe in the fold, how can we be satisfied when beyond the walls of our church are countless little ones whom Christ loves and for whom He died—and they have never heard His name?

In the boys nearby are untold possibilities. Not only is the soul of a child of inestimable worth, but each young life also presents a maximum of years that can be dedicated to the Master's service. What more opportune field could be offered to any church than the pliable minds, open hearts, and ready potential in boys.

Are we concerned for men only in our search for souls, or do we care for the boy as well? We may not admit it with our lips, but our actions often show that we count them as being of lesser value. Our emphasis on boys, or lack of it, indicates whether or not we honestly think the conversion of boys is important.

The attitudes of Jesus and of His disciples toward children were in open contrast. Matthew, Mark, and Luke all relate an important incident which illustrates this difference. When parents brought their children to Jesus for His blessing, the disciples openly rebuked them saying that He had no time for children.

Greater than the disciples' displeasure with those who brought the children was that of our Lord when He found out what they had done. He was highly indignant and said, "Suffer the little children to come unto me, and forbid them not; for of such is the kingdom of God" (Mark 10:14).

We stand in need of a crusade to win boys. This crusade should bring to its cause all the resources of the church, of human concern, and of divine power. To such a crusade let us commit ourselves with unswerving zeal and determination.

Panel Discussion and Open Forum

The key to winning boys lies in the hands of the pastor. A pastor must emphasize this need from his pulpit, and also become involved in activities that put him in personal contact with his boys. A camp-out with boys may have far more effect on them than what is said in sermons.

The Royal Rangers program is an ideal way of winning boys outside the church and a successful way of building the Sunday school.

Men must be shown the need and potential of winning boys so they will become involved in these outreaches. The best way to do this is through personal contact and by exposing men to activities that contribute to winning boys.

A recent national study on juvenile delinquency revealed that boys must have some man who will show them real interest and concern in order for them to adjust to today's society. The Royal Rangers program is a tailormade plan we can use to reach boys and to prepare them to face today's world. Royal Rangers is a preventive program designed to *conserve*, rather than *salvage*, our boys.

We must begin to teach boys at an early age more about what our church believes. The strong indoctrination emphasis of Royal Rangers will help meet this need. Because boys must be taught Christian principles and also be given practical outlets to express these principles, the Royal Rangers program is making an important contribution in the development of boys.

Men need training in the techniques of reaching boys. The Royal Rangers Leadership Training Course will train them for this ministry.

EVENING SEMINARS

BRIDGING THE GENERATION GAP

Speaker: **RAYMOND BROCK**
Moderator: **ROBERT WAY**
Panelists: **RICHARD BISHOP, KENNETH MAYTON, ERNEST MOEN**
Recorder: **WILLIAM HANAWALT SR.**

THE GENERATION GAP IS NOT NEW. Archaeological findings dated from the time of Abraham and Sarah predict, "The world is going to the dogs." That was four thousand years ago. In a recent commencement address Francis H. Horn of the university systems of New York said, "The generation gap has always existed but certainly not until our time has it been so apparent and its manifestations so widespread."

But the generation gap does not *have* to exist. A recent study by Vern L. Bengston at the University of Southern California found that 80 percent of the students felt no generation gap existed between them and their families, even though a gap did exist in the world at large.

I. The Gap

Why does a gap exist? I polled some of our young people across the nation to get their viewpoints. Their responses fall into four general areas.

1. "*A gap exists between people of any age who have stopped learning.*" We must keep up-to-date with technological changes, no matter what our age or where we live.

2. "*Too many people live in the past and thrive on its memories.*" Experiences that tie us to the past sever our relations with the present. The expression, "You can't trust anyone over thirty," has arisen because of this temptation.

3. "*We young people think for ourselves, but our elders are content to adhere to the ideas of others.*" Older folk are prone to assume that only age brings experience, forgetting that younger folk can be just as informed through study, travel, and the marvels of the mass media.

4. "*We young people want reasons, not rules.*" That is why some young people change so completely when they are away from the rules of home. The ideas which have been presented to them at home have been more in the form of ideals than a workable way of life.

In light of these observations, what can we do to bridge the generation gap?

II. The Tool

The primary tool at our disposal is *communication*. A cleavage develops when open communication fails to exist between two people, two groups of people, or two generations.

Three questions must be considered when communication is related to the generation gap.

1. *Do you understand yourself?* We can never understand others until we understand ourselves. When we do not understand ourselves, we project our errors into our attitudes toward others.

2. *Have you made yourself understood?* Self-understanding is not enough. We must make ourselves clearly understood. Have we presented ourselves in such a way that others, from their frame of reference with their unique set of experiences, can comprehend us? We must be sure

168

we are using the same meanings for the same words in the same emotional setting if we are to communicate. Otherwise, the gap broadens.

3. *Are you understandable?* What we have said must be clearly understandable, coherent, and meaningful. If the message is not intelligible, no matter how fervently we proclaim it, it will never get through. Enthusiasm, honesty, and devotion are not enough, even in communicating spiritual values.

These rules apply to both sides of the generation gap. That is why it is important to listen as well as to speak; that is why we must make sure we are speaking a common language with our youth.

III. The Home

It does no violence to Scripture to personalize Mark 8:36: "For what shall it profit a man, if he shall gain the whole world, and lose his own household?" If the generation gap continues, it can only result in the loss of young people to the cause of Christ. Experienced parents have discovered several attitudes essential to communicating Christ in the Christian home.

1. *Maintain a consistent example.* A child's first concept of God is much like that of his own father, clothed in security and safety. Gradually his concept broadens to reveal God as a sovereign Heavenly Father. If his concept does not mature, he will face desperate spiritual struggles as a youth. Parents must set before their children a positive example of Christian consistency.

2. *Respect individual value systems.* Each child must establish his own value system. One teen-ager expressed the feelings of his group this way: "We don't really have a faith of our own. We have taken what our parents believe and connected on to it. I guess you could call ours a 'connected experience.' " But "connected experiences" are not enough. Each child must have a vital, personal experience with Christ.

In the words of Walter H. Clark, each person must reach the level of "comprehensive integration" if his Christian faith is to become a way of life. When he does, Christ so permeates every segment of life that he says with Paul, "I live, yet not I, but Christ liveth in me" (Galatians 2: 20). A child doesn't inherit it; we can't give it to him. He must find it for himself through study, experience, and individual commitment to the values that constitute a philosophy of life.

If a value system is to be workable at any age it must be, in the words of James C. Coleman, a system marked by "integration and faith,"

a system framed in "realism and flexibility" and a system that has "personal meaning and satisfaction." The meaningfulness of such a value system is not marked by complacency. The Christian way of life is essentially being right with God, right with yourself, and right with your fellowman. What greater incentive could there be for creative involvement with the generation in which we live?

3. *Provide moral support.* We must never forget the frustrations and anxieties of our own adolescence if we are to be able to communicate with our young people as they experience the normal changes of growing up.

Youth is a perplexing time. It is a growing time, a doubting time. When questions in the classroom and community put religious concepts to the test, we must be equipped with answers. Patiently and prayerfully we must be close at hand as each young person works his way through his questionings: the existence of God, purported conflicts between science and the Bible, the dilemmas of philosophy, psychology, and sociology. At this time parents must keep their hands off and maintain faith in the Word they have planted in young hearts during the formative years.

A caution seems warranted here. A girl does not want her mother for a sister. Neither does a boy want his father for a pal. According to *Life* magazine (May 17, 1968), the younger generation also resents adults—even relatives—who experiment with their practices and frequent their clandestine hangouts. We must learn to stay in our own place and be available and reassuring, but not try to change into a role we are neither equipped for nor expected to play.

4. *Untie the apron string.* There comes a time in every home when parents must untie the apron string. If they hold too tightly, they force a break that is not necessary. It is more pleasant —and more Christian—to demonstrate positive faith in our young people to make right decisions as we untie the apron string than to force them to break it unilaterally.

IV. The Church

Let us turn our attention to the part the church plays in bridging the generation gap. This involves specifically our pastors, evangelists, teachers—all Christian workers. There are at least ten traits young people look for in their Christian leaders.

1. *Someone who is consistent.* One of the hardest crises a young person faces is when a

trusted adult falls short of his Christian profession. It doesn't have to be in the area of morals, just less-than-expected. A consistent personal life is essential in communicating with youth.

2. *Someone who strives to understand modern youth.* We must continually study our young people as individuals and as members of society, always keeping abreast of their problems, temptations, feelings, and challenges. We must develop the art of listening.

3. *Someone they can trust.* A friend of youth must prove he can be trusted. If they can trust you, they will come to you for guidance. Don't reject them, no matter how unimportant the question appears. No matter what they say, don't be horrified; don't show shock. If you rebuke or scold, you will no longer be eligible for their trust.

4. *Someone in whom they can confide.* Fortunate is the teacher or pastor in whom young people confide. It is in this relationship that many of life's most personal problems are examined and decisions made. When you are fortunate enough to be trusted with the secrets of others, hold the confidences as a sacred trust. A violation will irreparably damage young lives.

5. *Someone who shows concern.* We must show continuing concern for the problems facing our young people. The more we have experienced and the more widely we have studied, the more empathetically we will be able to relate to them. The more they feel our concern, without intrusion into their private world, the more we can assist them in their search for identity.

6. *Someone who is encouraging.* Encouragement from trusted adults is invaluable to youth. They may *feel* they are right, even *know* they are right, but they need encouragement from trusted adults. Don't overdo it, however, for nothing is more repulsive to young people than artificiality and insincerity.

7. *Someone who respects their reticence.* There is a time to talk; there is a time for silence. This is part of the teen-age code and must be respected. When they are silent, they are not ignoring you. They are simply using their energies on their problem. When they have clarified it enough to verbalize it, they will share it—that is, if they trust you. Until then, prayer and patience are your best approach.

8. *Someone who will allow them freedom of choice.* Every generation must sort through the opportunities of life and come up with its own way of life. We did in our day; our youth de-

serve the same privilege. The best gift we can give them is freedom to make choices.

9. *Someone who maintains positive expectation.* If the church has taught the Word and its leaders have interpreted it correctly, what is there to fear? We must maintain positive faith in our young people as they face the challenges of life in light of the values *they* have adopted.

10. *Someone who encourages creativity.* Creativity in religious expression is the right of every generation. New art forms and new music forms arise; so new ways of expressing devotion to God emerge with experience. This in no way implies doctrinal changes, for Jesus Christ is the same yesterday, today, and forever, and His Word is eternal (Hebrews 13:8; 2 Timothy 3:15-17). The church that is geared to youth will encourage experimentation with innovations to communicate the eternal purposes of Christ in changing times.

Lest this presentation conclude on a theoretical note, let me throw out some ideas which might serve as a springboard for discussion. They are not all original, but have been gathered from many sources in our constituency.

Currently we are striving for a balance of instruction, worship, and expression in our local church programs. To be more effective, have you tried a Sunday night vesper hour? Family night during the week? Why not experiment with group learning in large plazas using such techniques as team teaching, group dynamics, buzz sessions, and new audio-visual methods made available through technological advances. What about elective classes for those with special needs or interests?

Instead of letting your pupils go from school to an empty house, why not invite them to the church library to study and receive remedial academic help. For those with no pressing study needs, how about classes in doctrine, evangelism, and missions? How about instruction in arts, crafts, hobbies, and recreational skills, along with provisions for supervised indoor games and refreshments?

Why not try a covered-dish supper which climaxes in group guidance for the whole family. What about a Christian counseling service for families of the congregation *and* the community?

What are you doing to combat secularism in public education? One community may require a Christian day school or child-care center while another needs only a superior approach to released time or a Bible study club after school.

For students facing college, what about a

scholarship program to help them finance their studies on one of our Assemblies of God campuses? For those attending a secular college, what about Chi Alpha chapter houses staffed by Spirit-filled counselors? Further, what is the collegetown church doing to make the college student feel welcome the months he is resident in the city? How is your church utilizing the talents and meeting the special needs of recent college graduates who are just establishing their homes and becoming stabilized in their professions?

The value of this Council on Evangelism will not rest with the memories we relive or the theories we propound. The value will come in a new awareness of our strategic position as Christian leaders at this point in history and the courage with which we face the challenge of bridging the generation gap.

Panel Discussion and Open Forum

One panelist said that in this present age learning has accelerated; language has changed, and is changing; and fads change. When the older generation fails to keep up with the accelerated learning as well as language and fad changes, the generation gap exists.

Another panelist remarked that in searching for reasons for the generation gap, the following were contributing factors: (1) In the beginning the Pentecostal church was a culture of poverty; today, the Assemblies of God has a good share of the affluent. Youth of today have not experienced poverty. (2) We are living in an age of fatalism. (3) In attempting to respect the individual value system, we have reflected some ideas and methods of situation ethics. To counteract these influences, the church must teach the morals and ethics of the Bible.

The speaker then listed five steps in establishing a value system: (1) Value systems are received by example. (2) The youth accepts or rejects the parents' value system. (3) Values come from the example and what is accepted or rejected. The young person establishes his

system by personal experience and commitment. (4) The young person then attempts to verbalize his experience because it is meaningful to him. (5) Characterization involves bringing the life into a consistency with the value system which the young person is willing to accept. During this period, while the young person is attempting to arrive at a system, the parent must hold him steady, emphasizing the positive and not the negative. When the Bible is not clear on a value system, the person must work through on his own.

Someone pointed out that too many people are grandchildren of the faith; that is, they are Christians without a personal encounter and experience and are relying and depending upon the faith of their fathers.

A college youth challenged the idea that the church was God's voice. He further commented that in order to bridge the generation gap, perhaps the church and the youth should reason together. The church was not challenged as being God's voice where it clearly teaches and upholds what the Bible teaches; but in areas where the Bible is silent or does not give a clear message, there is room for the older and younger generations to sit down and reason together.

It was expressed that the cause of the generation gap, in many instances, was the lack of a personal salvation experience of the youth.

Question: If we in the Assemblies of God are attributing our failures to a lack of a personal encounter, why have not our youth had this personal experience since we have insisted and preached a personal salvation for a great number of years?

Perhaps the generation gap is not based on the lack of an encounter, but a failure to build Christian character through proper teaching and leadership after the encounter. Adults should humble themselves and admit they don't know it all. Very often they are too authoritarian. We listen to adults and don't take the time to listen to young people.

171

FROM HOUSE TO HOUSE

Speaker: **EDWIN COLE**
Moderator: **STANTON JOHNSON**
Panelists: **RICHARD FOTH, ROBERT STRAND, WILLIAM VICKERY**
Recorder: **BRENTON OSGOOD**

THE PHILOSOPHY OF GOING "from house to house" is scriptural. This is evident as we see the Early Church in its evangelistic fervor of the first century. Those early Christians were basically concerned with witnessing for Christ, rather than in inviting people to attend church. Naturally, after someone had accepted Jesus Christ as his Saviour, he was urged to join in the fellowship of believers.

There is a formula that seems to be rather accurate when applied in the spiritual world:

"The better a person is in his own eyes, the less the miracle of the Cross and the grace of God.

"The less involved in trying to reach others for Christ, the more prayerlessness of the life.

"The more concerned with witnessing, the more the need of the power of the Holy Ghost and His anointing. The less involved, the less need for the Spirit and power."

The sidewalks of our nation have been left in the main to those who preach not the gospel of Christ. We have allowed those who preach violence and hate to take the streets, while the church that began on the sidewalk and the street corner has retreated behind its walls.

Salesmen walk the sidewalks and knock on doors seeking to sell their products. Representatives of false cults make door-to-door calling a part of their weekly schedules. Others are using a Biblical principle for reaching men, while the church is weakest in this method.

Consider the importance of time. It can be an ally or an enemy. In developing a visitation effort, be sure to allow ample time for training. Remember that training is different from teaching. Training implies teaching by example. This takes time. Teaching without training is only getting the job partly done.

Time is also very important in being effective in visitation. We must know the proper time to reach people if we are going to obtain worthwhile results.

Another important ally is knowledge. What people do not understand, they are against. Unless they know what they are doing, they rebel against being asked to do it.

People want to know what to say when seeking to win souls through house-to-house visitation.

You can't push string, you pull it—and you don't push people around, you lead them. No one should teach what he does not practice. And none can insist that others go from house to house unless he has first done it himself.

There is an erroneous analogy used by some ministers to rationalize their failures in soul winning. They usually state, "I am a shepherd. The shepherd doesn't give birth to the sheep; sheep beget sheep."

It is tragic that these ministers seem to forget

that Jesus Christ, the world's greatest Soul Winner, called Himself the Great Shepherd. The disciples who associated with Him also became great soul winners, even though they recognized that they were under-shepherds.

Sheep follow their shepherd. Pastors who are great personal soul winners usually have congregations filled with people who practice soul winning. Conversely, pastors who fail to win souls personally usually unconsciously influence their congregations to lose interest in personal soul winning.

These are three basic ingredients for house-to-house evangelism. These questions must be asked: (1) Who is going? (2) What will they say? (3) Where are they going?

All materials, training, and other work involved in visitation is determined by the answers to these three questions.

When it is determined who will go, it will also determine in a large measure where they will go. The most important question, then, is, "What will they say?"

The soul-winning pattern should be simple, logical, and easy to present. If possible, it should be coordinated so that it can be both visual and auditory. That is, the soul winner should have something to say and something to show.

There are a variety of soul-winning conversations. Which conversation you use is not the important thing. The most important thing is that your congregation be trained, be given an example through its leaders, and be sent in systematic visitation. In short, the important thing is to stop talking and start doing.

Another important part of house-to-house visitation is the use of literature. What people see is perhaps more important than anything that comes to them through the other senses.

After hearing the plan of salvation, people want to read it for themselves. Thus literature used for house-to-house visitation should be coordinated with the conversational pattern of the visit. After you have left the home and the person reads the literature, he will recall your conversation. Those things you have emphasized will be emphasized again as he reads them.

Three pieces vital to visitation are: (1) general Scripture, such as American Bible Society's "Good News"; (2) your soul-winning pattern; (3) local church informational brochure.

Remember that the purpose of our literature is the same as the reason for calling on the home—to win people to Jesus Christ first. Secondarily, it is to invite them to church.

The axiom that "what people do not understand, they are against" is especially true of those who hear the message of Christ for the first time. We are endeavoring to bring people to understand the Person and mission of Jesus Christ.

Usually it is better to begin with teams making house-to-house calls. However, it is not mandatory that two people be together on all home calls. Once the soul-winning pattern is learned and experience gained, then confidence is instilled. Even though people may go into a neighborhood two by two, they may then visit homes alone. Sometimes personal witnessing is easier person-to-person. And it is not unlikely that two people witnessing to one unsaved person may make that individual feel somewhat outnumbered and overpowered.

There are some general things that house-to-house witnesses should remember about their conversation: (1) It should at all times be sanctified; (2) it should be very cordial; (3) it should never be tedious; (4) if the Spirit can inspire you what to say, He can inspire you when to stop; let Him; (5) it should be centered on the soul-winning pattern.

The basic materials to use in going from house to house are: (1) Master visitation summary sheet for the person coordinating or keeping records; (2) individual assignment sheets; (3) visitation wallets for assignment sheets and literature; (4) literature to be distributed; (5) a New Testament—marked for witnessing.

As you plan your own house-to-house visitation campaign, here is your checklist:

1. Set dates for your visitation effort and determine all the materials to be used.

2. Assign individuals (such as Sunday school staff) to map the entire area to be visited and to prepare individual assignments.

3. Coordinate your calendar for training sessions.

4. Enlist people in prayer.

5. Enlist people for visitation.

6. Train some workers privately and have them give testimonies at training sessions.

7. Be sure everyone is familiar not only with the soul-winning pattern but also with all literature and materials to be used during the effort.

8. Make follow-up assignments as the effort progresses.

9. Gratitude is essential.

10. Be a leader.

Panel Discussion and Open Forum

A verse of Scripture giving a basis for house-to-house witnessing is Luke 19:10: "For the Son of man is come to seek and to save that which was lost." Seeking is important because people do not come to public services as they once did.

The normal pattern of evangelism in the New Testament Church is recorded in Acts 20:20, 21: "I kept nothing that was profitable unto you, but have showed you, and have taught you publicly, and *from house to house*, testifying both to the Jews, and also to the Greeks, *repentance* toward God, and *faith* toward our Lord Jesus Christ."

Witnessing and soul winning are not synonymous. We are commanded to witness, but not all witnessing culminates in soul winning. We are to sow and water, but it is God who gives the increase.

Before a house-to-house witness can become a reality in many congregations, the philosophy of the congregation must be changed. Many Christians feel that this type of witness is the responsibility of the pastor or a few persons in places of responsibility in the local church. They feel that attendance and tithing are the sum of their responsibilities. Pastors must sell such congregations on the necessity of house-to-house witnessing.

Two types of door-to-door witnessing were mentioned: (1) concentrated, such as every night for a week; (2) week-by-week, a permanent part of the church calendar.

Question: How can we keep a witnessing program going?

1. Witnesses should be given recognition.

2. Sharing sessions immediately after each witnessing activity.

3. Report the results to the church.

4. Give witnesses and converts opportunity to share their experiences in the services.

5. Witnesses should be trained as to what to say—to overcome their fear and give them confidence. Most Christians are not ashamed of Christ, just afraid to witness.

It was observed there is a great need to use follow-up material in further contacts with new converts.

174

THE HOME—BULWARK OF EVANGELISM

Speaker: **MORRIS O. WILLIAMS**
Moderator: **KERMIT RENEAU**
Panelists: **JOSEPH FLOWER, J. ROSWELL FLOWER, EDDIE SCRATCH**
Recorder: **THOMAS SHEPHERD**

THE CHRISTIAN HOME is the bulwark of evangelism. Of all organizations and programs instrumental in propagating the gospel, none is more important than the home. This unheralded institution is the seedbed of evangelism.

In this twentieth century, we have transferred many of the functions of the home to public institutions and have relegated the home to a far too insignificant role. The Sunday school has been created to supply spiritual training for the child. The public school cares for his secular education. The hospital removes the sick bed from the home, while public parks and organized entertainment infer that the place to have fun is anywhere but home. Thus stripped of its original functions, home, in many unhappy cases, is a private hotel, finely furnished, where its owners can relax when they want to get away from the really significant things that are going on elsewhere. This ought not to be.

God intended the home to be a center of learning and He commissioned the parents to be the teachers in this all-important school. The children were to be trained in the way that they should go so that when they become of age, they would not depart from that way. This was, and is, the "reason for being" of the Christian home. For those who believe, the home's basic function must be to evangelize and train the children that are born into it.

Let us then look upon the Christian home as a school. It will have its extra-curricular activities, its times for eating and sleeping, its times for fun and relaxation; but basically and primarily it is a school, established specifically for the evangelization and training of the children born into it.

The program in the home must have as its goal the effecting of a decision for Christ by the child. This means that the program of the home must be a program of evangelism. While Assemblies of God people do attend Bible-centered churches, it is a question of some concern as to whether their homes are Bible-centered. Many parents would be hard put to point to any planned program in their daily schedule for the spiritual education of their children.

The curriculum of the home-school must include regular and well-planned activities that will lead the child to Christ.

If a parent is contending for the faith, a faith that he is absolutely convinced is necessary if his child is to be saved and without which his child will be everlastingly lost, then he has every right to use every legitimate means to propagate his message! A hands-off policy in this area would be immoral. Parents who leave the spiritual training of their children to the Sunday school teacher fail in their God-given duty.

The curriculum of the home-school must include regular and well-planned activities that will lead the child to Christ.

If a parent is contending for the faith, a faith that he is absolutely convinced is necessary if his child is to be saved and without which his child will be everlastingly lost, then he has every right to use every legitimate means to propagate his message! A hands-off policy in this area would be immoral. Parents who leave the spiritual training of their children to the Sunday school teacher fail in their God-given duty.

Day-by-day informal instruction in a Christian home, conducted by godly parents, will steer the child's heart toward a decision for Christ. The parent-teacher must always be an evangelist. Every Bible story will have its application, every event some meaning of significance with regard to discipleship. It is in the home-school that Christianity is learned to be a way of life, rather than a profession. It is there that serving Christ becomes relative to everyday living. It is a school in which the textbook is a combination of Bible and teacher—the former being interpreted by the life of the latter.

The curriculum has its formal teaching too. This will be concerned with establishing habit patterns in the child as well as seeking his evangelization. The father, in normal circumstances, must take the initiative in this formal education. He will make it his business to set up the home schedule to include personal and family devotions, setting specific times for church attendance, insisting that meals be eaten as a family unit where questions of general interest can be discussed, and finally, subtly arranging private encounters at bedtime where very personal and intimate problems can be shared.

The family altar is an ideal place to press the all-important question of decision. To encourage this family devotions should vocally involve each member. Devotions should be conducted in a comfortable and relaxed atmosphere where it is easy to converse and ask questions. Family altar must never be sporadic. An "on-today-off-tomorrow, do-it-when-we-remember" affair will never become a habit.

Bedtime prayers offer ideal times to press the matter of salvation. The mother and father should share in these occasions for reflection, repentance, and rejoicing over each day's activities.

Once it is clearly established in the minds of the parents that the function of the home is the evangelization and the training of the chil-

dren born into it, the building and every piece of its equipment will consequently be calculated to augment the purpose of the institution. The superfluous and the unrelated will not be allowed to clutter the scene or to hinder the fulfillment of the home's "reason-for-being."

When accessories in a home create the impression that its function is solely to provide pleasure for its occupants, then there needs to be some serious reappraising if evangelism and training are to be retained as prime objectives. While part of training is pleasant—and certainly physical health, sportsmanship, companionship, and competition all go into making up a well-rounded individual—pleasure for pleasure's sake is a precarious pursuit! That an activity provides pleasure is not enough reason to justify its practice. It must be related to the continuing and ultimate purpose of the home. It should, in some way, contribute toward the evangelization and training of the child.

As the environment of the world becomes less and less conducive to spiritual decisions, the home must become more and more a place where reverence toward God and tranquility of life provide a haven of sanity and decency.

The kind of house in which a Christian child is reared will surely affect his sense of values. I am not advocating poverty, but I am appealing to Christians in this affluent age to live frugally and to invest all the extra that God gives in furthering the Great Commission. Jesus said that it is harder for a rich man to go to heaven than it is for a camel to go through the eye of a needle. When a man makes the accumulation of wealth his goal in life, he should consider the odds against his making heaven.

Jesus lived very frugally and He taught His disciples that if any would follow Him, they must deny themselves. So whenever a Christian decides not to deny himself and to lavish his home with every conceivable luxury, he'd better be sure he has a special mandate from God to do so!

It is very difficult to teach a child to set his affection on things above while the parents are obviously enamored with things below. The furnishings of our homes may speak so loud to our children that they cannot read the plaque on the wall that says, "I surrender all"!

The evil of riches is not intrinsically in the riches themselves, but, more correctly, in the attitude in man toward riches. In attitude the poor can be as grasping as the rich. And this leads us to our final point—the teacher-parent.

More than curriculum, and more than buildings, the attitude of the parent toward God and toward the things that he possesses will determine the child's sense of values. Whether he will look for the things that are seen, or for the things that are not seen, will depend largely upon his instructors.

The depth of spiritual experience in the parents, their manner of life and speech will profoundly affect the lives of the children and are the surest single influence toward their evangelization.

When a child starts school, he must have prior training on which to fall back. This is such important training that it will require the co-operation of both parents. Teaching will become a full-time job of one of the parents while the other one works to bring in enough support to maintain the "schoolhouse" and to feed the "faculty and student body"! Of course, the husband will assume his teaching duties each day, after he has concluded his primary responsibility of providing bread and butter!

Home evangelism requires consistency on the part of the faculty. Nothing undermines the faith of a child more than to observe a double standard in his parents. It is the double standard in today's "Christian" home that is responsible for our current youth-in-revolt situation!

Assemblies of God young people are not prepared to accept the platitudes and pretenses of an older generation that professes one thing and then does another. There is no surer way of undermining evangelism in the home than this. If we are to win our children, we must be devout and godly in church and out of church, in sight of the children and out of their sight, in times of pressure and in times of relaxation. There can be no holiday from discipleship.

The necessity for consistency carries into the area of discipline. What is wrong today must be wrong tomorrow. Irregular reaction to regular wrong speaks loudly to the child. It says to him that it was the timing rather than the deed that was bad, for it caught Dad or Mom in the wrong mood. His concern, on another occasion, will center on the parent-teacher's frame of mind rather than upon correcting irregular activity!

The parent who punishes in the heat of irritation makes the child feel that he is the unfortunate victim of that irritation.

Children do not run away from God because there is discipline in the home. Neither do they develop dislike for parents who hold a standard and insist upon Christian behavior. It is when they see inconsistency in their parents that they become disillusioned. The desperate need today is for our homes to become a bulwark of evangelism—a place where truth, as Christ taught it, is demonstrated in the environment of the home by the example of a loving parent-teacher. Home must be a place of understanding—a place where the lines of communication are kept open between parent-teacher and child-pupil, a place where love is expressed and exchanged, a sacred place characterized by charity, confidence, and security.

Panel Discussion and Open Forum

It was pointed out that while a layman spends much of his time in an occupation away from the home, a minister because of his calling might spend more time in the home, thus allowing more time for his influence to be felt in the spiritual building of the home. A minister's home and a layman's home cannot be compared in this respect, but a layman is just as responsible for the spiritual upbuilding of his home as the minister is for his.

"Home Emphasis Meetings" were suggested. In these services whole families could be brought face-to-face with the subject of home evangelism.

The Bible must be the supreme Book of every Christian home. It must be given its rightful place. There must be a constant emphasis of the Bible's teachings in the home.

Question: Children desire the better things of life; but how do you make them understand, for example, that since a certain amount of this week's income is going for missions—and they will not be able to get some item they especially wanted?

It was suggested that children do not want everything they ask for. Many times simple love or affection will provide what a child is really trying to obtain through the means of a purchased possession.

Question: Two children are in the home. One responds to spiritual things; the other rejects them. What do you do?

It was first suggested that the case of the unresponsive child be studied and true answers sought as to why he was not responding to spiritual matters. Usually the reason can be found.

Question: What do you do about family altar when both parents work different shifts?

It was suggested that a definite time be set for family altar. If both parents are not present, then let the one present lead in the family devotions.

Question: What about the problem of working mothers?

Members of the panel believed that the mother's primary responsibility was in the home rather than working to help the family get "a few things extra in life." One must not get himself in debt over his means so that the wife is required to work and omit her primary responsibility of the home. Live within your means so you can let the mother remain in the home.

Question: Which is most important, the quantity or quality of time a parent spends with his children?

Quality of time was deemed more important. It was pointed out that John Wesley's mother spent one hour per week individually with each of her many children. Thus she was able to mold their lives for the kingdom of God. It is not how much time you spend with children, but what you do with that time.

MEN WINNING MEN

Speaker: **JOHN WALKER**
Moderator: **GLEN BONDS**
Panelists: **KEN ASPLUND, DOYLE BURGESS, CHARLES CAPPS**
Recorder: **EVERETT JAMES**

IT IS GOD'S PLAN that every Christian should be supremely concerned to make the Saviour known to as many people as possible—and as quickly as possible. God alone can save souls; but God cannot save souls alone, for He has ordained that this work shall be done through human instruments—through His own people.

What a responsibility this places upon those of us who know the Saviour is faithful. For in a very real sense the salvation of souls waits and depends upon our obedience and faithfulness.

There are a variety of ways to effectively witness for the Lord Jesus Christ. This is indeed providential, for we are all so different in temperament and gifts. And the fact that God has ordained that we may witness for Him in many different ways means that each of us may find at least one way of fulfilling this responsible ministry.

While some may be able to witness by preaching, the majority cannot witness this way. But we are all given the opportunity to witness through the variety of ways which God has provided. This leaves us all without excuse, for there will be at least one way in which we may effectively witness for our Lord and Master.

When Jesus uttered the words recorded in Acts 1:8, He was speaking prophetically. Ten days later His prophecy began to be fulfilled. Acts 1:8 is still the Lord's plan for world evangelization.

As a background for ways of winning men, I would suggest five marks of a true witness:

1. He must know the risen Christ personally (Acts 2:32; 3:15).

2. He must witness of the Lord Jesus Christ (Acts 1:8).

3. He must be no respecter of persons (Acts 26:22).

4. He must be willing to suffer (Revelation 20:4).

5. He must be spiritually equipped (Acts 1: 8; 20:23).

Here are six ways for men to win men to Christ.

I. Witness by a Consistent Christian Life

No witnessing will ever be successful if it does not proceed from a Christlike life. And no testimony is as powerful as the testimony of a changed life.

I believe the greatest proof to the world of the risen Christ is a Christian—one in whom the risen Christ lives and through whom His life is flowing (John 7:38, 39).

A consistent Christian life is a way in which every man can witness for the Lord. The Bible has many illustrations of the influence of a godly life—illustrations such as Joseph (Genesis 39:2, 3), Lazarus (John 12:11), the man at the Beautiful Gate (Acts 4:14). It is still true today: "Therefore if any man be in Christ, he is a new creature: old things are passed away;

179

behold, all things are become new" (2 Corinthians 5:17).

In a quiet, unpretentious way all of us must seek to witness for the Lord by what we *are*, what we *do*, and what we do *not* do.

II. Witness by Word of Mouth

Every Christian man should be ready to witness for the Lord by word of mouth. Yes, *every* Christian man. Psalm 107:2 declares: "Let the redeemed of the Lord say so, whom he hath redeemed from the hand of his enemy." Surely if the Lord has really saved us, we can tell others of His wonderful grace and power.

Our excuses for not speaking of and for the Lord are unreasonable and unworthy.

The rapid growth of the Early Church was due in part to the fact that the Christians went forth and told others about their wonderful Lord (Acts 4:20). I believe that every Christian should preach in the sense that Philip did in Acts 8:35: "Then Philip opened his mouth, and began at the same Scripture, and preached unto him Jesus." He must always be the theme of our witnessing.

What scope this kind of witnessing offers. Under all kinds of circumstances we can tell others of Jesus. And we should. There is such a thing as consecrating our conversation to the Lord (Psalm 50:23). This may lead to the additional privilege of public witnessing: of preaching to the crowd (Acts 8:5), of teaching a Sunday school class, of conducting services in hospitals and prisons. There is a tremendous need for men who will consecrate themselves to serve the Lord in this way, and the Lord has promised to supply the need of His servants who speak for Him (Jeremiah 1:4-9).

III. Witness by Open Association with God's People

Where it is at all possible, Christians should join a church. This is necessary for one's own spiritual welfare (Hebrews 10:24, 25), is helpful to other Christians (Galatians 6:2), and is a definite form of open witness to the Lord Himself (Acts 3:1).

IV. Witness by Literature Distribution

Many Christian men have found they can witness effectively for their Lord by prayerfully distributing suitable Scripture portions and tracts. There are some great promises to all who serve God in this way:

"Know now that there shall fall unto the earth nothing of the word of the Lord" (2 Kings 10:10).

"He that goeth forth and weepeth, bearing precious seed, shall doubtless come again with rejoicing, bringing his sheaves with him" (Psalm 126:6).

"Cast thy bread upon the waters: for thou shalt find it after many days" (Ecclesiastes 11:1).

No Christian need be idle while Scripture portions and gospel tracts are available for careful, prayerful, and widespread distribution.

V. Witness by Letter Writing

Another method of witnessing that many Christian men have found effective is that of letter writing. Christians deprived of the more public forms of Christian service have found great scope and blessing in this ministry.

Why not prayerfully write to people who are ill, in trouble, leaving the area, starting a new job, or getting married—urging them to seek the Lord. (See Isaiah 55:6.)

VI. Witness by a Variety of Silent Methods

Our homes should bear testimony that we are the Lord's. Such practices as grace at mealtimes and having a family altar bear effective testimony that we belong to Him.

Conclusion

We should regard everyone we touch as a potential Christian. (See Acts 20:6; Ezekiel 3:18.) Not all will accept Christ. A fisherman never catches all the fish available—only some. The most any servant of God can do is to save some. And God's plan is that we should all have the joy of seeing some saved.

Panel Discussion and Open Forum

Question: How do you get the men to witness?

Make the technique of presenting the plan of salvation simple so that everyone can do it. Be alert for opportunities to witness. Use wisdom in your approach. Ask the Holy Spirit's help just before you approach someone.

Make your presentation clear by using a simple tract or tool. The actual presentation of the plan of salvation should be as brief as possible but long enough so that the individual will see his need and know how to receive the Lord Jesus into his heart.

As a person is witnessing, he should pray for the guidance and presence of the Holy

Spirit. When the Spirit is present, a simple witness will bring results. The Holy Spirit Himself does the work of conviction and regeneration.

Question: How do you motivate your people?

The pastor himself is the key to motivating the people. If the pastor is not active in witnessing, he will find it very difficult to get his people motivated to witness. The only way he can lead his people is by demonstration.

Encourage people who do begin to witness. Workers should be given an opportunity to testify when they have won a soul to Christ. Their enthusiasm and joy will inspire and challenge others.

Witnessing is a stick-to, follow-through job. Witnessing regularly, consistently, and efficiently brings success.

A church should set aside a special night each week for witnessing. This is not to canvass, not to make a Sunday school visit, but to go out and talk to people about Christ. At least an hour of prayer should precede the witnessing program. Each pastor should make a soul-winning training program available to all desiring to be an effective witness.

Question: Are the days of evangelistic campaigns over?

No. However, it is foolish to call a meeting an evangelistic crusade when there are no sinners present.

Some churches now have two types of meetings: revival meetings for the Christians and special evangelistic meetings to reach sinners.

If the sinner is not coming to church, then the obvious alternative is for the church to go to the sinner. The days of evangelistic campaigns are not over, but the church must go out where the sinners are with the gospel.

THE MINISTRY OF THE ALTAR WORKER

Speaker: **ROBERT GATLIN**
Moderator: **OWEN CARR**
Panelists: **ROBERT CARRINGTON, E. ELSWORTH KROGSTAD, JOEL PALMER**
Recorder: **JAMES GRIGGS**

THE ALTAR IS A PLACE OF PRAYER. Most likely it will be in church; however, it could be anywhere.

Recently I have led seven men to the Lord on their sickbeds and then was called to conduct funerals for five of them. This has very forcibly emphasized to me that the altar is the place where man meets God—in the church, in the home, or in the hospital. As Spirit-filled believers we need to be ready to assist a soul in finding his altar anytime.

I. A Question of Procedure

Should personal work be done in a congregation while an invitation is being given? There is varied opinion. Many have been offended as a result of a careless invitation; but it is equally true that many are rejoicing in heaven today because they were approached.

We do urge caution. A worker should have a definite leading before approaching another person. To go from one person to another without leading from the Spirit will likely offend some. Always be led by the Holy Spirit.

If you are directed to someone by the Holy Spirit and he says, "Not now," it is best to express understanding and encouragement and then leave. To argue or plead can defeat your purpose.

II. A Principle of Priority

D. L. Moody wisely stated: "It is foolish to try to do the work of God without the power of God."

Paul tells us that our sufficiency is "of God . . . of the Spirit" (2 Corinthians 3:5, 6).

Acts 1:8 is a statement of fact, a fact for which we are responsible. "Ye shall receive power . . . and ye shall be witnesses." What a responsibility to have the power of the Holy Spirit—and not use it.

The Holy Spirit is the heartbeat and pulse of evangelism. He is the great Evangelist, the center and source of winning the lost. Like the underground spring leaping forth as a great surface river, so the Spirit is the great fountainhead of living waters to the believer and seeker alike. After such a well has been opened, you do not have to command it to flow; it is there bubbling forth. The believer's life should flow with prayer and compassion and the Holy Spirit.

Many today have been filled with the Spirit but have not retained that inner glow. The fire of the Holy Ghost will lay hold upon that which is cold and dead, making it sparkle and blaze. The love, the holiness, and passion for souls should make us shine as lights in the world.

Instance after instance in the Book of Acts bears out the importance of the leadership of the Holy Spirit when dealing with individuals. Much of the success or failure of the altar worker is determined by this.

As the Spirit leads, you will find yourself dealing with the poor, the outcast, the illiterate, the undesirable, and the transients. If we are going to gather fruit for the Master, it must be done His way.

The Holy Spirit will convict a man and make him want to be saved. Most drunkards know they are lost; they feel their guilt so they try to drown it with more drink; but the Spirit will convict a man of rejecting Christ and work through the believer to reprove him of sin, righteousness, and judgment. The Spirit provides the leadership and guidance needed by the worker at this crucial point. He will give you the words and testimony needed and enable you to apply the gospel to the particular need of the seeker.

Romans 1:16 tells us that "the gospel of Christ . . . is the power of God unto salvation to every one that believeth." A big part of the altar worker's responsibility is to determine the need and point to the remedy.

The worker must have a love for souls that comes from a heart of faith flowing out of a spirit of compassion.

The key to success, then, is absolute dependence on the Holy Spirit because God's Word teaches it is the Spirit that convicts, reveals truth, reveals Christ, and is agent of regeneration. The witness of salvation is by the Spirit.

III. A Personal Involvement

A personal, friendly word of encouragement is enough to get some people to the altar. It is more than an invitation; it is a bolstering of their courage, a stimulant to action. Many will be in heaven because of a few well-chosen words at the right time in the form of an invitation, or because of words of testimony that help the worker identify with the seeker.

Why is the person hostile, defiant, or indifferent? Search for a reason for the basic attitude. What heartbreak, disappointment, bitter experience, fear, or disillusionment formed it? If you can find this, it will give you an opening to his heart and a point for applying the Scriptures.

Listen to what he says and be ready to answer with Scripture if possible. Never argue.

This is one of the easiest traps to fall into. Avoid egotism, false pride, and denominational differences.

It will be helpful at this point if you have shown previous interest in the person's spiritual welfare. Establish the right to deal with him. On occasion it is good to sit with the person you hope to take to the altar with you. This would mean he has been on your prayer list and is not someone picked at random out of the congregation.

A soul winner is required to be clean and pure. He must have a fiery burden for the lost. His motive must be: "For the love of Christ constraineth us" (2 Corinthians 5:14). Spiritual work with spiritual results can only be accomplished by spiritual means.

It takes faith to produce results. This work must be done with absolute faith. If we are going to reach the most hardened cases, we must have Acts 1:8 power; then we can get a deep penetration of the sword of the Spirit with sure results.

IV. The Word in Action

When the unsaved person shows a desire to seek God, the worker's diligence in Bible study *will* be rewarded. It is God's Word, not our comment on the Word, that causes souls to be saved. Men shut up in an inner prison of sin cannot be loosened by the wrecking bars of philosophy or social reform; it takes the Scripture.

The Word converts (Acts 2:37); it discerns (Hebrews 4:12); it breaks the hard heart (Jeremiah 23:29); it enlightens (Psalms 119:130); it is faith-producing (Romans 10:17); and life-giving (Philippians 2:16).

The place the Word has in your life will help determine your place as a successful altar worker. God's Word generates faith as you speak. Be sure the sinner has an encounter with the Word of God.

Studying God's Word will cause you to walk closer to the Lord, reveal God's purpose, reveal Jesus, and enable you to work effectively and with compassion. Retain, mark, record, underline, number or use colored ink, but conserve the results of your study for that moment when a soul is ready to be shown the way.

Carry a New Testament or a small Bible; use a few meaningful Scripture verses; concentrate on the objective.

The seeker must understand the simplicity of salvation. "When any one heareth the word of the kingdom, and understandeth it not, then cometh the wicked one, and catcheth away that which was sown in his heart" (Matthew 13:19). The mind must be reached with the truth; that truth must be understood so as to grip the heart and change a life. A careless, prayerless, un-instructed worker can lose a soul for eternity at this point.

Salvation involves more than mental assent, and we must proceed to show the seeker:

That eternal life is in Christ (1 John 5:11).

To receive life he must receive Christ (1 John 5:12).

When he receives the Saviour, life will be imparted (John 1:12, John 1:4, John 14:6).

Receiving Jesus must be shown as a two-fold act of faith: *confess* with thy mouth, *believe* in thine heart (Romans 10:9, 10). This leads to a warm response to the love of God through Jesus.

The altar worker needs to be sure that the seeker takes two important steps: he must confess his sin; he must receive Jesus.

V. The Ultimate

The time of decision is the most important task of the altar worker—not only the seeker's decision to pray, but the decision to accept by faith Jesus Christ as his personal Saviour. The intellect and the conscience must be awakened. That deep sense of sin must be aroused. A strong desire for cleansing must be motivated.

You must be ready when the moment of decision comes.

Be sure the foundation has been laid (Romans 3:23; 3:10, 11; Ephesians 2:8; 2 Corinthians 5:17).

Show the way. Confess, repent, believe (Romans 10:9, 10; 1 John 1:9).

Explain the terms: serving the Lord, prayer, Bible reading.

Ask the all-important question; it must not be put off (2 Corinthians 6:2).

Assure him he will not stand alone (Jude 24; John 1:12).

Should the seeker, after a few moments of prayer, express a desire to delay the decision, deal with him from the Scriptures showing the urgency of positive action (Isaiah 55:6; Proverbs 27:1; 29:1; Matthew 25:1-12; Luke 12:19, 20).

If the reason is, "I must get started in my life's work first; then I will surrender to the Lord," apply Matthew 6:33. Usually one passage

of Scripture driven home will be effective.

When a person is at the altar and you have opportunity to work with him, be sure he understands clearly that:

Jesus is the sin-bearer (Isaiah 53:6);

Jesus is able to save to the uttermost. (Hebrews 7:25);

Jesus is both Lord and Christ (Acts 2:36);

Jesus will be his very own (John 1:12).

If the seeker is praying, let him alone for awhile. Pray along with him and encourage him to pray through. Determine the need as soon as possible. Give the plan of salvation, but not too many verses of Scripture. Confirm his experience by having him confess it to you.

As occasion permits, stress important Christian duties: Bible study, prayer, church attendance, water baptism.

There is too much hurried, superficial, indifferent altar work done today. May God help us to purpose in our lives that we will not allow souls to die at our altars for lack of skilled compassionate prayer, understanding, and counsel in the moment of decision.

Panel Discussion and Open Forum

It was suggested there be a training program for altar workers prior to an evangelistic campaign. This should not be merely to learn techniques and mechanics of altar work, but to understand the leading of the Spirit during the time of dealing with souls. Dependence upon the Spirit is vital. It was pointed out that Jesus met people where their needs were. To one He said, "Go and sin no more;" and to another He said, "Thy faith hath made thee whole."

The pastor must lead the way in training. He may do this by conducting a soul-winning class, or by preaching a sermon on it, or by other means.

In dealing with people it was suggested that one needed a positive faith in his approach. He could say, "You are coming to the altar with me tonight, aren't you?" It was noted that Romans was an excellent book to use in the step-by-step presentation of man's need for God.

The altar worker should not presume that all people know how to pray. If the seeker indicates he does not know how to pray, then the worker should ask him if he would like for him to help him. Often the Holy Spirit will help the worker touch the barrier that is between the sinner and the Lord.

The pastor should not take all the initiative

184

and responsibility of dealing with souls at the altar. (It was noted that he should be at the altar, however.) He should let the people do it. Then when the work is done, the people should bring the saved ones to him and tell him what God has accomplished. This brings confidence to the newly saved and assurance to the workers.

THE ROLE OF MUSIC IN EVANGELISM

Speaker: **IRA STANPHILL**
Moderator: **JOHN WANNENMACHER**
Panelists: **JOE NICHOLSON, ANZEL SHOULTS, PAUL TUTMARC JR.**
Recorder: **GWEN JONES**

MUSIC IS ONE THE MOST MAGNIFICIENT and delightful presents God has given to man, the only art of earth we take to heaven."

I have spent the major portion of my life in three related areas: evangelism, music, and the Assemblies of God. The music of Pentecost has been different just as its preaching has been different. There are few, if any, books written on the subject of the role of music in evangelism. Therefore, most of the thoughts of this seminar paper are those that have remained in my own heart after I have discarded many others.

I. Music in the Bible

As a good background let us look at the music of the Old and New Testaments. The Jews were great musicians. They played and sang in their homes and on all public occasions. They had a variety of expressions, using the harp, psaltery, trumpet, pipe, tambourine, cymbal, and voice. Josephus, in his account of the music equipment of the Temple, lists 200,000 silver trumpets and an equal number of coats for singers, plus 40,000 harps and psalteries. In both the Old and New Testaments, the people worshiped with solos, choruses, and congregational singing.

Great events in the Bible were celebrated with a song, i.e., the song of Moses, the song of Deborah, the song of Hannah, and the songs of Mary and the angels. David sang a lamentation over Jonathan, a song of victory at the defeat of Saul, and a song of praise on bringing the ark to Jerusalem. And the music of heaven—which the Bible says sounds "as the voice of many waters" —who can anticipate what its volume and quality will be?

I. E. Reynolds has said in *The Ministry of Music in Religion* that the words *music, musical instruments, musicians, song, singers,* and *singing* appear about 425 times in the Bible; *harps* and *viols,* 150 times; *shouting for joy,* 75 times; *joy,* 200 times; *happiness,* 25 times; *glad* and *gladness,* 150 times; and *rejoicing,* 300 times. The word *gloominess* appears in the Bible twice; and the word *despair* four times. Therefore, from a scriptural standpoint, we have every reason for emphasizing music in church worship and giving it its proper place.

II. Music in History

The early Christian churches used the Psalms with tunes handed down from the Hebrew worship. It was not until the second century that the early Christians began to compose their own songs, with a distinctly Christian sentiment.

In the fourth century, when the Catholic Church became the State Church, it saw the advantage of making music a part of its ritual; so it established schools of music for the sole purpose of training singers to take charge of that part of the service. For about one thousand years music was fostered entirely by Roman Catholic Church Fathers.

In the sixteenth century, during the Reformation, Martin Luther broke away from the old established Gregorian Latin chant, used at that time by the Roman church, and introduced congregational singing in the people's native tongue.

Soon after Luther two other men appeared who were to make a further contribution to the music of the church. They were Isaac Watts in the late seventeenth century and Charles Wesley in the early part of the eighteenth century. Following their writings the masses of the people began to use hymns and sing them enthusiastically. As in our times, the conservative element in the churches tried to stem the tide of this new order of song, saying it was of Satan; but on and on it went into every country wherever Protestants were to be found.

A further change in music came about in the middle of the nineteenth century in the introduction of the "gospel song." Dr. Breed in his *History of Hymns and Hymntunes* says that the gospel song made its appearance with the Moody and Sanky meetings in 1873; but Mr. Lorenz in his *Practical Church Music*, says that the gospel song was introduced several years before the Moody meetings by such writers as Bradbury, Lowry, Doane, Root, Bliss, and others.

III. Music Today

With great acceptance and some criticism, the gospel song, with its three or so verses and a chorus, has now become a prominent part of our worship services. A further development of this style was the introduction of the thirty-two measure sacred song in the style of popular music. Stuart Hamblen's song, "It Is No Secret," is an example of this type.

Never in the history of sacred music has there been a greater demand for music of all kinds. Sacred hymnbooks sell by the millions, as do the gospel songbooks. Sheet music sells in unbelievable quantities. The religious record companies do millions of dollars worth of business each year.

Music has played a major part in the inception of every great revival. I once spoke to P. S. Brewster of Cardiff, Wales, about the Welsh Revival, and he told me that praying and singing were major ingredients of that great move. Can you imagine a modern revival service where there is no singing or music? I have never seen one.

IV. The Purpose of Music

Music has a twofold purpose: to communicate with God in worship and to communicate with man in testimony. As with all other good things, this is another "good and perfect gift" that came down from the Father; therefore, it is to be returned to the Father in worship and used in this world for His glory. One man by the name of Mazzini said, "Music is the harmonious voice of creation, an echo of the invisible world, one note of the divine concord which the entire universe is destined one day to sound."

While holding our subject close to evangelism, let us notice the great possibilities of music. Moods can be created before the service by either vocal or instrumental music. The congregation can unconsciously be led to feelings of worship, praise, testimony, or rejoicing. By the direction of the Holy Spirit, this preservice music should be planned with a definite purpose to introduce the whole service.

The invitational song at the close of any service and the singing around the altar are of utmost importance. The right song can turn the tide to victory and the wrong one can prevent the same. Again, let us be led of the Spirit! Here music can be the vehicle, and the words of faith and surrender can be put into the heart and on the lips of those seeking the Lord with the effect of helping the seeker along the road to his goal.

Music in the church is great, but don't leave it there when you go out to your world. Paul tells us a Spirit-filled life consists of: "Speaking to yourselves in psalms and hymns and spiritual songs, singing and making melody in your heart to the Lord; giving thanks always for all things unto God and the Father in the name of our Lord Jesus Christ" (Ephesians 5:19, 20). Take a song to the dark, drab, discouraged world. This, too, is evangelism!

V. The Power of Music

Have you ever considered the great power of music and the things it can do? It can make women weep, men march to battle, and children let off steam. It can quiet the cries of a baby and convey the tenderest emotions of lovers. It can bring Christ to a sinner in words of poetry that are the words of love.

Did you ever notice how much theology we learn through songs? How about "Jesus Loves Me, This I Know"? This is the first thing we learn about the love of God. If repeated over and over during the early days of a child's life, it will be most difficult to forget. Other songs, such as "There Is Power in the Blood," teach some of the most powerful and necessary lessons of the Scriptures. "He Keeps Me Singing" further emphasizes the victorious life in all things. We may forget some of the verses of the Bible, but when put in rhyme, and to music, they have a way of staying with us.

VI. The Participants in Music

A. THE LEADER

I feel that something should be said about the participants in this great field of music. How about the leader? Should he be just anyone we can push into the job a few moments before the service?

If one is to render the greatest service in the most effective way, then the preparation of every church musician or director should be fourfold: (1) The first of these should be spiritual preparation. He should be a devoted Christian, loyal church member in regular attendance, interested in the whole church, generous in finance, and a soul winner at all times. (2) Then, there is the educational preparation. In order to be able to express himself properly, the leader should be trained in public speaking. (3) He also needs a good theological background in order to draw on the leading of the Spirit in all things. (4) He must also have as much musical education as possible to enable him never to be ashamed of his work before God or man.

B. THE CHOIR

If the leader is important, it follows that the choir is also important. Everything the choir does is observed from the moment they march in. Their actions can create or destroy the right spirit of the service. Let's not leave the congregation to sit and watch only; a good leader and a good choir will sweep up the congregation into its flow, and the whole sanctuary will consequently ring with praises to the Lord.

C. THE ACCOMPANIST

One of the well-known sayings of music directors is that it is easy to get an accompanist on the piano or organ bench but most difficult to get them off. Any song, arrangement, instrumental solo, or congregational song can be greatly assisted or easily killed by the proper or improper accompaniment. Watch your leader! Be ready on the spur of the moment! Know the choruses and their proper keys! Be able to transpose them into other keys if needed! Take time to practice whenever needed! Be dependable and be on time! Leave your heart open to the Spirit! You may have to play with your fingers, but your heart can and must be in tune with the Lord at all times.

Who, but the Lord, knows how many things converge to bring a soul to the knowledge of salvation. Music, especially vocal music, is one of the most important of these.

To quote a man by the name of Edwards, "God does not so much love to create, as He creates to love, and God sings while He creates . . . . From the morning of creation He ordained song and gladness for the redeemed prodigals of earth on their return to the Father's heart and home. . . . Music has every appearance of being a spiritual force, intended as a medium of communication between spirit and spirit, between God and men, and among men."

We expect every preacher to be anointed to speak. We should expect every singer or musician to be anointed of God to sing. I would rather have a prayed-up choir or soloist than an on-tune choir or soloist. Let's have the Spirit of the Lord in our music!

Panel Discussion and Open Forum

In the brief discussion period two key words were *ministry* and *flexibility*: the importance of keeping in focus that music is a ministry, not a time-filler, and the need for flexibility in types of music and techniques. Following is a summary of suggestions and comments:

CHORUSES

Know the proper keys. When the leader starts a chorus, instruct accompanists not to find the key unless they can do so without "stumbling around" on the instrument.

Seek the leadership of the Holy Spirit in selecting choruses. Realizing music is an "expression of feelings by tone," depend on the Spirit to generate those feelings in the right direction.

ALTAR CALL MUSIC

Pastors and evangelists will differ in their preference. The choir director and organist must take their cue from the leader as to background music during the altar call. Flexibility is the key.

Try lowering the altar call song a couple of keys.

There were pro and con comments on continuous organ during the altar service. This can become a crutch so that while the organ is playing, people pray; when the organ stops, the people stop. On the other hand, if it takes a crutch to keep people praying, is it bad? The organ can have a ministry of inspiration and encouragement.

TYPES OF MUSIC

Our people come from many different backgrounds and worship with different types of songs. A broad spectrum of music is needed to catch everybody. Include great hymns of the church.

Referring to the speaker's comment that "to communicate with our generation we must perhaps use their music," someone asked for a statement on having songs tempered to reach the world. The speaker responded: "Music itself is not moral or immoral; it is amoral. People are moral or immoral. I believe today we should not worry too much about what is sung, but what is our reaction to the song. It is something that should be used to glorify God. I have heard every type of rhythm used to glorify God. Communication is the important thing."

As to the use of classical music such as Bach and Mendelssohn, again the key word is *ministry*. Will it lead the people into worship? In some instances this would be the case; however, we need variety.

WEDDING MUSIC

Several comments stressed the use of sacred music in church weddings. The pastor can give direction to the couple in premarital counseling. The church might have a folio of suitable music available. A music committee might list music that is considered appropriate.

TAPE-RECORDED ACCOMPANIMENT

The question was raised regarding the use of tape accompaniment in the church. Would this hinder the freedom of the Spirit? The concensus of the panel was that where the accompaniment is appropriate and in good taste, it can be effective and certainly is the answer where "live" accompaniment is not available.

ORGAN DURING MESSAGE IN TONGUES AND INTERPRETATION

Responding to a question from the audience, the expression of the panel was that there should be nothing to distract during a message in tongues or prophecy. "The message of the Spirit does not need accompaniment."

MUSIC DURING YEAR OF REVIVAL

The seminar closed with a unanimous expression of concern that in the 1969 Year of Revival pastors and evangelists be inspired to give music its place, not as a preliminary or entertainment feature, but as a vital part of spiritual ministry.

THE SUNDAY SCHOOL TEACHER—
A SOUL WINNER

Speaker: **BRUCE MOTTER**
Moderator: **JOHN OHLIN**
Panelists: **SILAS GAITHER, MRS. G. W. HARDCASTLE II,**
L. B. KEENER
Recorder: **GARY LEGGETT**

MANY TIMES WE IN CHRISTIAN CIRCLES have spoken of teaching and soul winning as separate phases of God's work. This should not be so. Daniel 12:3 reads, "And they that be wise shall shine as the brightness of the firmament; and they that turn many to righteousness, as the stars for ever and ever." The meaning of the word *wise* in the King James Version is much more significant than it first appears. The word in the original means "teachers." In other words, "They that are teachers shall shine. These teachers that turn many to righteousness shall shine as stars forever."

Every Sunday school teacher who seeks to be effective in the soul-winning phase of God's work must ask himself a few basic questions: Just what is my role and purpose as a Sunday school teacher? Am I fulfilling or accomplishing that role? What kind of lives is my teaching ministry producing?

When we honestly evaluate our answers before God, we begin to understand our responsibility of giving the gospel to every creature.

What, then, is the role of the Sunday school teacher? To teach. But to teach what? Just what are we teaching, and how effectively are we communicating?

Secular education satisfies itself with the teaching of facts and theories. But can the Christian educator, the Sunday school teacher, be satisfied teaching just facts, theories, or even

principles? No! This is not the ultimate goal of the Sunday school teacher.

The ultimate goal of teaching is expressed in Romans 8:29, where we are admonished to "be conformed to the image of his Son." No matter what we have taught in the way of memorization of Scripture, retaining of facts, or knowledge of Christian principles, if we have not brought our students to conformity to the image of Christ by a personal commitment to Him, our teaching ministry has not realized its true and foremost goal. Doctrines, principles, and Biblical history become truly significant only *after* experiencing the "new birth" Jesus spoke about in the third chapter of John.

The question is sometimes asked, "Is it necessary to think of Sunday school as an evangelistic arm of the church as well as the teaching arm?" According to the National Sunday School Association, an estimated 85 percent of the church members in the average evangelical church were won to Christ through the Sunday school.

There may be a tendency on the part of Sunday school teachers and workers to look at a statistic such as this and pat themselves on the back, saying, "What a fine job we are doing for the cause of Christianity." But another statistic should shake us out of our complacency. Eighty out of every hundred pupils now attending Sunday school in the United

190

States will not be reached for Christ. They will leave their churches, never to commit themselves to Christ in a personal way.

A nationwide survey conducted in 1962 by the National Sunday School Association showed that one of the chief reasons young people drop out of evangelical churches is that the times of Bible study, particularly times in the Sunday school classrooms, are boring and irrelevant. In our own denomination our greatest loss of Sunday school students occurs at the junior high and high school levels. Many young people have sought for reality in other organizations because we have failed to challenge their intellect and motivate their desire to commit themselves to Christ.

Many American young people who revolt against the church are not rejecting Christ, for they don't really know who He is because they have never met Him. They are rejecting teaching, doctrine, and "churchianity" that has failed to give them the life-changing, life-producing part of the story.

But why is Sunday school so boring and irrelevant? Does it have to be so? Is it because the message we are trying to teach is antiquated as some have charged? No! This cannot be true! Even though the message is two thousand years old, the Word of God lives and produces life today just as it did two millenniums ago.

One of the tragedies of Christian teaching is that there is a tremendous confusion concerning the message and the methods. The message cannot change, but the methods we use to convey that message may change. Because many are unwilling to grasp this important truth and consider flexibility in their methodology, true Christianity has fallen behind in its attempt to keep up with the population explosion. The apostle Paul knew his methods had to be flexible when he said: "I am made all things to all men, that I might by all means save some" (1 Corinthians 9:22). We, also must continually evaluate and update our teaching methods in the Sunday school in order to have maximum effectiveness.

The cry heard from young people all over the world today is one calling for relevance and meaningfulness. With some this may be an excuse for nonconformity, but with others it is a sincerely valid appeal. Therefore, we must do everything within our power to make our methods present our message *with* relevance and meaning.

One advantage the Sunday school teacher in the classroom has over the preacher in the pulpit is that the teacher can be on a more personal basis with those with whom he is communicating. Capitalizing on this personal relationship factor may involve any one of a number of possibilities in or out of the classroom, but it certainly involves praying together with each student and showing concern for his spiritual welfare.

The Sunday school teacher must remember that he cannot leave his responsibilities in the classroom. In a very real sense the Sunday school teacher teaches every moment he is with his pupils. This personal relationship between teacher and pupil must be cultivated and maintained both in and out of the classroom. We then can present Christ and *His* personality in a more effective way.

The wise teacher must allot time somewhere in his weekly schedule to take advantage of this personal relationship. He must make time for a personal discussion with a pupil who needs counseling or for dealing with a pupil whom the Holy Spirit has been preparing for the experience of salvation. Often our attitude of teaching is to cram into the students as much of the lesson as time will permit, leaving no time for questions, counseling, or decisions. When this is done, we have lost sight of our true objective in teaching.

Another problem we face as teachers is that we are still using the lecture method as the chief means of communication. The best way of reaching the most students is to select a teaching method that will directly involve them in the lesson discussion. Only as that method is thoughtfully selected, carefully planned, and prayerfully led by the Holy Spirit is the final goal of winning the souls of our pupils going to be realized.

Individual participation is still the most effective method of learning available. Stimulating class discussions are enjoyed, accepted, and effective for almost any age group. Dramatic presentations of the lessons, though involving more work, can have a tremendous effect upon our pupils. The classroom must become a place of personal involvement if we are going to see our pupils won to Christ.

How about those activities outside the classroom? Again we must admit to the ineffectiveness of our methodology and our lack of motivation. We must be willing to change some of our preconceived ideas regarding methodology and become more sensitive to the moving of

God's Spirit in new methods and new ideas for new outreach.

All too often we criticize communication media when we should be using these media to further the gospel. We all recognize that television has been used to propagate many ungodly ideas and concepts, but how many of us have taken the time to discover new ways television could be used for spreading the gospel? Our entire evangelistic utilization of television has been to reproduce a church service for people to watch. Statistics prove that with this method we are reaching almost exclusively church-oriented people. Those that need it the most, those that we must reach, are simply not "tuned in." Kenneth Chafin in his book, *Help, I'm a Layman*, says a whole new world of evangelistic opportunity could be opened to us if we were willing to produce one-minute "Christian commercials," given at key times during key programs. Those who are watching a football game, for example, will not turn off their sets just because of a one-minute commercial.

Other possibilities exist. The most popular shows among teen-agers and adults today are "talk shows." Why can't we sponsor some "Christian talk shows," utilizing our high school or college-age Sunday school students? Here again we have a wealth of possible outreach to the ages that need it the most. Actually, getting to the people we are trying to reach is what it means to communicate our faith with relevance.

No matter what age group we are teaching, outside activities can be used to win pupils to Christ. Activities such as retreats, outings, camp-outs, and sporting events can be used as effective means of communication. Home Bible studies for young people and adults have been a tremendously effective means of soul winning outside the classroom.

Today there are organizations on our high school and college campuses that are attempting to communicate the gospel to these age groups. I do not disagree with these organizations, but the very need of their existence is proof that the church nationally, the church locally, and, most specifically, the local Sunday school, are all failing in their plans to reach and keep high school and college-age young people. We must look for new ways of extending our evangelism into these critical areas.

We must teach our Sunday school pupils themselves to be personal soul winners. For many years we have hidden behind the philosophy that evangelism is a Sunday night service with an altar call, or a two-week campaign with an evangelist. We have depended on people coming to us and to our churches to be saved. Maybe this worked at the beginning of the century, but it is by-and-large not working today. We must go back to the concept founded in the Early Church of going out to reach those all around us.

God needs the voice of committed Christians to be found in every area, vocation, and status or level of life. We do not have time to be indifferent. There are too many lives not being reached and slipping into eternity without hope. Sunday school teacher, renew your efforts and your thinking to meet the challenge of today's changing world. "They that are teachers *shall* win souls and shall shine." The Sunday school teacher must be, first and foremost, a soul winner.

Panel Discussion and Open Forum

We must be perfectly honest with ourselves. Two questions point up the area of motivation: (1) If you were being paid an adequate salary to teach, would you teach any differently? (2) If you were paid for winning souls, would you do differently?

An adequate guideline for all Sunday school teachers is found in 2 Corinthians 3:5, 6: "Not that we are sufficient of ourselves to think any thing as of ourselves; but our sufficiency is of God; who also hath made us able ministers of the new testament; not of the letter, but of the spirit: for the letter killeth, but the spirit giveth life."

Question: Regarding "Christian commercials" on TV, how would you finance such a project?

First, all TV stations are looking for good, wholesome commercials. Second, I feel we must evaluate our use of God's money for TV. Try to determine the potential you can reach by such means. When the church knows this, there should be little problem in financing such a project.

A Christian commercial might follow a dialogue pattern between two persons. One would ask: "What is the most meaningful thing in your life?" The other would answer: "My relationship to Jesus Christ." The rest of the dialogue would center on this theme. The commercial might be similar to those currently aired by the Heart Association regarding the dangers of smoking.

Talk shows might follow the format of a

round-table discussion with a moderator and several young people composing a forum.

Question: After a teacher has led a pupil to Christ, what follow-up would you recommend?

Personal counseling sessions with the pupil should occur at other times besides the regular class hour. Use other members of the class in follow-up if the age level permits this. Correspond with the pupil if he moves away from the city. Give the pupil a Bible and definite directions regarding the passages that will help him most as a new Christian.

Question: How and when should a teacher lead a pupil to Christ?

It is always best to seek the leading of the Holy Spirit in this matter. Perhaps one of the keys to knowing the best time is to be personally involved with each of your pupils.

Question: Why are we asking people to serve as teachers who are not qualified to win souls?

Sunday school teachers should be selected as carefully as pastors are chosen. Church and Sunday school leaders should plan to give instruction in soul-winning techniques and provide teacher training to qualify those who presently are unqualified.

A delegate stated his opinion that Sunday school materials need to include current events and a discussion of what is going on in the world around us.

A panelist suggested group dynamics as a means of involving the class in a study of the material. Teachers should try buzz sessions, panels, symposiums, etc.

The speaker mentioned he had found it helpful to use the undated manuals in his class. These can be chosen to meet the specific need in the class, and the teacher can take as much time as needed to complete the study.

He then stressed the most important factor in teaching and winning is to be sensitive to the moving of God's Spirit.

WOMEN WITNESSING

Speaker: **MRS. J. L. SCHAFFER**
Moderator: **MRS. MILDRED SMULAND**
Panelists: **MRS. LOUIS NEELY, MRS. KARL STRADER, MRS. DAVID WAKEFIELD**
Recorder: **MRS. L. GLEN AHLF**

B EHOLD, A SOWER went forth to sow" (Matthew 13:3). There is nothing profound or difficult about the task of planting seed. Even a little child can do it.

Jesus said the sower in His parable sowed the "good seed"; it was the Word of God. It will produce a harvest often in apparent unfavorable conditions. So we must plant it, sow it in every little nook and cranny, on rocky slopes and in grassy valleys. Keep sowing until the Husbandman comes to gather the harvest!

Do not sow mixed seed. Human concepts and vain traditions will not produce a harvest.

Jesus could just as well have said, "Pray ye the Lord of the harvest that He will send forth *sowers*."

Women Witnessing. These are two compatible words. They fit together so normally. Women will talk about the things that are most important to them. Neither monarchs nor dictators could threaten them to silence. This ability to be able to express themselves, to talk it out, to make things clear, to speak with emotion is God-given. What a potential for God if we channel it properly!

> *They talk about a women's sphere as though it*
> *had a limit;*
> *There's not a place in earth or heaven,*
> *There's not a task to mankind given,*
> *There's not a blessing or a woe,*
> *There's not a whispered yes or no,*

> *There's not a life, or death, or birth,*
> *That has a feather's weight of worth—without*
> *a woman in it.*   —*C. E. Bowman*

If you should be asking, "Where is my field of labor," I can best answer by saying, "Where you are and everywhere you go." Be a seed sower all day long, 365 days a year. This becomes a natural, spontaneous process that will produce an abundant harvest for our Lord.

We must be witnesses in our homes. Christian workers are constantly shocked at the irresponsibility of mothers today. Great mothers of faith produce great children of faith. Find the answer for your children's problems in God's Word.

Be witnesses to our children's friends. Healthy, normal children draw other children. In their associations at school, friends are often made with children from non-Christian homes. Even children from Christian homes will often respond to a word of advice, or guidance.

Let us love little children, dirty or clean, trained or untrained. Jesus loves them. He died for them. Are we too busy, too wrapped up in our own that we cannot catch the vision of this potential for God? Are we too busy to take time to gather them around and read carefully selected Bible stories or the Bible itself? Or to take time to invite and bring them to the house of God?

Witness to our neighbors. "As we have therefore opportunity, let us do good unto all men"

(Galatians 6:10). I read a statement the other day, "Neighborliness is out of style." Is it? If we must answer in the affirmative, we must remind ourselves that "good works" went out with it. True Christianity begins in one's own neighborhood.

The loss of loved ones, sicknesses, and many other neighborhood problems and interests can give women well-prepared soil in which to sow the Word of God. You might ask your neighbors to attend church numbers of times, and they will not respond; but show a special act of thoughtfulness and kindness in a crisis, and you will open the possibility of winning them to God.

Does it seem a little strange that we strain our imaginations to find new ways to do things for God when most of the time we ignore the ways God has devised for us through the Word. I wonder what would be the influence of the Church on the world today if we began to obey some of these divine injunctions to produce "good works?"

Witness to the people who come to your door. A young Christian woman keeps a supply of good tracts and *Evangels* near the door. After listening to a salesman talk, she then speaks to him about God and hands him a piece of literature. Newsboys, electricians, repairmen—she feels the Lord sent them her way so she can witness to them of His mercy and grace.

Witness to an employer or employee. This is a very challenging relationship for Spirit-filled women.

Here the Christian woman can be a "sign," which is one meaning of the word *witness.* In the daytime two signs may look alike, but in the dark one will glow and the other seems blank. This is because there is a glowing ingredient on one sign. Thank God for the Holy Spirit, the "glowing ingredient" in Spirit-filled Christians.

Witness in hospitals, nursing homes, and correctional homes. If you do not think you are needed, I would like to come to your community. I am positive we could find those who will laugh when we come and weep when we leave. You can become the only sunshine in many precious lives. Life can take on new meaning for you as you realize, "Here is a neglected field." People do not become saintly just because they are old. Many old people are not ready to meet God.

Then there are the correctional homes and homes for unwed mothers. Oh, how marvelous to be able to unlock heaven's gates for souls burdened with the guilt of sin! The only way lives can be washed clean is in the "fountain filled with blood." Jesus is His Name, we tell them, as we stand at the crossroads of their lives.

There are many other places we can sow the seed—such as PTA and civic affairs where volunteers are needed. But let us beware of a common tendency to become involved in a carnal way and not be doing the service "heartily, as unto the Lord." Time is very precious, and what many people call being "involved" can be mere "entanglement." We must invest our time in the causes that will bring the greatest dividends for the Master.

Let us consider how to "sow the seed." We must sow in love. On the dry-land farms in Colorado, where the rainfall is very light, I've seen a farmer soak his seed corn to make it germinate faster when planted. This is a dry and barren field in which we labor—let's soak the seed in *divine love.* There is a great difference in pity and compassion. We can feel sorry for someone and go on our way and forget them, but divine compassion will make us do something.

Natural love is not enough. Womanly tenderness is not sufficient. Our souls must be bathed—and our emotions touched—with the living flame of love.

Sow in tears. Remember the promise, "He who goeth forth and weepeth, bearing precious seed, shall doubtless come again with rejoicing, bringing his sheaves with him" (Psalm 126:6). The ministry of tears is so essential. Can we really be moved and not weep?

What do we weep about? To be able to weep is a blessing if we weep for the right cause. The next time you feel like crying, ask God what He wants you to cry for. Weep for your sons and daughters; weep for thousands of homeless children; weep for fallen girls, broken homes, barren altars, empty churches, lukewarm church members, the lonely, and the forgotten.

Sow in prayer. As you pray, the Holy Spirit will work. He will direct you. Pray until you tremble with excitement. Pray until you groan in pain, and let your tears flow down and soak your altar. Pray and weep until your eyes are washed clean and you can see each little boy and girl, each teen-ager, and each man and woman as the one for whom Christ died.

Panel Discussion and Open Forum

Question: What is the real motive for personal witnessing? Does a guilt complex enter into one's thinking, making him feel, "I must tell someone"?

Compassionate love for lost and suffering humanity is a main incentive in an individual witnessing to the love of God and His redeeming power. Empowering of the Holy Spirit provides needed impetus for the effort. It was pointed out that the most retiring, timid persons can commit themselves to the Spirit in such a manner as to be among the most effective soul winners. No method or procedure, no program, will be successful without Holy Spirit conviction in the heart of the worker.

One panelist suggested that American women of the twentieth century are better prepared to participate in a ministry of personal witnessing than women of any other generation because they have more time—due to work-saving devices and, generally, more education. Also, present-day living—traveling, business associations, civic and social opportunities—provides more witnessing opportunities.

Question: What kind of witnessing program can a church institute for women?

One panelist reported that in her church women meet for a day's preparation for soul winning. Baby sitters are provided. Two of the group are designated to prepare the noon lunch. Workers are provided with a packet containing city or area maps; cards for needed information; pamphlets; and a scheduled procedure.

A team consists of one experienced worker and one novice—thus new persons capable of becoming leaders are constantly being trained. Participants are taught how to bring people to a decision and do the soul winning themselves, not merely invite the people to church. Workers return with a written report. "Souls are won every week," said the panelist.

Question: How can we help train the women in our assemblies as soul winners?

Short training sessions of concentrated study held consecutively for a week or ten days can be offered periodically to those interested in this ministry. A specialist in the field can be invited to teach the art of soul winning.

A panelist suggested that having an outside instructor lent importance to the training course.

At the end of the class instruction, participants should be sent out to put into practice the things they have learned. Two workers should be sent out together—one for a "buffer," to baby-sit or converse with other members of the family if necessary so the needy one can

be segregated for soul-winning conversation.

A panelist suggested kaffeeklatsches as a natural way in which a Christian woman could reach her neighbors in a soul-winning effort. She described the kaffeeklatsch as an hour when women of the area are invited to have coffee with the hostess. During the time everyone would be led to share in free discussion of some contemporary subject such as, "How may we become better mothers?" "Should women work?" and related topics. Bible discussions and reading might occur at the first meeting or follow later. The alert hostess or Christian friend would be prepared to tactfully take advantage of the slightest opportunity. A Bible study introducing an undated quarterly or approved books dealing with a certain subject could be introduced at the proper time, perhaps at the request of the group.

Question: When you invite the unchurched to a kaffeeklatsch, do you tell them there will be a Bible lesson?

No, for other activity is offered. In some cases such an announcement would defeat the purpose of the invitation. Such a meeting, though it is never held without the pastor's knowledge and the guidance of qualified leadership, is not identified as a meeting of the church.

Question: How does one start a coffee hour?

Just start. Invite one or two guests for a social time. Gradually others will be added. This project will grow with patience and time.

A panelist, the wife of an evangelist, said that during a revival she used the kaffeesklatches with women of the congregation as hostesses to reach different neighborhoods. She said, "Not only are women of the city influenced by the meeting in progress, but the lay women, seeing the plan of witnessing work, will be interested in continuing the outreach after I am gone."

Question: Of what value are children's story hours?

Children's story hours are a most versatile outreach toward the homes of the community. They are considered a door to similar meetings on the adult level with the mothers and, finally, other women of the area.

Question: How can a children's story hour be initiated?

The club may begin with a mother allowing her children to invite playmates to share a game and storytime after school. The circle of interest will grow.

A sign, "Kid's Club" or "Story Hour," and the time, placed in a conspicuous place in the yard will arouse interest. Children will come to inquire. Bible stories may be included in program. Printed helps are available.

The club may be held in a garage, on the floor in a home, or on a patio or a lawn.

The length of meetings should be one hour after school or on weekends. Refreshments are considered an attraction.

YOUTH SEMINAR: PHILOSOPHY

Speaker: **JAMES D. BROWN**
Moderator: **JOHN GARLOCK**
Panelists: **VIRGIL NICHOLSON, GEORGE WOOD, DWIGHT COLBAUGH**
Recorder: **HARRIS JANSEN**

PHILOSOPHY MAY BE DEFINED as "a critique of the facts of experience." Thus it considers Christian faith, which it classifies under religious experience, fair game for investigation. Because there are times when certain teachings of philosophy clash with one's experience with Christ, many Christians ask, "Is my faith in Christ intellectually defensible?"

I. Four Philosophies

The teachings we shall consider are taken from the philosophies of positivism, pragmatism, empiricism, and existentialism.

A. POSITIVISM

The positivism of Auguste Comte says essentially that man has crossed three states of development: (1) theological, (2) metaphysical, and (3) positive. In the first stage man explains natural phenomena in terms of spirits, gods, etc. In the second he explains natural phenomena as the working of principles referred to as scientific laws. In the third stage anything called reality must be verified by sense experience.

Actually there are a number of weaknesses in the doctrine that nothing is meaningful that cannot be confirmed by sensory experience. Its basic tenet undercuts itself. For if one says that only what is observed by the senses is reality or truth, then by what sense experience can he justify this statement itself?

The biggest weakness of positivism is that it contradicts the Word of God. "Whom having not seen, ye loved," says Peter of our relationship to our invisible Christ. "By faith we understand," says the writer to the Hebrews.

One variant of logical positivism is scientism, which holds that knowledge is obtained through the scientific method. By definition scientism excludes faith. But one principle the scientific method insists upon is that each discipline use the tool most nearly assisting the investigative function for which the discipline exists. If we utilize faith as our major tool in religious knowledge, then it can hardly be said that we are not scientific, since faith is the tool which best assists our religious pursuit.

Either the scientific method includes or excludes faith. If it excludes it, then science cannot insist on each discipline using the tool best suited for the subject matter peculiar to that discipline. If the scientific method *includes* faith, then scientism is wrong in saying that knowledge comes solely by the scientific method which makes no room for faith.

B. PRAGMATISM

Pragmatism is the philosophy of practical consequences. To the pragmatists only that which is practical has value.

One of the facets of pragmatism which conflicts with the Christian world view is the pragmatic criterion of truth. If an idea works, it is true. Its truth is tested by its consequences.

For several reasons a Christian young person should not make workability the ultimate test of God's truth. Not every idea which appears to be working is true. The ideas of Simon the Sorcerer appeared to be working at Samaria. But if he possessed truth, then how can we ever draw the line between the genuine and the counterfeit?

Another serious objection to the pragmatic criterion of truth is that there are times when a particular truth in the Bible is working and we do not perceive it. The pragmatic criterion would mean we must suspend judgment on such truth until we perceive it working out in practical consequences. Thus Mordecai could not have accepted the truth of God's protection as long as Haman seemed to hold the upper hand.

The third objection is that even if we grant that the truth of an idea is its workability, we must still select a criterion of workability. In the pragmatist's scheme of things workability is ascertained through sense experience or experimentalism.

C. EMPIRICISM

The upshot of this is that we are thrown back to empiricism, the doctrine that knowledge stems from experience. According to this view there is no room for spiritual transmission and reception of truth.

Furthermore, if we follow empiricism to its logical conclusion, then we are led into the philosophy of idealism. This philosophy says that if all knowledge comes from experience, then whatever cannot be experienced cannot exist. Thus if God cannot be experienced through the senses, then God cannot be said to exist. If God cannot be said to exist, then the Bible which assumes His existence cannot be true. So if we follow this philosophy to its logical conclusion, we deny the Bible as the source of ultimate truth.

D. EXISTENTIALISM

Existentialism holds that "existence precedes essence." According to the existentialist, truth cannot be discovered through reasoning but only through paradox. There is no objective truth; truth is in us.

The theological expression of existentialism, originally conceived by Soren Kierkegaard, is now called neoorthodoxy. It postulates the existence of God solely on the basis of faith—not reason. Neoorthodoxy's rallying point is the old Augustinian position of "faith seeking understanding." In a word, we believe in order that we might know.

The basic weakness of neoorthodoxy is that it reduces God's Word to the subjectivity of man's experience, making man's experience the critic of the Bible. According to the writer to the Hebrews, however, it is the other way around. "For the word of God is quick, and powerful, and sharper than any two-edged sword ... and is a discerner of the thoughts and intents of the heart."

Although there may be a measure of truth in the idea that God's Word is only true to me personally as I appropriate it, nevertheless the very fact that it exists and is eternally true, irrespective of my acceptance or rejection of it, constitutes the very grounds on which I can appropriate it. Unlike the neoorthodoxist who denies an infallible Bible and accepts only those Scriptures as inspired which he says the Holy Spirit illuminates, we come to the Word with the assurance that "*all* scripture is given by inspiration of God and is profitable...."

II. Helps for Our Young People

A. AUTHORITY

Let every Christian settle what he considers his ultimate authority. The Christ's Ambassador who will make the Word of God his ultimate authority will not succumb to attacks on his faith.

For the Christian there appear to be only four choices outside the Bible as our source of ultimate authority. They are reason, religious experience, tradition, and the church. Each of these options contains truth, but none is equal to the Word of God which *is* truth.

Now let us suppose that a Christ's Ambassador chooses one of these as an alternative to the Word of God as the source of ultimate authority.

If he chooses reason, it must begin with an irrational faith in reason. The rationalist must have faith that reason works. Then, our thought patterns and observations are shaped by our perspective. We draw our conclusions on the basis of our world view. Third, reason cannot possibly handle paradox or apparent contradiction without looking to that which transcends itself.

There are difficulties, also, with religious experience as the source of ultimate authority. First, we have the grave problem of deciding what is meant by "experience." When do you decide that an experience is religious? Second, it is an anarchistic view, because there is no authority common to you and me. Third, religious experience justifies the status quo. Protestants never see visions of the Virgin Mary. Buddhists have Buddhist religious experiences. Fourth, the subjectivity of religious experience leaves man at the mercy of his own sinful tendencies. He tries to have the experience he wants to have. Fifth, the content of the experience is often eclipsed by the emotion of the experience itself.

Tradition—or the belief that something is true because it has stood the test of time—is also limited as a source of ultimate authority. Traditions are often contradictory. Thus we need some authority outside tradition to show us which is correct.

The Church is hardly a valid option as our source of ultimate authority. It is argued that if the Church wrote, gathered, and decided the canon of Scripture, then it is illogical to claim that Scripture alone is authoritative. But the burning issue is this: Do we have the witness of Scripture because of the Church or was the Church born in response to an objective event? Because the Word of God called the Church into being, it is the judge of the Church.

We are now back to our point of departure—the Word of God as our ultimate source of authority.

B. Honest Doubt

We must distinguish honest doubt from unbelief. Satan will often tell a youth in a sincere intellectual struggle that he has become a rank unbeliever. To help our youth, we need to ask ourselves if it is a problem concerning his faith or one concerning his reasoning. If it is the former, then we must walk the tunnel with him and literally feel with him to victory. If it is the latter, then we must show him in diplomatic fashion where the fallacy lies.

I suggest further that the pastors of our Fellowship keep in mind that our young people are exposed basically to inductive reasoning in college, whereas their religious orientation is based on deductive reasoning. Thus, we tell them that evolution is untrue because the Bible suggests it is untrue, and that is that! But the Christ's Ambassador goes to college and hears a professor begin with the "facts"—as he calls them. After piling these alleged facts upon each other, he then concludes that the hypothesis of evolution is tenable. And since inductive reasoning has become a "god term" in many of

our universities, it seems to invest the so-called facts themselves with validity.

C. Consensual Validation

The final suggestion I would offer is that we take cognizance of what sociologists call "consensual validation." Essentially this concept says that if a person's faith is to withstand attacks, it must be validated periodically by the person being in the presence of others who share his views. If we disassociate ourselves from others of like faith, the probability is increased that we will become intellectually identified with someone whose views are contrary to Christianity.

There are several implications. First, we must have pastors in college towns who can minister to both the spiritual and intellectual needs of our students. Second, the pastor at the student's home church should communicate as much of the church's atmosphere as possible by mail. Third, such organizations as Chi Alpha should have our prayerful and financial support.

None of this is meant to imply that our pastors need to be top heavy on education to minister to our students. Neither should they try to refute the teachings of philosophy with philosophy. Only a few are called to be apologists. Most of us are called to be witnesses.

Furthermore we must never underestimate the great preserving power of the Holy Spirit. But let us remember that we have a warrant for this only as we can say with Paul, "I kept back nothing that was profitable unto you."

Panel Discussion and Open Forum

Christians are primarily called to be witnesses: this principle should guide Christian young people as they face unchristian philosophies on college campuses or elsewhere.

This conclusion was based upon the New Testament example of both Jesus and the apostle Paul. For instance, when Jesus sent out the disciples in Matthew 10, He specifically instructed them not to argue; but if their words were not received to go on to another house or city. Paul told the Corinthian church he did not come to them in great wisdom, but simply declared the Word of God (1 Corinthians 2:1). It was not up to him to defend it; rather, the Holy Spirit would affirm it.

Yet the church generally has not kept pace with the issues and problems facing today's Christian college or university student. The panelists urged that pastors of churches located in college communities be conversant with ideologies current on the college campus. Students are asking for more relevant involvement of the church in areas of student interest.

Because of the openness of the college student to truth, it was urged that Assemblies of God churches take a clear and positive attitude toward the contemporary educational scene. Spirit-filled leaders who know the issues will lead Christian students to synthesize basic Christian concepts into their philosophy of life.

It was agreed that students on the secular campus are generally tuned against the gospel and believe the church has not kept pace with trends as they exist today. Unfortunately, mass media of communication have done much to create this poor image of the church. While Assemblies of God students on the secular campus retain their respect for their church, there is the feeling the church did not prepare them properly to face the ideological conflicts they experience in the secular college classroom.

Today's college student is more idealistic than ever. When he observes inconsistency, he rebels against the institution he believes responsible for the inconsistency. His active involvement in today's critical issues rises from his strong compulsion to practice what he believes.

It was pointed out that one of the great contributions the church could make to college students is to hold before them a high view of the Bible as authoritative truth. Show that God is ultimate truth, it was recommended. Show them they do not need to be afraid of faith. They should be given opportunity to test the theories of the classroom against the fact of Scripture. Truth will provide its own best defense.

While Christians especially are witnesses, there will be some occasion for debating, as did the apostles in the Book of Acts (Peter and John in Acts 4; Paul in Acts 17). It should be recognized God has called some to be apologists, to work with truth; but others should avoid the attempt at apologetic.

As for the Christian college student, it is foolish for him to take issue with the secular professor, for the weight of the professor's years of training and experience would quickly overpower the student. However, the freshman student may be able to demolish another freshman's argument.

Finally, the church should listen to what the student has to say. Churches and adult Christians should reexamine their role to be sure they are contributing meaningfully to finding solutions for the ills fostered by misguided and inconsistent philosophies such as are common to the secular campus.

YOUTH SEMINAR: PSYCHOLOGY

Speaker: **T. F. ZIMMERMAN III**
Moderator: **ANDREW NELLI**
Panelists: **DAVID DRAKE, DELMAR GUYNES, DAVID WIGGINGTON**
Recorder: **RICHARD CHAMPION**

To PURSUE SCIENCE and be simultaneously religious has often been construed as contradictory. People within the church have reacted to my interest in and study of psychology with attitudes ranging from mild curiosity to head-shaking apprehension. The question frequently puts the topic sharply in focus: "How can you be a psychologist and be Pentecostal?"

This question succinctly frames the doubt that people in our churches still have. Psychology and Pentecost are seen in conflict.

It is my thesis that this conflict is more apparent than real. It is further my firm conviction that psychology can support faith. My personal experience has demonstrated the validity of this conviction to my satisfaction.

This paper will simply be saying: (1) I understand why people of the church are defensive about psychology; (2) this defensiveness is unnecessary; and, (3) the pursuit of scientific knowledge, psychology included, is an important part of the First Commandment, "Thou shalt love the Lord with all . . . thy mind."

I. A Historical Perspective

It is true that science and scientific enterprises are frequently skeptical about religion, but this skepticism is somewhat understandable. It was the church and its leaders that contributed to the near total suppression of scientific advancement during that tragic period of history now known as the Dark Ages. Men were hanged for belief that the earth was round. In our present society, where science and technology have become dominating factors, we can only be thankful that scientists are more humane in their relationships with the church.

During the last century evangelicals have neglected to relate the Bible to current knowledge. Pentecostals specifically have been lax and defensive in regard to scholarship. I would like to discuss two reasons which, in part, can help us understand why this has come to be.

First, it is partly due to the aggressive anti-Christian attitude characteristic of the origins of modern science and philosophy. Again I would remind you it was at great price and sacrifice of life that men won their freedom from the church so they could admit fact. The anti-Christian character and flavor of science led many to think it wiser not to take such studies, their belief being that science would undermine religious faith.

The second reason for the lack of scholarship among Pentecostals is what I call an anti-intellectual habit of mind. At times we may have exalted strong emotion at the expense of clearheadedness. It has not been difficult for one to gain the impression that right feeling is more important than right thinking.

This lapse into fear and intellectual laziness is a modern form of one of the oldest thorns in the church's flesh—Manichaeism. Very simply, the Manichaean idea is something as follows: (1) The material world is evil and worthless; (2) one's dealings with it should therefore be cut to a bare minimum; (3) true spirituality means living as much out of direct contact with this world as possible; (4) holiness is defined in terms of abstinence from needless traffic with created things; (5) nothing is gained from the study of anything here below.

In summary, the less interest one has in the world around, the better for one's soul. This Manichaean theme has consistently recurred in the history of the church, and it seems that the Pentecostal movement has been the vehicle for one of its more recent appearances.

Given this historical context and perspective, it is simple to understand why the issue of the psychologist versus the Christian is raised.

II. The Unity of God and His Works

I propose that ultimately there can be no conflict between the facts of honest science and Biblically founded religion. The same God is the origin of both the Bible and the world of creation. As theology attempts to comprehend the nature of God, so psychology attempts to comprehend the nature of man. In what is both a very humorous and at the same time a rather tragic approach, the church has attempted to help God out by vigorously opposing both the facts and the theories of science and philosophy. It strikes me as somewhat conceited for man to imply that God and His Word cannot stand sufficient in themselves.

God forbids Christians to lose interest or turn away from *His* world. Genesis 1:28 establishes that man was put into the world to have dominion over it, to use it, and to use it for God's glory. It therefore seems obvious that man's duty is to study the contents of the world and to try to cope with its problems. Never forget that the Creator cares about His creation; so must we.

It would be naive to imply there are no conflicts between science and religion. There are many apparent conflicts. But it is my contention that when all the facts are in and man has constructed a valid and reliable theory, it will be consistent with and, in fact, positively support the truth of the Scriptures. The discipline of wrestling with the problems of relating two sets of facts, natural and Biblical, leads to a greatly enriched understanding of both.

It should not be the mission of a vigorously evangelistic church to stifle the minds of men. The Bible is one long march of disciplined scholars grounded in the science and knowledge of their day who evangelized their worlds. It is abundantly clear that we are in the midst of a scientific age, witnessing an unbelievable explosion of knowledge. If our Pentecostal movement is to speak to its day and reach its generation, it must achieve scientific competence.

III. The Utility of Psychology

One cannot view psychology as a modern substitute for a meaningful personal relationship with Christ. Psychology is not a religion. It is a tool that by itself is neither good nor bad. As with any other tool, it becomes the extension of the person using it. A hammer can be used for either building up or tearing down. There is ample evidence that the facts and theories emanating from psychology have been applied to destroying religious faith; but these tools have also been used to illuminate and stimulate faith. In the limits of this brief paper I can only cite a few examples of how psychology can be applied to contribute to a more effective evangelistic thrust in our church.

1. *We can develop an awareness of and appreciation for the group mental health of our churches.* Social psychology gives us real insight into the destructiveness of what the Bible plainly calls sin. I am personally concerned about the poor interpersonal relationships existing in most of our churches.

2. *Psychology can help us understand what constitutes an evangelistic personality.* We need to be made vitally aware that witnessing is not something you *do* but something you *are.*

3. *The knowledge of the social sciences can help us be aware of our upward social mobility* and the danger of losing our compassion for those who are less fortunate in our society.

4. *As individuals we can gain insight into our motivations.*

5. *Psychology can assist us in understanding what the baptism in the Holy Spirit can mean* as an experience of the total personality.

These are only some of the subjects to which the tools of psychology can be applied.

The nature of our technological age demands that we become proficient in all sciences. Evangelism means that we must penetrate the world; and if we are to do this, we must equip ourselves with all available knowledge of the creation of God. Our church cannot afford any anti-intellectualism or academic laziness. We must study both the Word and world of our Lord.

I would like to make the following recommendations:

1. *It is essential to become mentally vigorous* —"Study to show thyself approved unto God." We need to cease our anti-intellectualism.

2. *Do not overestimate science or psychology.* People tend to give the sciences too much significance. There is more we don't know than we do know. Psychology is the youngest of the sciences and proceeds with theories.

3. *Don't underestimate your faith.* Read and study the Bible; be thoroughly grounded in the Word. Problems in college come because students are not grounded in the Bible. This is not the fault of the university; it is our fault.

4. *Don't attempt apologetics with three general psychology credits.*

Panel Discussion and Open Forum

Psychology is still in the experimental stage. It is hard to study because of the variables. When we say, "We accept psychology," we do not necessarily accept all views because these views do not agree among themselves.

The Bible cannot be used as a text on the physical sciences, but it is a basic text on human behavior. It lays out the causes of human behavior, so there is no better text than the Bible for understanding man.

All people use a lot of psychology—even those who fight it. But faith is a higher faculty than reason, so that we don't need to fear psychology. Understanding ourselves will help us reach others.

Question: Since psychology gives insights into our motivations, how can we get the amount we need?

The speaker suggested college courses, correspondence courses, or getting a good bibliography and studying the books recommended.

Although man has always sought to understand himself, it was stressed that the sophistication in modern medicine is similar to what is happening in problem solving today. Yet the extent of the church's involvement too often has been only, "We'll pray for you." Many people have written off the church because of our failure to understand.

One panelist cited statistics showing that sixty to eighty percent of those chronically ill have nothing organically wrong with them. But he cautioned that a person must exercise care in applying psychology for he may blunder and thus alienate people.

The Christian student will be battered around in college, but he can face conflicts. Nothing in psychology offers hope or faith. The most complete "theory" of life is the Bible. Religion is not a science—it involves the supernatural; and psychology cannot account for the supernatural.

YOUTH SEMINAR: ARCHAEOLOGY

Speaker: **ROBERT COOLEY**
Moderator: **JERRY SANDIDGE**
Panelists: **RALPH HARRIS, MEL SHAW, DAVID WOMACK**
Recorder: **CLARE ROSE**

THERE ARE THOSE WHO assert that the Bible is nothing more than a human book, subject to human limitations. In questions of history, geography, and the like they say it contains errors and cannot be expected to be scientifically accurate.

On the other hand, we assert that the Scriptures are the Word of God, written by holy men borne along by the Holy Spirit. The result was the written record of God's mighty deeds in time and space, a record of God's self-disclosure in Jesus Christ, a record through which the Creator speaks to the creature. The Christian may place his confidence in the written record and need not be dismayed by the many attacks made upon it.

I. The Influence of Biblical Criticism

The science of Biblical criticism has played an important role in scholarship for nearly two centuries. Bible scholars felt compelled to suggest answers to the questions concerning the truthfulness and authenticity of Scripture. Numerous theories resulted. We shall note two.

A. THEORIES CONCERNING THE AUTHENTICITY OF THE SCRIPTURES

After the middle of the eighteenth century scholars began to question a unified Pentateuch, authored by Moses. In 1753 a French physician, Jean Astruc, called attention to the fact that there were two names used for God, *Elohim* and *Jehovah*. He tried to account for this by saying it represented the combinations of two documents into the Genesis record, while, at the same time, maintaining Mosaic authorship. Astruc's "clue" furnished the first tenet of the documentary theory: the criterion of divine names.

Johann Eichhorn in 1779 pointed out that certain characteristics of style could be traced in the sections which used the different divine names. This idea and the criterion of divine names were carried through the whole Pentateuch by later critics. Mosaic authorship was now challenged. In 1805 W. M. L. DeWette assigned Deuteronomy to the seventh century B.C. on the ground of peculiarities of style and content. This added the concept of a third document to the original two-document theory proposed by Astruc and elaborated by Eichhorn.

Several other theories were subsequently proposed; however two important additions were to come. The first was made by Herman Hupfeld in 1853. He set forth the idea that there are two Elohist documents (E) in Genesis. The first Elohist document is formed in the first 19 chapters of Genesis, and the second Elohist begins with chapter 20.

Karl Graf proposed the second important modification. In his essay on "The Historical Books of the Old Testament," published in 1866, he claimed that the first Elohist document was the latest one written. The first Elohist document is characterized as being of a legal nature and was written by the priests. Thus, the symbol P (priestly document) came to be generally used to describe it and E was used for the second Elohist. So according to Graf, the order of the documents was: J E D P, written between 850 B.C. and 400 B.C.

The JEDP theory was popularized by Julius Wellhausen in his book, *Introduction to the History of Israel*, published in 1878, and aside from minor variations is the theory accepted among those who deny the Mosaic authorship of the Pentateuch.

The division did not stop with the Pentateuch. The other books of the Old Testament soon came under the attention of the critics. The whole result of the critics' labors was to discredit the traditional authorship and date assigned to most of the Old Testament books. Such an approach to the Bible has resulted in a "modernistic" view that it is a human religious book containing a conglomeration of myth, legend, history, and spiritual lessons.

B. The Date of the Acts

The New Testament has not been exempt from such attacks. It was contended that Acts was produced about the middle of the second century to reconcile the Pauline party, which advocated Gentile liberty, and the Petrine party, which held to a strict observance of the Law.

C. Underlying Premises of the Critics

The critics based their approach upon three underlying premises.

1. *A rejection of the supernatural.* While the critic rejects the supernatural, he does try to hold on to the "religious values" of the Bible.

2. *An adherence to religious evolution.* According to the liberal critic, Israel's worship of God, like that of every other religion, had a very primitive beginning, and Israel's religious institutions were to be explained as a product of evolution. According to this, monotheism evolved from polytheism, and there can be no such thing as a supernaturally revealed religion.

3. *A skepticism concerning the historicity of much of the Bible.* Throughout these decades of critical study was the emergence of a marked skepticism toward the historical data of the Old Testament. The critic's attitude is that the Biblical record presents all the graduations between pure fiction and genuine history.

During the century in which the critical theories were being formulated, the inerrancy and the authority of the Scriptures were not questioned by the comman man. The critical attacks gained momentum from the fact that no adequate defense for the Bible's authority was available. Thus the people's faith in the Bible was shaken.

D. Reversals in Biblical Criticism

At the turn of the twentieth century archaeology in the Bible lands made spectacular progress in developing scientific techniques. As a result a phenomenal amount of material has been discovered, and the judgments of the critics have proved to be without foundation.

In a recent book John Elder states: "It is not too much to say that it was the rise of the science of archaeology that broke the deadlock between historians and the orthodox Christian. Little by little, one city after another, one civilization after another, one culture after another, whose memories were enshrined only in the Bible, were restored to their proper places in ancient history by the studies of archaeologists.... Contemporary records of Biblical events have been unearthed, and the uniqueness of Biblical revelation has been emphasized by contrast and comparison to newly discovered religions of ancient peoples. Nowhere has archaeological discovery refuted the Bible as history" (*Prophets, Idols and Diggers*, 1960, p. 16).

We can echo the Psalmist, with assurance, "For ever, O Lord, thy word is settled in heaven." Let us note a few of the best known and most significant discoveries.

II. The Bible and Modern Discovery

A. The Pentateuch

Basic to the Documentary Theory is the rejection of Mosaic authorship. It was assumed that writing was unknown in fifteenth century Palestine, and that the Pentateuch could not, therefore, have been written until after the ninth century B.C.

A calendar found at Tell Gezer was written about 925 B.C. and is the earliest Hebrew document thus far discovered. It was a schoolboy's exercise, itemizing the various months and activities of the agricultural year. Thus the skill of writing was so well known and widely practiced in Israel during the tenth century B.C. that even the students were being taught this skill. Further, the Ras Shamra tablets (dated from about 1400 B.C.) are written in a thirty-letter alphabet, closely related to Hebrew. These tablets represent the religious literature of the Canaanites and indicate that writing was so widely diffused among the Semites of the Mosaic Age that even the common people could read and write. Moses could write "in a book" (Exodus 17:14)!

1. *Nuzi Tablets.* In the past scholars have denied the historicity of the Hebrew patriarchs. Through excavations at Alalakh, Nuzi, and Mari it has become clear that the historical, social, legal, and economic background described in Genesis is very old and is an accurate reflection of the cultural milieu of the early second millennium B.C. Let us consider some of the evidence from the Nuzi Tablets.

The Nuzi Tablets constitute one of the outstanding discoveries of the Patriarchal Age. These tablets throw a flood of light upon the customs which figure in the patriarchal narratives.

a. Adoption. Abraham refers to his servant, Eliezer, as his heir and calls him "son of my house" (Genesis 15:2, 3). At Nuzi a childless couple would adopt a son who would serve them during their lifetime. However, if the couple should later have a son of their own, then the adopted son would step aside and give to the real son the privilege of being chief heir. No doubt, Abraham and Sarah adopted Eliezer to be their son. This would explain Abraham's words in Genesis 15:2, 3, prior to the birth of Isaac.

b. Giving of a handmaid. The Nuzi marriage regulations required that the wife who did not bear children give her husband a handmaid to raise family heirs. This explains why Sarah gave her servant Hagar to Abraham and why Rachel gave Bilhah to Jacob. The Nuzi regulations further stipulated that if the wife should afterward have a son of her own, she was not to expel the offspring of the handmaid. No wonder Abraham was reluctant when Sarah was going to expel Ishmael. This was contrary to the old law, and Abraham doubtless would have refused to do so had not a divine dispensation overridden the law.

c. Rachel's theft of the images. Before Jacob secretly left Laban, Rachel stole the family images which belonged to her father. When Laban discovered the loss, he pursued Jacob's company for seven days. Laban searched but could not find the images because Rachel had hidden them in a camel saddle on which she sat (Genesis 31:34). Why was Laban so anxious to find these images? The Nuzi Tablets showed that possession of the father's images played an important role in inheritance. Since Jacob possessed the images, it meant he had the right to inherit Laban's wealth.

d. Oral blessing. When Isaac was nearing the end of his life, he desired to bestow his blessings on Easu. When Isaac discovered that Jacob received the blessing through deception, he was filled with remorse; yet he did not revoke his oral blessing. Why? One of the Nuzi Tablets shows that an oral blessing had legal validity in patriarchal times.

Critics have denied the possibility of the early existence of a code of laws like that given through Moses in the Pentateuch. Assuming the evolutionary development of religion, they felt that the laws attributed to Moses were too far advanced for the time of Moses (1500-1400 B.C.) and must, therefore, be dated much later in Israel's history—say the eighth century B.C. Such criticism has been silenced by the discovery of the Code of Hammurabi by Jacquest deMorgan in 1901-1902 at the site of ancient Susa. This code was written several hundred years before Moses, and yet it contains some laws similar to those recorded by Moses. In the light of this discovery the critics can no longer say that the laws of Moses are too advanced for his time.

B. The Historical Books

Omri, the sixth king over Israel, built Samaria as the capital city of the northern kingdom. Harvard University excavated the site, uncovering six successive Israelite levels, and confirmed Omri's building by finding the native bedrock a large palace identified as Omri's (880-874 B.C.).

In summarizing the acts of King Ahab, the Bible mentions his ivory house (1 Kings 22:39). In the excavations at Samaria the remains of Ahab's palace were discovered, complete with walls faced with white marble, which would give the appearance of an ivory house. Also, numerous ivory decorations were found. The white gleaming walls and the ivory decorations give double reason for calling this palace an ivory house.

Until 1843 the name Sargon could not be found anywhere except in Isaiah 20:1. Some critics and historians, therefore, dismissed the Biblical reference as completely worthless historically. However, the whole picture was changed when Paul Botta was digging at Khorsabad. There he found the remains of a great palace covering some 25 acres. As was the custom among kings of his era, Sargon had his name stamped into many of the sun-dried clay bricks with which the huge palace was built. Further work by the Oriental Institute of the University of Chicago in recent years has added to our knowledge of this notable king of Assyria.

It is obvious that archaeological investigations have done much to vindicate the truth worthiness of the Old Testament record. The same can be said for the New Testament.

C. THE ACTS

Luke, more than any other New Testament writer, relates his story in the context of contemporary events. Archaeological discoveries have corroborated his use of the proper titles for contemporary officials, his use of geographical terms and description of cities. Sir William Ramsay, after devoting his energies to the thorough study of the antiquities of Asia Minor, maintained that the most reliable guide to this region during the first century was the Book of Acts. What is significant is that Ramsay began his investigations firmly convinced that Acts was a second century A.D. production. He was compelled to completely reverse his views by the factual evidence he uncovered in the course of his research.

Consider these examples: Gallio (Acts 18:12) was assigned his correct title by Luke: "proconsul of Achaia." An inscription found at Delphi records a proclamation of Claudius which indicates Gallio became proconsul of Achaia in July, A.D. 51. Luke usually called the Province of Achaia by its more ordinary name Greece (Acts 20:2) but departed from his usual procedure when giving a governor's official title, and so calls Gallio not "proconsul of Greece" but "proconsul of Achaia"—his official title.

A bewildering variety of titles were held by men of official positions in various parts of the Roman empire. Luke used the term *politarchs* to denote the civic authorities at Thessalonica. This term is not found in any classical author, but nineteen inscriptions from Macedonian cities show it was an official title for magistrates. Five of these inscriptions come from Thessalonica. Similarly, Luke calls Publius, the chief man in Malta (Acts 28:7), "The first man of the island." Greek and Latin inscriptions from the island show that "first man" was indeed his proper title.

Luke's description of salient traits of Ephesus has been amply corroborated through the numerous discoveries at the site.

Conclusion

Archaeological data have contributed to an increased understanding of Bible history. Against this background we can read the Scriptures with enhanced comprehension and appreciation. However, by the very nature and limitations or archaeology as a science it cannot confirm the great theological truths. Archaeology can illuminate the historical context of God's manifestation in the flesh; it can add understanding to the circumstances of Christ's death, burial, and resurrection; but it is not the means whereby the significance of these acts is apprehended as truth. God has ordained that simple faith shall always be necessary in dealing with Him or His revealed truth, "For we walk by faith, not by sight" (2 Corinthians 5:7).

The contributions of archaeology can never take the place of faith. However, scientific attestation may act as an aid to faith. Build your life on the firm foundation laid in His excellent Word!

Panel Discussion and Open Forum

Question: Did Moses use documents and other writings as research material for his writings or was his only source of material from God?

It was pointed out that "Moses was learned in all the wisdom of the Egyptians, and was mighty in words and in deeds" (Acts 7:22). Therefore, his education made various documents at his disposal, but "the Lord said unto Moses, Write this for a memorial in a book" (Exodus 17:14), and God made his writings correct. God used human instrumentality under His divine direction.

Question: How old does archaeological evidence show man to be?

There is no agreement. Regardless of when you set the beginning of man's existence, it is not contrary to the Scriptures.

Question: How do archaeologists go about their work?

The people built walled cities on hills for defense. When a city was destroyed, they would level the rubble and build new cities on top of the rubble. Archaeologists excavate both vertically and horizontally.

Another interesting fact in archaeology is that one can never rework his experiment.

In summary, many of the skepticisms, criticisms, and theories regarding the divine inspiration, truthfulness, authenticity and historical accuracy of the Scriptures have been answered by archaeological findings. These findings may serve as an aid to faith and contribute much to our understanding of Bible history. However, Christian faith is the essential ingredient in apprehending the great truths of the Scripture.

DECLARATION AT ST. LOUIS

DECLARATION AT ST. LOUIS

Recognizing the end times in which we live and the evident hand of God which has rested upon the Assemblies of God for these times, and having engaged together in prayerful study in this Council on Evangelism concerning God's purpose in the world today and our place in His purpose, we make the following declaration.

Declaration

Because the Assemblies of God came into being as the Holy Spirit was poured out in prophetic fulfillment at the turn of the century and a body of like-minded Pentecostal believers voluntarily joined together in worship, ministry, and service; and

Because the Assemblies of God has accepted the Bible as the inerrant Word of God and has declared it as the whole counsel of God, giving emphasis to the full gospel; and

Because the Assemblies of God has grown rapidly both at home and abroad and has continued to experience the blessing of God as it has sought to do His will and to be an instrument of divine purpose; and

Because the Assemblies of God determines to remain a body of believers responding fully to the divine working in these last days; therefore, be it

Declared, That the Assemblies of God considers it was brought into being and built by the working of the Holy Spirit as an instrument of divine purpose in these end times; and be it

Declared further, That the Assemblies of God recognizes God's purposes concerning man are:

1. To reveal Himself through Christ to seek and to save that which was lost,

2. To be worshiped in spirit and in truth.

3. To build a body of believers in the image of His Son; and be it

Declared further, That the Assemblies of God recognizes that its mission is:

1. To be an agency of God for evangelizing the world,

2. To be a corporate body in which man may worship God,

3. To be a channel of God's purpose to build a body of saints being perfected in the image of His Son; and be it

Declared further, That the Assemblies of God exists expressly to give continuing emphasis to this mission in the New Testament apostolic pattern by encouraging believers to be baptized in the Holy Spirit, which enables them:

1. To evangelize in the power of the Holy Spirit with accompanying supernatural signs,

2. To worship God in the fullness of the Spirit,

3. To respond to the full working of the Holy Spirit in expressing His fruit and gifts as in New Testament times, edifying the body of Christ and perfecting the saints for the work of the ministry.

Response

LEADERS: In response to this declaration of mission of the Assemblies of God, we affirm that God is not willing that any should perish but is revealing Himself through Jesus Christ and is seeking to save the lost, calling man to Himself in Christ.

CONGREGATION: *This we affirm!*

LEADERS: We affirm that God desires to build a body of believers in the image of His Son, separating them unto Himself.

CONGREGATION: *This we affirm!*

LEADERS: We give ourselves to be an agency of God for evangelizing the world through Jesus Christ.

CONGREGATION: *We give ourselves to Him for this mission.*

LEADERS: We give ourselves to be a spiritual body in which man may worship God in the beauty of holiness and may be separated unto Him.

CONGREGATION: *We give ourselves to Him for this mission.*

LEADERS: We give ourselves to build a body of saints being perfected in the image of His Son, conforming unto Him.

CONGREGATION: *We give ourselves to Him for this mission.*

LEADERS: We dedicate ourselves to Spirit-filled living and teaching, to encourage believers likewise to be baptized in the Holy Spirit, knowing this will enable us to evangelize in the power of the Spirit with signs following.

CONGREGATION: *We dedicate ourselves to this mission.*

LEADERS: We dedicate ourselves to be filled with the Spirit so we will worship God in the fullness of the Spirit and minister before Him in spirit and in truth.

CONGREGATION: *We dedicate ourselves to this mission.*

LEADERS: We dedicate ourselves to respond to the full working of the Holy Spirit, praying He will use us mightily even as He worked in the New Testament Church, granting expression of fruit and gifts and ministries for the edifying of the body of Christ.

CONGREGATION: *We dedicate ourselves to this mission.*

LEADERS: This purpose of God and this mission of the Assemblies of God we affirm this day, and to this mission we dedicate ourselves, praying always to be kept in the faith, to evangelize in the power of the Spirit, to worship in spirit and in truth, and to conform to the image of His Son—so help us God!

CONGREGATION: *To this purpose of God and to this mission of the Assemblies of God we give ourselves this day—so help us God!*

APPENDIX

COUNCIL SPEAKERS

Messages and Seminars

Seth Balmer, Pastor, Bethel Assembly of God, Lincoln Park, Michigan

Earl Blythe, Superintendent, Tennessee District

Raymond Brock, Faculty, Evangel College

James Brown, President, South-Eastern Bible College

Cordas Burnett, President, Bethany Bible College

G. Raymond Carlson, President, North Central Bible College

Edwin Cole, Men's Fellowship Director, Northern California-Nevada District

Robert Cooley, Faculty, Evangel College

Norman Correll, Secretary, National Christ's Ambassadors Department

Donald M. Cox, Evangelist, Mobile, Alabama

Billie Davis, Missionary, Miami, Florida

Richard Dortch, Secretary-Treasurer, Illinois District

Richard Dresselhaus, Pastor, Summit Avenue Assembly of God, St. Paul, Minnesota

Paul Ferrin, Music Director, First Assembly of God, Memphis, Tennessee

Joseph Flower, Superintendent, New York District

Marcus Gaston, Pastor, Calvary Temple, Seattle, Washington

Robert Gatlin, Pastor, First Assembly of God, Panama City, Florida

U. S. Grant, Pastor, First Assembly of God, Kansas City, Kansas

Arthur Graves, Former President, South-Eastern Bible College

James Hamill, Pastor, First Assembly of God, Memphis, Tennessee

Ralph W. Harris, Editor in Chief, Church School Literature

Cyril Homer, Pastor, Gospel Tabernacle, Edina, Minnesota

D. V. Hurst, President, Northwest College of the Assemblies of God

Donald F. Johns, Dean, Central Bible College

Sam Jordan, President, National Action Crusades Council, Ottumwa, Iowa

Otis Keener, Pastor, First Assembly of God, Pacific Grove, California

Paul Lowenberg, Superintendent, Kansas District

Murray McLees, Pastor, First Assembly of God, Eugene, Oregon

Eugene Meador, CA President, Oklahoma District

Bruce Motter, Faculty Member of Western Reserve

Hal Noah, Pastor, Oak Cliff Assembly of God, Dallas, Texas

Robert Pagett, CA President, Oregon District

Haskell H. Rogers, Superintendent, West Texas District

Mrs. J. L. Schaffer, Woodlawn Assembly of God, Knoxville, Tennessee

Kenneth Schmidt, Pastor, First Assembly of God, Santa Cruz, California

216

Raymond Schoch, Pastor, Faith Center, Glendale, California

Gene Scott, President, Wescott Christian Center

Ernest Shores, Pastor, First Assembly of God, Phoenix, Arizona

Ira Stanphill, Pastor, Rosen Heights Assembly of God, Fort Worth, Texas

Hardy Steinberg, Secretary, Department of Education

Floyd Thomas, Pastor, Glad Tidings Tabernacle, San Francisco, California

William Thornton Jr., Pastor, Bethel Temple Assembly of God, New Orleans, Louisiana

John Walker, Pastor, First Pentecostal Assembly of God, Ottumwa, Iowa

E. S. Williams, Former General Superintendent

Morris O. Williams, Missionary, Republic of South Africa

Ward Williams, Faculty, Evangel College

T. F. Zimmerman, General Superintendent

T. F. Zimmerman III, Associate Professor of the School of Medicine, Kansas City, Missouri

NOTES

NOTES

NOTES

NOTES

NOTES

NOTES